TROUBLESOME WORDS

LANGUAGE WORLDS is a unique series that explores the cultural histories of the world's languages as evolving expressions of human experience. Each volume traces a language's journey across time – its origins and transformations in written and spoken form, and the communities that have shaped and sustained it. Language Worlds offers readers a vivid portrait of how languages both shape and are shaped by the societies that use them. Richly contextual and globally minded, the series invites readers to see languages not as static systems, but as dynamic sites of communication – each with its own rhythms, struggles and creative possibilities.

Troublesome Words

A Cultural History of Russian

Simon Franklin

REAKTION BOOKS

In memory of Natasha:
without whom this book could not have been written;
with whom it would have been so much better

Published by
REAKTION BOOKS LTD
2–4 Sebastian Street
London EC1V 0HE, UK

www.reaktionbooks.co.uk

First published 2026

EU GPSR Authorised Representative
Logos Europe, 9 rue Nicolas Poussin, 17000, La Rochelle, France
email: contact@logoseurope.eu

Printed and bound in Great Britain
by Bell & Bain, Glasgow

A catalogue record for this book is available from the British Library

ISBN 978 1 83639 266 8

CONTENTS

A NOTE ON TRANSLITERATION AND DATES

ALMOST ALL RUSSIAN words in this book are represented in transliteration into the Latin alphabet. Cyrillic lettering is used only in a few instances where it is necessary to illustrate a point. The transliterations generally adhere to the 'modified Library of Congress' system. The most noticeable feature of this convention is that it uses 'i' where some conventions use 'y': so, Tolstoi rather than Tolstoy, Maiakovskii rather than Mayakovsky. The so-called 'soft sign' (') is retained in transliterations, except when the relevant word (usually a proper name) is part of the running text as a normal rendition in English: thus, for example, Gogol in the text, Gogol' in transliterated Russian in a footnote reference.

With regard to rulers, this book sticks to the illogical custom of referring to emperors and empresses through the anglicized forms of their names (for example, Peter I and Catherine II, not Petr and Ekaterina), while most subsequent leaders keep the transliterated Russian forms (hence Mikhail Gorbachev, not Michael). A standard exception is Stalin, who is always Joseph rather than Iosif. I have no idea why.

As a guide to pronunciation for those who know little or no Russian, the stressed syllable is indicated (with an acute accent) in the transliteration of words from the late nineteenth century onwards. In the transliteration of earlier vocabulary stress is not indicated, since it can often be uncertain, especially in imported words.

Common Era dates are given according to the system in operation in Russia at the relevant time: that is, according to the Julian calendar up to the end of January 1918, and subsequently according to the Gregorian calendar. The switch of systems involved a 'loss' of thirteen days such that, officially, 1–13 February 1918 never happened.

Dating according to the Common Era was adopted in Russia from the start of 1700. Before that, it was more common for events to be dated according to the number of years since the Creation. As was well known, the world was created 5,500 years before the birth of Christ – although, because of an ancient glitch in calculation, Russian *anno mundi* dates generally convert to *anno domini* dates by subtracting 5,508, not 5,500. For convenience, however, pre-1700 dates are given according to the Common Era.

Introduction

What is the (or a) cultural history of a language? The title is not a clear pointer to the content. In principle, there is almost no limit to what could be included. Language is cultural. Virtually any aspect of the study of language could have a cultural dimension. In terms of conventional disciplines, should a cultural history of a language be conceived principally as a contribution to historical linguistics? Or to sociolinguistics? Or is it something less technical, to do with the history of culture? That is to say, is it mainly about language history with a focus on culture, or mainly about cultural history with a focus on language?

The cultural history of language(s) is not an established disciplinary label either in linguistics or in cultural studies. The phrase crops up from time to time, but with no consistent definition. For example, in the preface to his book *A Cultural History of the English Language*, Gerry Knowles stated that his intention was to write 'an outline history of the English language for linguists and for students of linguistics and modern English language'.[1] In practice, this meant a concise history of language development in relation to its contexts and contacts. The focus was on the role of culture in language change: in effect, a branch of historical sociolinguistics.[2] In this respect Knowles's 'cultural history' was not so different from, say, Dick Leith's *A Social History of English*, whose second edition was its almost exact contemporary.[3] Besides historical linguistics with a cultural slant, there is also the newer field of cultural linguistics, or 'linguocultural studies'. This is quite different. It is concerned with the analysis of conceptualization, of cultural concepts embedded in languages; like a branch of semantics.[4] Since the 1970s Russian linguists have developed the related field of *lingvostranovédenie* – the study of a country and its culture through key concepts in its language.[5]

Neither of these models – the impact of culture *on* language, or the expression of culture immanent *in* language – quite fits the approach of the present book, which is mainly about the culture *of* language. Its central theme is the history of the Russian language as an object and instrument of purposeful cultural reflection. Each chapter explores different ways in which cultural (and to some extent political) change has served as a framework for changes in the culture of language; and ways in which the language has been cultivated and contested, crafted and reconceived, in pursuit of cultural (and to some extent political) agendas.

The questions themselves are not new. This general history could not have been written in a vacuum. On the contrary, it draws heavily on a strong tradition of particular studies of cultural contexts in the history of Russian. For example, in the preface to his excellent study *After Newspeak: Language Culture and Politics in Russia from Gorbachev to Putin*, focusing on the late twentieth and early twenty-first centuries, Michael S. Gorham does refer to the work as 'a cultural history of the Russian language' for the relevant period, drawing on 'cultural studies, sociolinguistics, and new media studies'.[6] Gorham's choice of tools is multidisciplinary, although the contextual emphasis, as is made plain in the book's subtitle, is political. By contrast, and at the opposite end of the chronological spectrum (mainly medieval and early modern), Viktor Zhivov's monumental *History of the Language of Russian Writing*, though deeply rooted in formal and technical historical linguistics, is also a major work of cultural history. To cite another preface – in this case the preface to Zhivov's book by the linguist A. M. Moldovan – Zhivov conceived of his subject not as a self-contained linguistic phenomenon but as developing according to 'scenarios created in cultural processes'.[7]

The title of Viktor Zhivov's book was a modification of a traditional category. General histories of Russian tend to have followed one of two paths: on the one hand, histories of, say, the structures of grammar and sound, that characterize Russian and distinguish it from other languages;[8] and, on the other hand, histories of a particular register of language that is termed the *literatúrnyi iazyk*.[9] *Literatúrnyi iazyk* is often rendered into English as 'literary language', but this can be misleading. Literature has played an important role in the development of the *literatúrnyi iazyk*, but the *literatúrnyi iazyk* is not limited to the language of literature, nor even to the language of writing. It includes educated speech. When Russians refer to the literary language, they tend to mean, more broadly, the norms of what is reckoned to be correct usage: the 'standard' language. Insofar as the present book is concerned with language as an object of cultural reflection, and with norms and normativity, it draws to some extent on studies of the *literatúrnyi iazyk*. However, in places it deals as much with challenges to norms, or with the non-normative, or with what might be called alternative normativities. A cultural history of Russian is not, therefore, just another way of framing an account of the Russian literary language.

When does the story in this book begin, and what are its principal contents? The definition of the subject determines both its scope and its limits. For present purposes the cultural history of Russian starts when the Russian language becomes an object of reflection and discussion: an idea, an aspiration, something to be crafted and debated. That means roughly from the late seventeenth century. It has no natural end, only the unavoidable hiatus at the point where history would (at the time of writing) transmute into prophecy: that is, the mid-2020s. The narrative therefore spans approximately three and a half centuries.

This is not a traditional chronology for histories of Russian (or of the *literatúrnyi iazyk*), which tend to begin a great deal earlier.

Typically, they start with the language situation in Early Rus of the late tenth to thirteenth century and the relations between Church Slavonic (the written register that was adopted along with Christianity) and varieties of vernacular East Slavonic. Some go back further and place both these registers of language in the context of their derivation from Common Slavonic. This is because, in histories of Russian, the emphasis has tended to be on tracing its emergence: its origins, the processes of linguistic change and differentiation that produced, over a protracted period, distinct registers of Slavonic, then distinct registers of East Slavonic, which in turn became the foundations of the modern Russian, Ukrainian and Belarusian languages. The emphasis on origins and the processes of language differentiation is nicely captured in the title of the handbook on the subject by Tore Nesset: *How Russian Came to Be the Way It Is*.[10] Here and in similar works, Russian is the culmination of the story, not its main subject. Similarly, for example, Zhivov's *History of the Language of Russian Writing* takes over a thousand pages getting from the tenth century to the early nineteenth century, but characterizes the period from circa 1830 to the present in just 25 pages. Almost all of the book, therefore, is about the medieval precursors of Russian, and about the formation of a standard language of culture (a 'literary language') in the eighteenth and early nineteenth centuries. In other words, a lot of works that call themselves histories of Russian could more accurately be labelled its *pre*histories.

The focus on Russian as an object of culture and cultivation also determines the book's principal sub-themes. Two topics, in particular, permeate the narrative: the question of norms, and the question of authority: what ought the language to be? What constituted proper Russian, correct Russian, good Russian, prestigious Russian? Members of language communities recognize and affirm themselves through a sense of shared norms. Normativity is necessary but also artificial. Norms exist to be asserted, modified, expanded, contracted, contested and undermined, parodied, challenged, broken. Even the breaking of norms depends on a shared sense of their existence: transgression is only expressive in relation to the norm. Sometimes, norms in Russian have been imagined to be intrinsic and immutable, guarantors of continuity in preserving the essence of the language. But norms have also changed and adapted in response to political, cultural, social and technological challenges. Both the existence of norms and the challenges to norms have induced anxiety, argument, reaction and creativity. A cultural history of Russian is a tale of continual dialogue or tension between normativity and disruption. Today's rebarbative innovation may – or may not – turn out to settle into tomorrow's tradition.

Such processes are not self-contained. Ideas about norms do not form and re-form randomly. They reflect assumptions about linguistic and cultural authority and status. Who validates the norms? Who decides what the language of culture ought to be? The church? The state? Intellectuals? Publishers? Educational and academic institutions? Creative individuals? Political parties? Media organizations? Or, in the networked age, decentred informal chat groups? And what are the criteria for the validation of norms? The claimed (or imagined) sources of linguistic authority and status can be very varied: political, institutional, ideological, historical, communal. In the cultural history of Russian, norms tend to have been challenged out of a sense of frustration about their limits, because they have not been reckoned adequate for new tasks or changing values and ideas and cultural stimuli, or because their resources have been too restricted to fill the cultural spaces opened by new technologies of communication (print, radio and television, computers and the Internet). Behind the question 'what is the proper language of culture?' lie questions of what, or who, the language of culture is *for*. Diverse sources of normative authority can also coexist or overlap, both in harmony and in conflict. Arguments and fluctuations can be regarded as necessary conditions for a cultural history. In part, this cultural history of Russian is structured through tracking the aspirations, anxieties and tensions around successive sources of perceived authority for language norms.

Norms of what? One should distinguish cultural norms from merely formal notions of linguistic correctness. Language learners have to worry (or *should* have to worry) about prescriptive norms for correct spelling, for example, or about the 'rules' that relate to the case-endings of nouns. However, formal correctness is only one part of cultural normativity in the uses of language. There are many kinds of boundary, which are continually tested and renegotiated. Where should lines be drawn? Is it axiomatic that the language of received culture should be preserved and protected? To what extent is it enriched – or diluted, undermined and threatened – by extending its boundaries to include, for example, colloquial speech, or jargons of non-elite social groups? Or regional variations? How appropriate are concepts of decency and indecency? Are taboos essential or absurd? Or – a particularly contentious and recurrent theme in the history of the culture of Russian over the past three centuries – are foreign words to be embraced as enhancements to the expressive capacity of the language, or resisted as contaminations, even abominations? Or, still more fundamentally, is language itself too frustrating, too restrictive, too inherently normative to be accepted as adequate as a means of true expression? Most challenges to norms involve experimentation and innovation *within* language; some demand experimentation *beyond* language.

The cultural history of Russian has been played out in a shifting social and political landscape. It began when people started to identify, define, codify and reflect on Russian as a medium and instrument of culture. Initially, these were the concerns of a tiny elite in a peasant country of mass illiteracy: a country with (at the turn of the eighteenth century) no universities, and with fewer printing houses than could be counted on the fingers of one hand. Yet this tiny elite developed ambitions to shape and establish a Russian language that might stand with dignity alongside the cultured languages of Europe, a language worthy of an empire. Peasant language as such (that is, the speech of the vast majority of the population right through into the twentieth century) entered the story only when and to the extent that the linguistic culture-makers decided that it should. Over the course of three centuries, through cultural reorientation, educational expansion, political reforms and upheavals, and technological transformations, the questions of norms and boundaries, of authority and transgression, spread their tentacles ever wider: to a language of or for the masses, a standard national language, a transnational language as an instrument of assimilation within a multi-ethnic state, an imperial language, a global language.

This overview of the cultural history of Russian cannot pretend to be comprehensive. It picks out some key themes and episodes, and at each stage it attempts to convey a flavour of what was involved, both at the level of broad ideas and at the level of language practice. Its general direction is linear and chronological, but its narrative is also shaped by a kind of recurring cycle: a cycle of solutions achieved and dissolved, of solutions that turn out to be illusions because the problems themselves mutate, because the world changes, because cultural values and hierarchies are persistently questioned, because the necessary artifice of norms can be felt as irksome and restrictive. The awkward thing about language is that it lives. In the preface to the first edition of his great dictionary in 1755, Dr Samuel Johnson nicely catches the ambiguity: we want fixity but we also know that fixity is stagnation.

> Those who have been persuaded to think well of my design, require that it should fix our language, and put a stop to those alterations which time and chance have hitherto been suffered to make it without opposition. With this consequence I confess I flattered myself for a while, but now I begin to fear that I have indulged expectation which neither reason nor experience can justify . . . The language most likely to continue long without alteration, would be that of a nation raised a little, and but a little, above barbarity.[11]

In the preface to a subsequent edition Johnson famously likened the lexicographer's quest to 'chasing the sun': the sun is just over the horizon; but when you reach the horizon it is no closer – just over another horizon.[12]

Language users can take equal delight in being either ahead of or behind its trajectory. The lure of innovation is obvious, but we should not underestimate the opposite. Linguistic nostalgia, or sometimes merely frustration that the language refuses to sit still, is an essential part of the texture and tensions of language culture. Normativity can be caricatured as oppressive or reactionary, but it would be hard to find a language user whose own practices and prejudices do not at some level depend on some form of normativity. Although we know that, over time, usage determines correctness, many (most?) of us enjoy the occasional bout of cantankerousness about corrupt usage in the face of what we like to think should be correct. In English it may be split infinitives, or egregiously random apostrophes, or the lack of differentiation between 'disinterested' and 'uninterested', or between 'repudiate' and 'refute', or a thousand other such niceties.

Here, a confession: for me, in historical accounts of language, a trigger for curmudgeonly grumpiness is the notion of 'loanwords' and lexical 'borrowing'. A loan is something that one is expected to repay. Lexical 'borrowings' are used with no expectation of being returned. True, the idea of lexical 'loans' and 'borrowing' has been hallowed by near-universal usage, whether in English, in French (*emprunt*, *mot d'emprunt*) or in Russian (*zaímstvovanie*, *zaímstvovannoe slóvo*). This widespread mislabelling perhaps originates in a false calque from the German *Lehnwort*. No matter. In this book there is no loaning. Languages may appropriate or assimilate or take or import from one another. They are neither lenders nor borrowers of words.

This is trivial. Such lexical fastidiousness is obviously misplaced. It changes nothing. I mention it as a reminder that, in the experience of language culture, triviality matters. This general history of the culture of Russian unavoidably deals with large processes and with somewhat schematized choices and conflicts. Some of those involved in and affected by such processes may indeed have imagined them in broad terms, in the general sweep of their development. But, as often as not, real people's perception of language change has been more granular, less panoramic, more personal, sometimes more contradictory, even capricious – less historical, more human.

1

Prehistories

Russian has no beginning. There was no 'before and after' moment of its birth or creation or completed formation. Nor, more subjectively, was there an instant of sudden recognition, when its features were first perceived and named. Both as a set of linguistic practices and as a cultural idea, elements of Russian, as it might now be recognized, emerged unevenly. We should not project its present onto its past, but features of its past can be detected in its present. Aerial photographs of fields can reveal subtle lines and contrasts of colour and contour in which archaeologists detect traces of how those fields were worked or inhabited centuries ago. Similarly, linguists surveying patterns on the surface of a modern language can find traces of its substrata in deep history. This chapter begins with examples of such features in contemporary Russian. They provide a way in to the question of what Russian emerged from. Some familiarity with this is necessary if one is to understand the early debates about what Russian ought to become. As an aside for non-linguists: the first section of this chapter is the *only* part of the present book that focuses on technical issues such as historical phonology and morphology.

Digging for Roots

Start with some sounds. On the surface, the combinations of letters *-olo-* and *-la-*, or *-oro-* and *-ra-*, may not seem particularly close to each other. Put them into Russian words, however, and it becomes clear that they are related. For example: ***golová*** means 'head', and ***glavá*** also means 'head'; but not the same kinds of head. The difference is that *golová* is physical, the head as a part of the body, while *glavá* is more abstract or metaphorical: the head of an organization, the section headings or chapters of a book. This contrastive affinity is carried over into derivative forms such as adjectives. ***Golovnáia bol'*** is physical: 'a headache'. ***Glávnaia tsel'*** is more conceptual: the 'main aim'. Similarly, ***górod*** means 'town', a physical place, whereas ***grad*** means 'town' in more elevated style, including compounds such as *Lenin**grád***. As for derivatives: ***gorozhánin*** is a townsperson, while ***grazhdanín*** has the more conceptual meaning of 'citizen'.

What lies behind such phenomena? If we were to travel back far enough, more than a millennium, we would find that the remote ancestors of today's Slavs made no such distinction: that, in Common Slavonic, today's *-oro-* and *-ra-* were both more like *-or-*, while *-olo-* and *-la-* were both more like *-ol-*. Over time, different phonological shifts produced different regional articulations: *-ra-* and *-la-* among South Slavs, *-oro-* and *-olo-* among East Slavs.[1] So why does Russian – an East Slavonic language – have both of them? The reason is Christianity, and the culture of writing that came with it. In the mid-ninth century, as part of the missionary activity associated with the brothers Constantine (better known by his monastic name of Cyril) and Methodius, Christian devotional texts began to be translated into Slavonic. The regional base of the translators was mainly South Slav, so the sacred texts – in a register now labelled Old Church Slavonic – reflected the *-la-* and *-ra-* forms. These texts later made their way to the East Slavs of early Rus, whose official adoption of Christianity was in the late tenth century; and thence to later Muscovy; and thence into the age of the formation of modern Russian. Until the seventeenth century the majority of high-prestige written culture was, in a broad sense, devotional. Thus the two sets of forms, which had originally been just variant regional articulations – regional accents, in effect – came to be differentiated in style and meaning and function.

In linguistic terms, phonological differences became lexicalized. That is why, in the above examples, the *-olo-* and *-oro-* forms convey concrete meanings from everyday usage in the East Slav vernacular, while the *-la-* and *-ra-* forms reflect centuries of book culture, more elevated in style and often more abstract in meaning.

In the story of the emergence of Russian, features such as the *-la-* and *-ra-* forms are known as Slavonisms. Other types of Slavonism similarly echo ancient differences in sound-structures. One could produce an equivalent excursus, for example, on the origins and semantic implications of modern words with *-shch-* (щ) as opposed to *-ch-* (ч), or with *-zhd-* (жд) as opposed to *-zh-* (ж). Other Slavonisms were lexical from the start – words and concepts that reached the East Slavs through the Christian scriptures and that became assimilated through centuries of familiarity in the tradition of Christian devotional writing. Besides sounds and words, there were also Slavonisms in the structures of expression. Most translators believed in sticking as closely as possible to the shape of their originals. Old Church Slavonic was created principally for the purpose of transmitting texts whose originals were in Greek. This meant that sentences in Old Church Slavonic were often constructed according to patterns of Greek. Typical signs of this would be the regular use of subordinate clauses and participles, and of rhetorical devices that were habitual in the Greek (or Latin) bookish tradition, but which were probably rare in East Slavs' speech.

Before going further into the prehistories of Russian, we should clarify some terminology. *Old* Church Slavonic is a self-contained artifice devised by linguists. The term conventionally refers to the language that can be extrapolated on the basis of surviving texts written in the tenth and eleventh centuries. These texts – it has been assumed – provide the closest achievable reconstruction of the register of language that was created in the mid-ninth century for the sole purpose of making Christian devotional texts accessible to converted Slavs. The full list of what are often called the 'canonical' sources for Old

Church Slavonic contains just a couple of dozen items, of which only seven are substantial manuscript books, while the rest are fragments of manuscripts or brief inscriptions.[2] This is the traditional, purist version, although in principle it is also possible to mine later manuscripts for features of early texts. The 'canonical' textual witnesses to Old Church Slavonic were written in two different scripts. Some are in Cyrillic: a script based on Greek, and the remote ancestor of today's Cyrillic alphabet. Others are in the script known as Glagolitic. The names can be confusing, since the script invented by Cyril himself was probably – we cannot speak in certainties – the one now known as Glagolitic, not Cyrillic.[3]

The point of the Cyrillo-Methodian mission, and of subsequent translation activity, was to make the scriptures available to Slavs in their own tongue. In principle, therefore, Old Church Slavonic was supposed to be a version of a vernacular language.[4] Self-evidently, it was closer to a Slavonic vernacular than was Greek or Latin, let alone Hebrew. But it was a lofty, bookish form of discourse that was created for a world without lofty bookishness. At its core were many, many ideas and *realia* for which Slavonic vernaculars had no words and which were far removed from any version of everyday Slavonic orality. If not entirely an invented language, it was an invented register.

Old Church Slavonic, though not wholly uniform, is broadly homogeneous by design, because it is chronologically circumscribed. Take away the adjective 'old' and the character of the phenomenon changes. Church Slavonic is a blanket label for what happened to Old Church Slavonic over the next thousand years, as the texts were copied and re-copied, edited, distorted and imitated; as new texts were created; as regional traditions evolved in contact with a range of vernaculars across the lands in which they were used. Church Slavonic thus developed somewhat divergent local variants – a process that has continued into modern times.[5] If there is one constant about Church Slavonic, it is that the source of its authority lay in books. It owed its existence to written texts. That is not to say that it existed *only* in writing. Church Slavonic could not be a language of casual chatter, but its texts were often delivered and received orally. Liturgy is, after all, an oral performance. Already from the early period of the dissemination of Church Slavonic, liturgical pronunciation has tended to adapt to the sound structures of local speech.[6] And, as we have seen even in the relatively small example of *-ra-* and *-la-* forms, Church Slavonic could and did migrate from devotional books into general speech. However, there was no doubt as to its fundamentally bookish nature.

East Slavonic is a trickier and more fluid concept. One could even view it as a convenient fiction. The term 'East Slavonic', like Church Slavonic, can also be prefixed with the adjective 'Old'. Old East Slavonic is a generalized representation of linguistic features that are assumed to characterize speech across what are broadly defined as East Slav areas (approximately the areas of modern Ukraine, Belarus and European Russia) between about 1000 and 1400. An increasingly popular – if not wholly felicitous – alternative term in English is (Old) Rusian, with a single 's': an adjective created to refer specifically to Rus, not to Russia.[7] If Church Slavonic is a language of real books that to some extent affected and was affected by speech, Old East Slavonic is the opposite: a language of hypothetical speech, whose features are only deducible from their very limited (by comparison) refractions in books and inscriptions. We can see and analyse church books, but we cannot see or hear early East Slavs speaking. We can extrapolate some likely features of some of their speech in some geographical areas. For example, through an accident of source survival and retrieval, we happen to have an exceptional quantity of evidence for some structures of sound and phrase in medieval Novgorod. The evidence is provided by the extraordinarily direct and diverse texts scratched on fragments of birch-bark which continue to be excavated from the saturated mud in which they have been embedded for between 500 and 1,000 years. The earliest of them date from the first half of the eleventh century; the latest are from late fifteenth century. Scratched messages on birch bark have been excavated in about a dozen sites across the northern Rus lands, but the overwhelming majority are from Novgorod (and nearby Staraia Russa).[8] These reflect what is labelled the Novgorodian 'dialect'.[9] The term is fine, so long as it is understood that *every* local usage (including Kyivan, for example) was in the same sense a dialect, not a deviation from some retrospectively constructed standard version of spoken Old East Slavonic.

We have to assume that the real spoken range of East Slavonic vernaculars was more capacious and varied than has been preserved or reflected in any tradition of written texts. Apart from the birch-bark documents and similarly informal specimens of writing such as graffiti, East Slavonic is most conspicuously reflected, in a limited and formulaic mode, in some administrative texts such as law codes; and partly in non-devotional bookish texts such as chronicles, whose linguistic register has been described as hybrid.[10]

Church Slavonic and East Slavonic interacted with each other in two main ways. On the one hand, through prolonged mutual contact, each assimilated some features of the other: that is, there were signs of limited convergence. On the other hand, despite acquiring some East Slavonic colouring, Church Slavonic was in principle conservative in form and in cultural function, while, as we shall see, East Slavonic changed significantly. In some respects, therefore, the two became more distanced. Even where words appear to be the same, meanings have often diverged. Eloquent examples include *rabóta*, which in Russian means 'work' but in Church Slavonic means 'slavery'; *pozór* in Church Slavonic was 'a spectacle', but in modern Russian it has become 'a disgrace'; *prélest'* in Russian means 'charm' in a rather mild and positive sense, alongside its adjectival derivative *preléstnyi*, 'charming', while in Church Slavonic it is 'deception', 'temptation', 'deviance', in an unequivocally negative sense.[11]

In origin, and for the centuries of its dominance in written texts, Church Slavonic was a language of prestige culture by definition. Old

East Slavonic was not. The emergence (or creation) of Russian as a language of culture and social prestige radically shifted the linguistic ecology. As a fully operational register of language, Church Slavonic was confined to its niche in devotional practice. Beyond that, elements of Church Slavonic remained and still remain productive in the Russian linguistic toolkit: partly providing means of stylistic and semantic variation, and partly as materials for word-formation.

Not everything that came to be perceived as a Slavonism was characteristic of Russian Church Slavonic *as opposed to* East Slavonic. There are also features that were originally shared but have disappeared from vernacular East Slavonic. Thus the notion of a Slavonism has tended to include forms that could equally be parsed as East Slavonic archaisms. If we return to skimming the surface of the modern language in search of chronological fault lines, we can pause to look at two of them: first, a curious inconsistency in the way Russian verbs express time; and second, the letters of the alphabet most dear to the hearts of new learners, the so-called 'hard sign' and 'soft sign'.

In the present and future tenses, Russian verbs conjugate properly, so to speak; in a manner acceptable to classically trained grammarians. That is, their endings change in order to differentiate between first, second and third person singular and plural (I, you, he/she/it, we, you, they). In the past tense, however, they operate a different system, with endings that indicate number (singular and plural) and – in the singular – gender (masculine, feminine, neuter) rather than person. In other words, the past tense of the verb looks rather like an adjective agreeing with the subject of the sentence. The form is in origin a participle. This was at one stage more logical than it now appears. It is a relic of an earlier compound past tense consisting of a past participle that did indeed agree with the subject, plus a form of *present* tense of the verb 'to be', which carried the expression of person. Between them – past participle plus present of 'to be' – they expressed the perfect tense, which conveys a present state as a result of a past completed action: 'I have done' – or, here, literally, 'I am having-done'.

The conjugated form of 'to be' dropped out, leaving just the seemingly incongruous participial form to express the past tense all by itself.

That is only half of it. In the modern language the originally participial form does not just express the perfect tense. It is standard for all modes of past action. Why? Here the modern language differs fundamentally from Old East Slavonic and Church Slavonic, both of which had other forms of conjugated past tense: imperfect for continuous or repeated action, aorist for single or completed action. Modern Russian conveys such modes of action (repeated, continuous and so on) by other means: not through a system of endings, but either through changes to the stem or through prefixes, which indicate the type of action, or the 'aspect' ('perfective' and 'imperfective') distinguishing single or completed action from repeated or continuous action. So, the old participial form has transmuted into the standard means for expressing action in the past, while the old conjugated past tenses – aorist and imperfective – have disappeared from standard Russian, leaving learners to fret instead about aspectual pairs. Church Slavonic (even Old Church Slavonic) and Old East Slavonic had various means of differentiating modes of action – that is, of conveying aspect[12] – but the systemic importance of aspectual pairs is a feature of the modern language. The transition from the dominance of tense to the dominance of aspect was a long process, but it was fairly comprehensive.[13] Again, therefore, the surface archaeology of the contemporary language reveals deep fissures which take us into its prehistory, and at the same time help to explain something of its specific character.

From ways of conveying time, we return to sounds and their encoding in writing. Two letters in the modern Russian alphabet are unpronounceable: not in the sense that they are difficult for foreigners, but, quite literally, they do not represent any distinct sound. These are the so-called 'soft sign' (ь) and 'hard sign' (ъ). In Latin-script transliteration they are usually represented by single or double quotation marks or primes – which are useless to anybody who does not already know what they mean. These signs cannot be articulated alone. Instead, they provide information about the articulation of the preceding consonant. A consonant followed by a soft sign is, not surprisingly, 'soft' – or, technically, palatalized. A consonant followed by a hard sign is 'hard', or unpalatalized. In practice the hard sign is rarely necessary: 'hard' is the default pronunciation for the majority of consonants as written, unless followed either by a soft sign or by one of the vowels that also indicates that the preceding consonant is palatalized ('e', 'и', 'ю', 'я'). A hard sign is informative only in one context: when a prefix ending in a hard consonant is added to a word that begins with one of these vowels. So, contrast *sest'*, 'to sit down', and *s"est'*, 'to eat up': in the former, the initial 's' is palatalized as part of the stem of the word; in the later the 's' is a prefix, whose unpalatalized quality before the 'e' has to be indicated with the hard sign.

The pairing of hard and soft consonants, like the aspectual pairings of perfective and imperfective verbs, is a feature of modern Russian. It was not always thus. Let us go one stage back. Open any book printed before 1918 and two visual features stand out. First, the text will almost certainly include two letters that were later abandoned – 'ѣ' and 'і', and it may also include occasional instances of two others ('ѵ' and 'ѳ'). And second, every word ends either in a vowel, or in a soft sign, or in a hard sign. The regular use of the hard sign in final position was redundant as a guide to pronunciation, and it was also abandoned. But why was it there in the first place? Going much, much further back – a thousand years or so, to Old Church Slavonic – these letters were not hard or soft signs. They had independent value. They represented reduced vowels, or semi-vowels: syllabic but weakly articulated like, say, the middle 'a' in 'putative' by contrast with the 'u' and 'i' on either side of it; or both the 'o's in 'collaborate'. In the implied pronunciation of Old Church Slavonic (as well as in the earliest period of Old East Slavonic), all syllables were open; that is, no syllable or word could end in a consonant, but all must end in a vowel. Starting from around the eleventh century, in the East Slav areas, these two reduced vowels were dropped. Or, more accurately, they ceased to be reduced vowels. Some of them, in what linguists term 'strong' position (in the syllable preceding another reduced vowel) transmuted into full vowels ('e' and 'o' for 'ь' and 'ъ' respectively). The rest disappeared, or ceased to have syllabic value. In writing, however, in some positions they survived. The front semi-vowel turned into the soft sign, retained where the preceding consonant was palatalized. The back semi-vowel was normally dropped in writing, except – by curious inertia – at the end of words, despite the fact that, by definition, a reduced vowel at the end of a word could not be in a 'strong' position and hence was not pronounced. The redundant hard signs at the end of words in pre-1918 spelling are visual relics of that very distant age of open syllables.

However, dropping semi-vowels had consequences far more diverse and profound than merely a long-standing anomaly in conventions of spelling.[14] Not only the vowel system was affected. The radical shift away from open syllables had implications for the quality of consonants. If you remove reduced vowels, then consonants find themselves in new situations: they may be isolated at the end of newly closed final syllables; or they may be brought together in unaccustomed clusters: consonants that had previously been separated by reduced vowels now rubbed up against one another. In many situations this also produced adaptations in the ways in which those consonants were articulated, as they assimilated to (or differentiated themselves from) the characteristics of their new neighbours. Most notable are two kinds of change, both of which involved the emergence or spread of binary pairings in the consonantal system. One such pairing enhanced the opposition between voiced and devoiced (aspirated) versions of a consonant ('g' and 'k', 'b' and 'p', 'd' and 't'). The other binary pairing that became more extensive, as we have seen, is between palatalized and unpalatalized versions of consonants: their 'soft' and 'hard' versions; which takes us again to the two unpronounceable letters in the modern Russian alphabet.

Back on the surface of the modern language: it is all very well to delve into ancient distinctions between Church Slavonic and East Slavonic sounds and forms, but, as any learner of elementary Russian instantly discovers, the language is full of *words* that are not of Slavonic origin. Lots of words in Russian look (or at any rate sound) quite familiar to an Anglophone observer: from *futból* to *teátr*, from *bráuzer* to *kofe-bréik*, from *realízm* to *post-modernízm*. Foreign words have rolled into Russian in successive waves over the centuries. They have been loved and loathed, embraced and resisted, welcomed as enrichments of the language, condemned as corruptions of the language. Several layers of imported vocabulary will figure in later chapters of the present book. The oldest, and perhaps the least recognized as such, are actually embedded in Church Slavonic itself, which, as originally a language of translation, absorbed a great deal from Greek. However, the first massive influx of western European words dates from the early eighteenth century and is associated mainly with the policies of Peter I.

Peter's expansion of the secular sphere, in technology as well as learning, had an impact on language. New skills and new concepts brought new words. It is estimated that approximately 5,000 words of western European origin entered Russian during the Petrine era.[15] They included military and naval terminology (for example, *batal'on*, *marsh*, *fel'dmarshal*, *signal*, *flagman*), terms used in commerce (for example, *kommerts*, *manufaktura*, *bankir*), administrative vocabulary (for example, *artikul*, *lakei*, *ministr*) and diverse scientific and technical terms ranging from *professor* to *problema*, from *metall* to *okulist*. The source languages included Dutch, German, Polish, English, French, Italian and Swedish. The lexical pathways into Russian could be both direct from the language of origin, or via one or more of the other languages as intermediaries (for example, from Swedish via German, from German via Polish and so on).[16]

These are just a few examples of how the surface archaeology of contemporary Russian reveals strata of its prehistories.

The Emergence of a Culture of Language

The prehistories of Russian cannot be reduced to formal features such as its phonology and morphology. A culture of Russian developed not just because of the ways in which Church Slavonic and East Slavonic happen to have diverged or converged. It grew out of a culture of thinking about language. Among the Orthodox East Slavs, Church Slavonic had always been esteemed as the language of high culture, a language with an aura of sacrality. However, towards the end of the medieval period (or the start of the early modern period) – roughly in the seventeenth century – the culture of language began to develop features that one can regard as precursors of the emergence of a culture of Russian. This section outlines four ways in which the Church Slavonic-based bookish register began to be increasingly objectified and held up for scrutiny: visual representation, rhetorical manipulation, parodic defamiliarization and grammatical formalization. All four strands were relevant to the subsequent development of Russian itself as a bookish register. They converged towards the latter part of the seventeenth century.

An important context for change – both as one of its products and as one of its catalysts – was educational. Before the mid-seventeenth century it had been traditional for Muscovy's rulers to hire specialists from abroad as and when their skills were required: architects to work on the churches and walls of the Moscow Kremlin, translators to render texts from Greek or Latin or to serve at the Ambassadorial Chancery (*posol'skii prikaz*) responsible for foreign relations, trained medics to staff the Apothecary Chancery (*aptekarskii prikaz*) responsible for the health of the tsar and his family, and so on. However, there was a persistent reluctance to support and develop the institutions and systems of learning on which such skills were based. From the mid-seventeenth century this began to change. Initially the pattern might have looked conventional. There was an influx of learned men: in this instance, mainly from Ruthenia (a label for the Ukrainian and Belarusian lands within the Polish–Lithuanian Commonwealth). These were polyglot scholars who, though Orthodox, had been trained in schools that had adopted Jesuit-style curricula. And, in the second half of the century, key centres of such an education – most notably Kyiv itself – were subjected to Muscovite control. Bookmen from Ruthenia were critically important in the service of the Muscovite state and church in the late seventeenth century. Now, however, the import of skills went beyond merely hiring highly educated individuals. For the first time, formal institutions of higher education and learning began to be established in Moscow itself. In the early 1680s the Moscow Print Yard was a location for a school that has been described as Russia's first public educational institution. In 1687 the brothers Ioannikii and Sofronii Likhud (that is, the Greeks Ioannikios and Sophronios Leichoudes) founded the Slavo-Graeco-Latin Academy in premises constructed for the purpose.[17] The appearance and growth of institutionalized education are an indicative context for our four key strands in the immediate prehistory of the culture of Russian.

The first strand is visual,[18] and it is characterized by two seemingly opposite tendencies: on the one hand, a kind of fetishization of form, a belief in a direct relationship between appearance and substance; and, on the other hand, a distancing of form (letter form, word form, text form) as an artefact – polyvalent, beautiful, cryptic, expressive, rather than simply informative or correct.

Church Slavonic was a sacred language. It is not surprising that, over the centuries, its custodians were solicitous about how it was presented. There were periods of heightened attention to the culture of forms such as the shapes of letters and the spelling of words, periods of what Viktor Zhivov has called 'de-adaptation', or attempts to cleanse the language of accretion and restore pristine form.[19] The most explosive episode of de-adaptation – explosive because of the reaction to it – occurred in Moscow in the mid-seventeenth century. Patriarch Nikon (1605–1681) initiated a process of the 'correction' of devotional texts. The was the catalyst for a schism in the Russian church that continues to this day.[20] Nikon claimed that he was cleansing the texts of corrupt accretions by collating them with early Church Slavonic manuscripts and with the corresponding texts in Greek. The schismatics (Old Believers, Old Ritualists) saw his work as a diabolical corruption of true tradition. Among the contentious issues were ritual practices such as whether one should make the sign of the cross with two fingers or with three; but they included disagreements over spelling. For example, in Nikon's reforms, the name of Jesus was written with two 'I's at the beginning (Iisus, reflecting the Greek spelling); for the schismatics the only correct version of Christ's name was Isus. The problem was exacerbated by technology. In medieval manuscript culture, a certain amount of orthographic variability was inevitable and was impossible to monitor in detail. Nikon fixed and distributed the authorized texts in print. Indeed, the Nikonian reforms were a landmark in establishing print as a medium of cultural authority in Russia.

The other type of visual objectification of language was aesthetic. Again, attention to the aesthetics of lettering was not in itself new. There was a strong medieval tradition of elegant form, of decorative and sometimes figuratively illustrative (historiated) initials. A style of interwoven lettering called *viaz'* was common in manuscript headpieces, whence it migrated to a broad range of luxury inscribed objects in the sixteenth and seventeenth centuries. Though formed of letters, *viaz'* was not meant to be easily deciphered. It was somewhere between cryptography and purely decorative graphic design; a sign of lettering rather than letters as signs. Here, too, however, one can observe a qualitative shift over the course of the seventeenth century. This can be illustrated by contrasting materials from both ends of the century. In 1604 the scribe Fedor Basov produced an extraordinary manuscript. It consisted entirely of alphabets and specimens of letter forms (illus. 1).[21] In principle, it was functional: it was a kind of reference work, providing a comprehensive range of examples for use by other scribes. So: its variations on the letter 'L' (illus. 2) consist of

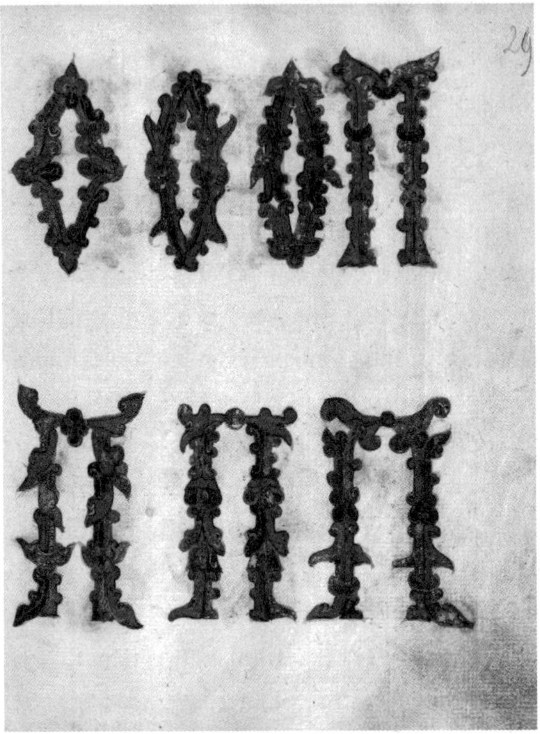

1 Specimen alphabets from a manuscript by Fedor Basov, 1604: variants of the letters 'O' and 'P'.

a long sequence of syllables beginning with 'l' in cursive scripts, preceded by a monumental encryption of the name for the letter: *liudi*. Cursive (*skóropis'*) developed in Muscovy, mainly in administrative documents, especially over the course of the sixteenth and seventeenth centuries. A characteristic feature is indeed the wide range of forms for the same letter, both in itself and in various combinations.[22] The four letters of the word (люди) are interlaced in a way that, at first sight, looks like an abstract graphic design. In fact it is a kind of monogram, whose de-encryption is in the colour scheme: focus on the lines in the separate colours, and it turns out that each represents a single, quite legible letter of the word.

Despite the potential practicality of such specimens as a guide to producing manuscripts, it is difficult to escape the impression that Basov's calligraphic contortions went far beyond the professional needs of scribes, as he delighted in abundant display itself. Out of context, one might think it almost Baroque in spirit.[23] Indeed, it foreshadows Baroque visuality of the later seventeenth century – the difference being that the latter made no pretence at mundane functionality. In 1667, for example, the prolific court poet Simeon Polotskii (1629–1680) prepared a special manuscript of a cycle of poems, *The Russian Eagle*, for presentation to the tsar's family. In addition to the elegantly penned verses, he included letter-pictures: forty lines of verse written out as a continuous ribbon that twists around itself in the shape of a heart; a picture of the Russian eagle (symbol of the state and its ruler) surrounded by a representation of the sun that consists of 48 rays, each of which contains a word indicating the many virtues that shine forth from the eagle-tsar (illus. 3), a kind of graphic sign of a sun-king, contemporary with Louis XIV.[24] From the 1690s, with an even closer resemblance to Basov's alphabets, there are the openly ludic multiple letter forms in the primer of the poet and

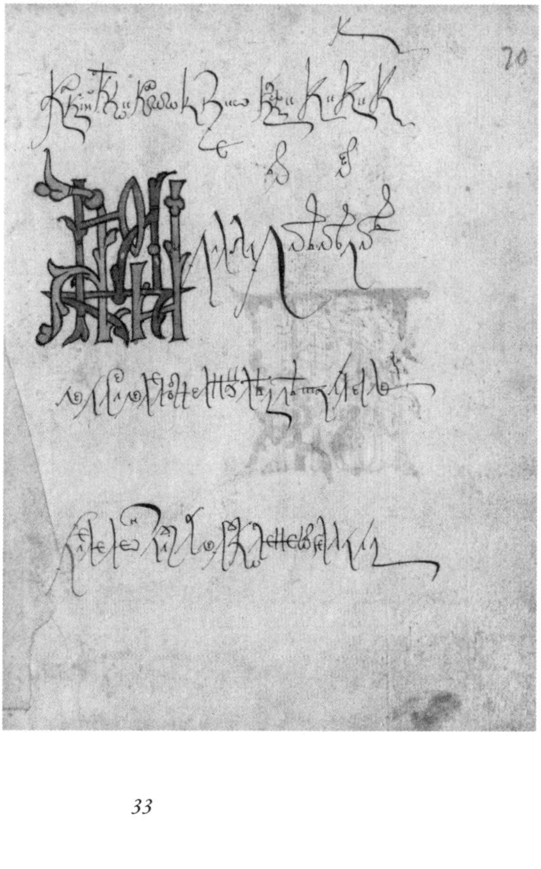

2 Specimen alphabets from a manuscript by Fedor Basov, 1604: variations on the letter 'L', and a quasi-cryptographic design for the name of the letter.

3 *The Russian Eagle*, manuscript by Simeon Polotskii, 1667.

educator Karion Istomin (1640–1718). This was first produced in manuscript for the royal children, and then in multiple copies as an engraved book. Each page of Istomin's primer presents one letter of the alphabet and includes illustrations of objects whose names began with that letter, some verses about the letter, and a string of examples of different ways in which the letter might be written, sometimes as many as twenty variants (not unlike Fedor Basov's manuscript of specimens) (illus. 4).[25]

4 Variations on the letter 'Iu', from the alphabet book (*bukvar'*) of Karion Istomin, 1690s.

By the end of the seventeenth century, therefore, in the Church Slavonic tradition, letters could be essentialized as bearers of intrinsic meaning, but they were also being heavily aestheticized as material for cultural creativity.

The second strand in the emerging culture of language was rhetorical. As an example, we can consider one form of structured rhetoric: verse. Church Slavonic had a strong tradition of practical rhetoric – that is, of rhetoric that was embedded in textual and performative tradition, if not in formal theory and training. Church Slavonic rhetoric could also include much that was in a broad sense poetic, but little or no formal verse. It could be rhythmic and assonantal (mainly through the repetition of identical syntactic structures), without being consistently metrical or rhyming. The tradition of formally structured verse developed from the early seventeenth century.[26] Typically, verses were put together in rhyming couplets, made from lines with regular numbers of syllables. By the late seventeenth century, verses can be found in many contexts: in correspondence, in prefaces and dedications to printed books, in captions to illustrations, in cycles of poems produced for special occasions, in commemorative inscriptions. Verses ranged from terse aphoristic couplets through to major compositions of several thousand lines.[27] Verse was also prominent in a new area of elite entertainment: theatre. Court theatre in Moscow dates from the early 1670s, and the most substantial surviving text, which is based on the biblical book of Esther, is partially written in verse.[28] Examples of verse 'school drama' – a form that reached Moscow with curricula from Ruthenia – include plays on the themes of the Prodigal Son, and on Nebuchadnezzar, by Simeon Polotskii.[29] Polotskii was the most prominent of several seventeenth-century versifiers who, in contrast to the often anonymous authors of the earlier Church Slavonic tradition, signed themselves as individuals and used verse as a display of personal literary accomplishment.

The third strand was parody (also, of course, a type of rhetorical device). Parody creates a mismatch between form and its conventionally expected content. For example, the *Liturgy to a Tavern* (*Sluzhba kabaku*) was written in the form of a service for Vespers. In its overall structure, as well as in its style and devices, it masqueraded as a conventional piece of Church Slavonic writing – except that its subject, drunkenness, was the very opposite of pious devotion. Another satirical text, purporting to be an exposé of the misdeeds of a priest named Sava as written by one of his trainees, included a parody of a liturgical hymn that in fact catalogued Sava's vices. Parody was a new (in Russia) form of the manipulation of language, in which the sacred tongue was used to undermine itself. Like the visual games, and like the emergence of verse, parody distances language, holds it up for inspection and turns it from a means of direct expression into an object for cultural reflection.

The fourth strand was grammatical. In order to use a language, one does not necessarily have to engage in the systematic study of its grammar. Church Slavonic was a learned register, but for much of its history it was most widely familiarized through habit and practice rather than through analysis. A 'grammatical approach' to language became more prominent and controversial in the mid-seventeenth century.[30] In the textual reforms that provoked the schism, Patriarch Nikon's leading translators and correctors had a formal training in grammar and a systematic approach to language. Among the most notable, for example, was Epifanii Slavinetskii (*c.* 1600–1675), another scholar with a Jesuit-style education, who had been brought to Moscow from Ruthenia. Besides his work on translation, Epifanii compiled a Greek–Slavonic–Latin lexicon.[31] His epitaph, written at the start of the eighteenth century, calls him 'a man greatly learned in grammar and rhetoric'.[32] Indeed, grammar became a topic of argument on *both* sides of the argument about Nikon's reforms, as each belittled the accomplishments of the other: according to a prominent schismatic, Nikon's scholarly textual reformers had 'no understanding of grammar whatsoever'.[33]

Grammar had not conventionally figured in the basic study of Church Slavonic. Elementary alphabet books, as well as more extensive primers, were the most frequently reprinted products of the Moscow Print Yard in the seventeenth century.[34] However, they were generally brief guides to reading, not textbooks of grammar. Nevertheless, through the seventeenth century there were signs of an emerging culture of formal grammar. The 1634 and 1637 printed primers of Vasilii Burtsov contained, besides the usual alphabets and syllabaries, information on the conjugation of verbs and the declension of nouns, following precedents from earlier primers printed in Ruthenia.[35] Elementary Church Slavonic elicited some curiosity even outside Russia. A brief primer (without grammar) was printed in Sweden in the late 1630s or early 1640s under the title *Alfabetum rutenorum*. It consisted of specimen alphabets, syllabic exercises and a few religious texts in Church Slavonic, with Swedish translations in parallel columns.[36] This was one of a cluster of booklets printed in Stockholm by the German type-founder Peter von Selow, who was invited to Sweden specifically for the purpose of creating a Cyrillic typeface.[37] The first Muscovite version of a detailed grammar of Church Slavonic was published in 1648. It was adapted from the grammar of Meletii Smotrytskyi, first published in what is now Vievis in Lithuania in 1619 – a product of western and central European grammatical thinking. In the latter part of the century, leading bookmen produced more substantial primers. In 1679 Simeon Polotskii printed a 320-page primer, whose prototype was perhaps intended for the seven-year-old future tsar Peter I. Karion Istomin's shorter primer of 1694 is remarkable not just for its multiple illustrations of letter forms (in various scripts including Latin and Greek), but for the fact that its preface stated that it was aimed at the education of girls as well as boys, women as well as men.[38] Two years later Istomin produced a larger and more conventional primer in two hundred pages.

All these schoolbooks by the learned elite were littered with syllabic verses. Indeed, the introductory verses addressed to the young reader in Burtsov's primer of 1637 – in rhyming couplets, though not isosyllabic – were the first formal rhymed verses in Russia to appear in print.[39] All of the authors were heavily involved not just in the world of print culture in general but in the practical business of printing. The sequence reached a kind of culmination in 1701, with the appearance of the 318-page trilingual (Slavonic, Greek and Latin) primer by Fedor Polikarpov (*c.* 1670–1731), which drew on several of its predecessors while producing something quite new in Russia.[40] Polikarpov himself had been one of the earliest students at the Slavo-Graeco-Latin Academy, and he eventually became the director of the Moscow Print Yard. Polikarpov's work was designed for children learning all three of these book-based languages. The rigorous method of instruction is shown in one of the illustrations, above verses on the importance of diligent study (illus. 5). The primer included extensive Greek and Slavonic syllabaries, as well as specimen texts with Church Slavonic, Latin and Greek in parallel columns,

5 The discipline of learning to read and write: from the primer of Fedor Polikarpov, 1701.

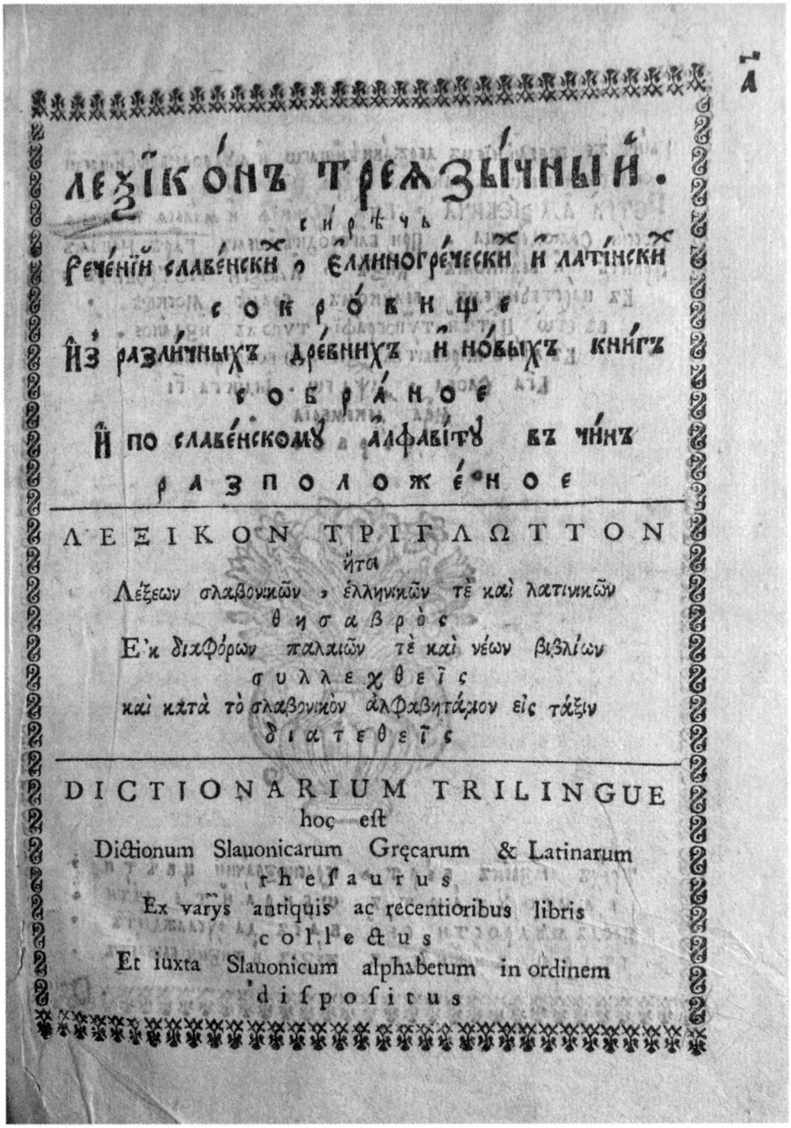

DICTIONARIUM TRILINGUE
hoc est
Dictionum Slauonicarum Græcarum & Latinarum
thesaurus
Ex varys antiquis ac recentioribus libris
collectus
Et iuxta Slauonicum alphabetum in ordinem
dispositus

6 Fedor Polikarpov, *Trilingual Lexicon* (1704), title page.

and word lists. Three years later Polikarpov published a companion volume: a trilingual lexicon in around 750 pages (illus. 6).[41] Together, Polikarpov's primer and lexicon were by some way the most ambitious published guides to language and languages to have appeared in Russia.

Such, in outline, were the four strands in the prehistory of the culture of language that merged over the second half of the seventeenth century. Woven around the language of prestigious book culture, Church Slavonic – albeit in the sometimes heavily hybridized register that had evolved locally – to an extent unprecedented in Russia they brought language itself into culture as an object of representation, discussion and dispute, analysis, defamiliarization, manipulation and systematic education.

'Russian' before Russian

Where, in all of this, was the Russian language? It is all but invisible. Phonologists and morphologists might posit structural features, but people do not speak morphology or phonology; they speak words and phrases and idioms and nuances. A remarkable lexicographical project, devised in the early 1960s and still in progress at the end of the first quarter of the twenty-first century, tries to reconstruct the vocabulary of 'the everyday Russian language' of Muscovy of the sixteenth and seventeenth centuries. According to the theory, this is the vocabulary of the 'supradialectal system of conversational speech'.[42] The words of this hypothetical conversational register, that supposedly transcends the diversity of locality, are inevitably extracted from written sources, most of which are bookish in nature. The result is a monumental multi-volume dictionary of a kind of 'everyday Russian language' that may never have existed as such.

If early modern 'Russian' is elusive (or uncomfortably hypothetical) even with all the resources of modern academic historical linguistics, imagine putting the question 'what is Russian?' to witnesses at the time – say, in the late seventeenth and early eighteenth centuries. What did *they* have in mind when they referred to a Russian language? In the previous section we looked at strands of a changing and more open culture of language that was broadly within the tradition of Church Slavonic. That does not mean that the concept of 'Russian' did not exist; nor does it mean that nobody used elements of a linguistic register that we would today recognize as Russian. But there was no consensus about what it was, or what it should be, or what it should be *for*. What did 'Russian' mean before schools and academies took control of its definitions and descriptions? There were several answers. We can illustrate the range with three prominent examples. They were not directly in dialogue with each other, since they were produced in different places for different purposes, several decades apart (the gap from each to the next was approximately twenty years). Yet between them they nicely frame the field of possibilities.

'I love my native Russian language' (*liubliu svoi russkii prirodnyi iazyk*), declared our first witness, the archpriest Avvakum (1621–1682), in the preface (or perhaps afterword) to the final version of his account of his own life, written in the mid-1670s.[43] A leading and charismatic figure in the schism of the Russian church, and an indefatigable Old Believer polemicist, in 1682 Avvakum was burned to death in a log cabin in remote northern exile. And indeed, Avvakum's autobiography – which, in the light of his subsequent martyrdom, has acquired the aura of an auto-hagiography – is noted for its pithy colloquialisms. So, is Avvakum, already in the 1670s, proclaiming the status of vernacular Russian? While contesting the hegemony of the official hierarchy of the church, was he also contesting the hegemony of its official language of culture, Church Slavonic? This might be an obvious inference, but only if the quotation is taken out of context. In fact, however, Avvakum's point (and his practice) is different. He continues: 'I am not accustomed to adorning my speech with philosophical verses . . . God does not seek from us the Latin language, or Greek, or Hebrew, or any other . . . therefore I am not concerned with eloquence and do not belittle my Russian language.' Avvakum takes up the same theme in an aside to Tsar Aleksei Mikhailovich: 'say, in the Russian language, "Lord, have mercy on me, a sinner", and forget about *Kyrie eleison*! That's what the Hellenes say. Spit on them. You, Mikhailovich, are a Russian (*rusak*), not a Greek. Speak in your native Russian language . . . God loves us no less than the Greeks.'[44]

Avvakum's objection is not to Church Slavonic, but to Greek, and Greek-inspired learning. In fact, he does not distinguish Russian from Church Slavonic.[45] The passage continues: '[God] gave us letters in our own language, through St Cyril and his brother.' This implies that, for Avvakum, 'my native Russian language' *included* Church Slavonic. His own writing supports this view. Alongside the colloquialisms, much of his autobiography drew heavily on Church Slavonic vocabulary and grammar. To modern sensibilities this can feel incongruous: an extreme version of stylistic hybridity. For Avvakum, it was all one. Avvakum can be depicted as both behind his time and ahead of his time. In a sense, his attitude echoes the maxim of a chronicler from early Rus: that 'the Slav tongue and the Rus tongue are one'.[46] On the other hand, Avvakum seems to foreshadow the notion of an integral 'Slaveno-Russian' (Slavenorussian) language (although he does not use the term) that, as we shall see, became almost axiomatic in the mid-eighteenth century.[47] But in no way should he be seen as advocating Russian *as distinct from* Church Slavonic.

Avvakum would have detested our second witness: Heinrich Wilhelm Ludolf (1655–1712). A German who spent much of his later life in England, Ludolf was in Russia from January 1693 to June 1694. His main passion was for evangelism (he was one of the founders of the Society for the Promotion of Christian Knowledge),[48] but he was also a keen linguist, whose most celebrated work was his *Grammatica russica*, printed in Oxford in 1696 (illus. 7). By contrast with Avvakum, Ludolf did make a clear distinction between Russian and Slavonic. The distinction is encapsulated in an aphorism from his preface: 'among them [the Russians] it is said that Russian is for speaking, and Slavonic is for writing (*apud illos dicitur, loquendum est Russice, et scribendum est Slavonice*).'[49] This was his justification for producing a grammar. Ludolf's book was the first printed grammar of Russian: a grammar of the spoken language, for the benefit of foreign visitors such as himself. Ludolf was aware that the aphoristic contrast was not absolute. Hybridization was possible. For example, he states that, since

HENRICI WILHELMI LUDOLFI
GRAMMATICA RUSSICA
QUÆ CONTINET
Non tantum præcipua fundamenta
RUSSICÆ LINGUÆ,
Verum etiam
Manuductionem quandam
AD
GRAMMATICAM SLAVONICAM.
Additi sunt in forma dialogorum modi loquendi communiores, Germanice æque ac Latine explicati, in gratiam eorum qui linguam Latinam ignorant.
Una cum
BREVI VOCABULARIO RERUM NATURALIUM.

OXONII,
E THEATRO SHELDONIANO, A. D. MDCXCVI.

7 Heinrich Wilhelm Ludolf, *Grammatica russica* (Oxford, 1696), title page.

Slavonic was the language of religion and learning, those wishing to appear more learned might pepper their speech with Church Slavonic. However, Ludolf reports that such pretentiousness in spoken discourse would by some be considered ridiculous.[50] For him, the exception proves the rule. By contrast with Avvakum, in whose perception the relation of Russian to Church Slavonic was unitary whether in speech or in writing, in Ludolf's perception it was binary.

After a dissident archpriest and a foreign missionary, our third witness is the tsar himself, Peter I (1672–1725). In 1716 Fedor Polikarpov – author of the trilingual primer and lexicon and head of the Print Yard – offered for Peter's inspection the draft of his translation of the *Geographia generalis* by Bernhardus Varenius. This was a huge work, and to translate it was an enormous labour. In his preface, Polikarpov proudly explained how he had striven not merely to convey the sense (he uses the word *sens*[!]) of the original, but to reflect its aesthetic dignity, 'the loftiness and beauty of the author's style'. And, in order to achieve this, he had deliberately avoided the 'common Russian dialect' (*obshchenarodnyi dialekt rossiiskii*), but instead had attempted 'as far as possible to preserve the rules (*reguly*) of grammatical order'.[51] Peter was not happy. He wrote to Polikarpov: 'I am sending to you the *Geography* in your translation, which, whether through lack of skill or some other reason, is very bad. Correct it; but not in high Slavonic words, but in the simple Russian language.' The contrast could hardly be plainer. Despite parading some modish foreign imports (*sens*, *reguly*), Polikarpov still assumed that the language of learned writing should be Church Slavonic. This was precisely what Peter wanted to undermine. He was carving out a space for secular culture, and did not want it recolonized by devotional culture through linguistic inertia. Polikarpov's preface declared that he had deliberately avoided the 'common Russian dialect'. Peter turned traditional prestige on its head.

What did this mean in practice? What was the substance of the revisions that Polikarpov introduced after Peter's intervention? Most of the changes were morphological and syntactic. For example, the old-style aorist and imperfect past tenses were replaced with the -l- form past tense that distinguished gender and number, but not person; the old final '*i*' disappeared from infinitives and from second-person singular forms of verbs in the present tense (i.e. *-ti*>*-t'*, *-shi*>*-sh'*). There were also regular modifications to participial forms and constructions, and to pronouns, conjunctions and particles, including a range of lexical substitutions (for example, *izhe*>*kto* or *kotoryi*; *obache*>*odnako zh*; *iako*>*kak*; omission of *ubo*). This was not an isolated episode. There is evidence that Peter repeatedly intervened in translations in a similar way.[52] The outcome, in Viktor Zhivov's formulation, was to move towards a language of learned books without the traditional linguistic markers of learned bookishness.

How can we suggest that there was as yet no such thing as Russian if the tsar himself so plainly asserts that there was? We need to be more specific. What did Peter actually mean when he said he wanted Polikarpov to render his translation into the 'simple' or 'plain' (*prostoi*) Russian language? It might be natural to assume that he wanted the language of the learned text to be based on the language of speech; that he was breaking down the dichotomy asserted by Ludolf's informants: Russian should be not *just* the language of speech, but a language of writing. However, Peter went on to clarify his demand. He was not asking Polikarpov to imitate the vernacular speech of simple folk. On the contrary, his model was an existing written register: 'use the words of the Ambassadorial Chancery' (*Posol'skogo prikazu upotrebi slova*).[53] Presumably Peter reckoned that this register would be more widely comprehensible, but for him it had the additional virtue of being secular, not Church Slavonic, not redolent of devotional book culture. The new scholarly learning should not be permeated with the whiff of incense. The practical work of the Ambassadorial and other chanceries was indeed conducted in a written but non-bookish register that drew more heavily on the vernacular.[54] For Peter, that was its 'simplicity'. It may be relevant that in Ruthenia, where many of Peter's literati had been educated, the term 'simple' or 'plain' language (*prosta mova*) designated a written register used mainly for administration. But regardless of whether or not Peter's appeal to the 'simple Russian language' was a hidden Ruthenianism (one which would have been well understood by Polikarpov), the underlying point is that, in place of the linguistic authority of the church, Peter prescribed the linguistic authority of the state.

Thus, our three witnesses imply three radically distinct views of what 'Russian' was or ought to be. For Avvakum, Russian and Church Slavonic were in essence the same thing, and this was his native language by contrast with anything foreign. For Ludolf's informants, Russian was a spoken register by contrast with the Church Slavonic written register. For Peter I, 'simple' Russian was the written register of his state administration, by contrast with the written register of ecclesiastical learning. The three witnesses may not agree with each other, but in their disagreements they map out the ground.

However, the significance of their utterances was not purely linguistic. It relates to the *culture* (or cultures) of language. Whatever one thinks of Peter's notion of the 'simple Russian language', his criticism of Polikarpov reflects his wider cultural project: to differentiate clearly, on all levels – verbal and visual – between devotional culture and secular culture. His preference for the language of the Ambassadorial Chancery looks limited and eccentric in retrospect, but the underlying point was sharper and more far-reaching: it was no longer acceptable to assume that linguistic and cultural status resided in Church Slavonic; secular culture should develop a language for itself, with its own dignity and prestige.

Peter's concern to delineate a secular culture of language was not restricted to vocabulary and style. It extended to the visual representation of language: to the very shapes of letters. In 1708 Peter introduced a new typeface, known as his 'civil type', specifically for the printing of secular texts.[55] Civil type was partly derived from western European humanistic typefaces, but was also close to some styles of contemporary handwriting used in administration. Visually, therefore, it contrived to be a signal both of Westernization and of administrative continuity. The first book printed in the civil typeface was a work on geometry. The implication was clear: books of science should not look like books of theology – just as Peter later insisted to Fedor Polikarpov that a translation of a book about geography should not be rendered in the same register of language as, say, a collection of the lives of saints.

No Russian ruler has been so thoroughly mythologized as Peter I (illus. 8), Peter 'the Great' (the epithet spread abroad even in his own lifetime). He became an emblem of radical change, the man who, in conventional representation, transformed Russia's cultural orientation, visual appearance, modes of governance, global status, historical

8 Jean-Marc Nattier, *Peter I*, 1717, oil on canvas.

path, destiny. In the imagery of *The Bronze Horseman*, a poem of 1833 by Aleksandr Pushkin (1799–1837) and inspired by the 1782 equestrian statue by Étienne Falconet, Peter 'raised Russia onto its hind legs', and 'cut a window onto Europe'. Born in 1672, he became joint tsar with his half-brother Ivan in 1682 (at first under the regency of his elder half-sister Sofiia). He was sole ruler from 1696 until his death in 1725. He built Russia's first fleet, founded a new capital city, travelled through Europe in search of technical knowledge, and recruited huge numbers of foreign engineers, architects, shipwrights, doctors and scholars in order to realize his goals. His innovations were eclectic, both in micro-management and in global vision: whether taxing beards, or experimenting in dentistry, or imposing western European styles of dress, or importing classical statuary, or marking his military victories with parades through triumphal arches adorned with classical imagery and inscriptions, or establishing Russia's first printed newspaper, or assembling his cabinet of curiosities, or founding the Academy of Sciences, or restructuring the state administration by abolishing the agglomeration of disparate chanceries (*prikazy*) and replacing them with small number of centrally coordinated 'Colleges', or declaring, in 1721, that his tsardom was now, officially, an empire. Peter has come to represent a kind of seismic fault line in history, the divide between epochs: Russian history is either 'pre-Petrine', 'Petrine' or 'post-Petrine'.[56]

Pendulums of interpretation swing. Historians contest the received image of Peter's achievements and significance. 'Great man' constructs of history become unfashionable, conventional claims about radical change are challenged by counter-claims about underlying continuities. On the one hand, many of the innovations attributed to Peter had earlier roots, developing from the second half of the seventeenth century. On the other hand, Petrine reforms were often skin-deep, changes in appearance more than in substance. Rather than being the pivot around which Russian history turns, Peter becomes just one phase in Russia's long early modernity.[57]

Among the policies often attributed to Peter is the secularization of culture. This is misleading. Peter did not ban the liturgy, or turn churches into concert halls or military barracks, or declare God to be a myth, or appropriate vast tracts of monastic lands. The centrepiece of his new city of St Petersburg was a monumentally prominent church – albeit demonstratively with a western-style steeple instead of the traditional Russian-style domes. Rather than secularization as such, Peter's policy was the rapid expansion of the secular sphere of high-status culture, and its demarcation *as* secular. The expansion of the secular meant that devotional culture, though not in itself secularized, was reduced to a smaller role in the overall ecology of elite culture. The visible demarcation of the secular *as* secular accentuated the distinction between the two. So also in the culture of language: Peter shifted the balance of linguistic status.

This was fundamental to the crafting of an authoritative Russian language but it was not in itself sufficient. For the next stage in its cultivation, a Russian language of culture needed a new cultural purpose. Administration and education were not enough. By demanding that their register be 'simple', Peter made a virtue of accessibility, but the relevant areas of usage provided limited scope for suppleness, subtlety and expressiveness. Many of the prerequisites for a Russian secular language of culture were in place, but the most productive stage in the crafting of it began only when the focus shifted to a new function for it: literature.

2

A Language Worthy of Empire

In the late seventeenth and early eighteenth centuries Russian was not widely acknowledged, even within Russia, as a language of high cultural status. It was not treated as a language whose dignity and prestige were in any way comparable to the established ancient and modern languages of western European literature, learning and polite conversation. On a scale of esteem, few, if any, would have ranked Russian remotely close to German or French, let alone Greek or Latin. Mid-century scholars and writers were on a mission to close this gap, to raise Russian to the place worthy of its potential, to a status that befitted the language of an empire among empires. The project was principally enabled through two institutions: the patronage of the imperial court and the scholarship of the Academy of Sciences (the latter founded by Peter I in 1724); and it was principally realized through two forms of language-focused activity: grammatical and lexicographical systematization, and the production (and fractious discussion) of exemplary works of literature. The mood and movement that provided the cultural frame of reference was, broadly speaking, Classicism. As for the language itself: a characteristic feature of the mid-eighteenth-century project is its conceptualization of the relationship between Church Slavonic and East Slavonic traditions. Instead of representing the 'Slavonic' and 'Russian' elements either as functionally distinct opposites (like the informants of Wilhelm Ludolf) or as essentially the same thing (as implied by Avvakum), they reimagined Slavonic and Russian as overlapping zones on a linguistic continuum, which was sometimes characterized as the 'Slavenorussian' language.

Here, as often, it is important to distinguish, on the one hand, the cultural conceptualizations of Russian as it ought to be from, on the other hand, any historically systematic analysis of Russian as it actually was.[1] Thus, for example, a curious consequence of this scheme was that it allowed no space for non-Slavonic components of the language. Despite the strong western European presence permeating mid-eighteenth-century elite culture, including literary culture, and despite the flow of foreign words into educated usage, the 'Slavenorussian' image of the literary language had, in theory, no means of accommodating imported vocabulary.

Literature, 'Slavenorussian' and the Authority of Genre

Some of the groundwork for Classicist approaches to literature appeared in the Russian Empire somewhat earlier than Classicism gained a foothold in Russia itself. For example, in 1705 Feofan Prokopovich (1681–1736), then a teacher at the Mohyla Academy in Kyiv, composed an *Ars poetica* – in Latin. A decade later Prokopovich was summoned to St Petersburg, where he became the leading rhetorical eulogist and ideologist for Peter I. The genre was ultimately derived from the *Ars poetica* of the Roman poet Horace. Almost as authoritative in Russian Classicism was the French treatise *L'Art poétique*, written by Nicolas Boileau in 1674. However, anyone wanting to transfer such lessons and exemplars to literary culture in Russia and in Russian quickly came up against a devastatingly awkward fact: the lack of literature to which it might be applied. Classicist poetics provided a framework for an *idea* of Russian *belles-lettres*, but its substance was yet to be created.

The interplay of idea and nascent substance can be illustrated through the contributions of three of its protagonists from the generation after Feofan Prokopovich: Vasilii Trediakovskii (1703–1769), Aleksandr Sumarokov (1717–1777) and Mikhail Lomonosov

(1711–1765). All three were both theorists and practitioners: writers *of* literature and *about* literature. In the very small space of mid-eighteenth-century Russian literary culture, they repeatedly crossed paths and swords with one another. Their disputes could be bitter and hence entertaining. However, they argued because they fundamentally agreed about what was worth arguing about. Though their activities converged, their backgrounds were diverse. Only one of them – Sumarokov – was born into the elite. Trediakovskii grew up in Astrakhan on the lower Volga, the son of a provincial priest. His early education was at a local Catholic school founded in 1713 by Capuchin monks from Italy. After a couple of years at the Slavo-Graeco-Latin Academy in Moscow, from 1726 to 1730 he continued his studies in western Europe, mainly in Paris. Lomonosov was the son of a peasant – a fisherman – from a village in the northern Arkhangelsk region. He received his early education from a local priest, and from his own avid reading. He remained in the village until, in December 1730, he went on foot to Moscow. There, with forged documents (it was illegal for peasants to travel far from their villages without permits), he too enrolled in the Slavo-Graeco-Latin Academy. In the second half of the 1730s he also studied abroad, but in Germany rather than France: three years at Marburg, then in Freiburg. Sumarokov, by contrast, was from the hereditary service nobility. His career was outwardly much more like what one might imagine to be stereotypical of an officer and a gentleman. Educated at the Cadet Corps, he rose up the appropriate ranks, first on the military scale (eventually becoming a brigadier), then transferring to the equivalent civil scale. Unlike both Trediakovskii and Lomonosov, he had no immersive experience either of a Russian non-gentry provincial upbringing or of life and education in western Europe.

In 1730 Vasilii Trediakovskii published a translation of Paul Tallemant's sentimental and allegorical novel of 1663, *Le Voyage de l'isle d'amour* (*Ezda v ostrov liubvi*). In the same volume he printed a selection of his own poems – thirteen in Russian, eighteen in French.

This has been taken as the emblematic initiation of a new phase in Russian writing, and in thinking about what Russian ought to be. Tallemant's allegorical journey seems to have had as much literary resonance beyond France as within it. In the 1680s it and its sequel were adapted into English verse by Aphra Behn. Indeed, by a generic coincidence, Behn, like Trediakovskii, published the *Voyage* alongside some of her own occasional poems.[2] Trediakovskii's preface articulated his apprehension that a Russian public may not yet be attuned to his approach to the language of literature and literary translation:

> I humbly beseech you, be not angry with me (those who are still devotees of the verbal profundity of Slavonism (*slavenshchizna*)), that I have translated this book not in the Slavonic language but in almost the simplest Russian speech – that in which we speak among ourselves. I have done this for the following reasons. First, the Slavonic language is, for us, the language of the church, and this book is secular. Second, in the present age the Slavonic language is very obscure, and many of us who read it do not understand it; and this book is about sweet love, so should be comprehensible to all. Third – the reason that may seem to you the most superficial, but for me is the most important: that is, that the Slavonic language now sounds harsh to my ears.[3]

This seems to echo several traditional ideas but with a fresh twist. Trediakovskii's preface includes the notion of Church Slavonic and Russian as functionally distinct registers, the contrast between ecclesiastical culture and secular culture, and the Petrine advocacy of 'simple' Russian. However, for Trediakovskii, simplicity does not derive from the written language of administration but – ostensibly – from the Russian 'that we speak among ourselves'. Trediakovskii's 'we' (despite his own provincial background) refers to an elite steeped in European culture; it is not the language of the common folk. Beyond that,

Trediakovskii declares that his criterion for choice is not merely social but *aesthetic*. On this he appeals both to the oral and to the aural: Slavonic is harsh on the ear. Elsewhere in his writings Trediakovskii regularly returned to the aesthetic contrast between 'harsh' Slavonic and 'tender' Russian (usually *nezhnyi* or *nezhneishii* – probably reflecting the French *délicat* and *élégant* respectively).[4]

This is among Trediakovskii's first programmatic statements about the language of literature, but it was by no means his last word. Over the next 25 years his views became more nuanced and complex, honed in multiple polemics with equally passionate and opinionated theorists and practitioners. He was aware that a great deal of preparatory work needed to be done if his broad programme was to become realized. In particular, writers in Russia still lacked the basic tools of the trade. On 14 March 1735 Trediakovskii gave a speech 'on the purity of the Russian language' at a conference of translators at the Academy of Sciences, urging the necessity of producing a grammar and a dictionary. This was apparently the first rhetorical address delivered at the Academy in Russian. One of its aims was to encourage the establishment of a section of the Academy with the function of overseeing language, like the French Academy. As is fitting in a formal panegyric, Trediakovskii framed his desiderata in terms of praise for the ultimate patron, the empress Anna Ioannovna (r. 1730–40). He started by representing her as the inspiration for the gathering and for his proposal: 'Gentlemen, in the blessed dominion of our great monarch Anna we have reached this joyous state that acknowledges concern for the perfection of the Russian language.'[5]

More importantly, in Trediakovskii's rhetoric, Anna herself was not just a benevolent patron; she was the very the reason why the language needed attention. In the Classicist canon of genres, the panegyric ode was in the highest category; yet the Russian language lacked the resources to praise the empress fittingly. In this speech Trediakovskii imagined languages as repositories on a scale of completeness, as vessels to be filled:

> In truth, gentlemen, the deeds and virtues of this crowned heroine are so great – as is known around the entire globe – that not even the most perfectly replete language could find words equal to the task of describing them. And what of our language? Our language, which is not only not replete, but which to this day has not even begun to be filled? Precisely for this reason we are now entrusted with the duty of bringing our language to perfection, so far as is possible, so that thus we might obtain the means, however moderate, to glorify the deeds and virtues of our sovereign empress.[6]

Trediakovskii was here addressing the problem of rhetorical resources for the purpose of imperial panegyric, but the implications of what he said were felt to be far broader, as can be seen from some of the responses to his speech. In an extensive letter to Trediakovskii, dated 18 February 1736, the historian Vasilii Tatishchev (1686–1750) expressed his joy that the subject had been raised, and gave his own thoughts on several areas in which he felt that Russian was in need of attention.[7] Among his desiderata was that 'laws should be written simply and comprehensibly, in the language that its subjects speak, so that even the very simplest man might correctly understand the meaning of the law and the will of the lawgiver.'[8] Here Tatishchev picks up on the notion that simplicity should be grounded in speech. However, unlike Trediakovskii in the preface to *Voyage to the Isle of Love*, he explicitly refers to common speech, the speech of 'the very simplest man'.

Trediakovskii's longest publication on language was his book *A Dialogue between a Foreigner and a Russian on Ancient and New Orthography and All That Pertains to This Matter*, printed at the Academy of Sciences in 1748.[9] On the title page the author declares his qualification for the task as a 'Professor of Eloquence' (*professor elokventsii*). The *Dialogue* digs deep into history while advocating what its author regarded as a simpler and more rational version of

Russian orthography than was current. It had little resonance except to enhance Trediakovskii's growing reputation for pedantry. From the late 1740s he was engaged in almost continual dispute about technical questions of versification, especially about the propriety and semantics of metre and genre. His principal antagonists and critics were Lomonosov and, in particular, Sumarokov.

Aleksandr Petrovich Sumarokov was a versatile writer and translator, an innovator (in the Russian context) across a wide spectrum of genres, especially in verse.[10] His poetic forms ranged from the lyrical to the epic and included sonnets, epigrams and madrigals. For the theatre he wrote comedy and tragedy (his devotees represented him as Russia's Racine). In 1748 he published his version of *Hamlet*. Though heavily modified (the cast of characters is much reduced, and Hamlet and Ophelia do not die), this was the first version in Russian of any play by Shakespeare.[11] And he was the author of fables. For much of this there was little or no precedent, little or no tradition either of how to mould the relevant genres to Russian, or of how to mould Russian to the respective genres. Sumarokov's ideas about how it should be done were honed in practice, not through theory. He was notoriously irascible and cantankerous. He quarrelled with everybody. The subject of his arguments was, as often as not, language; and many of his sharpest polemics were themselves formulated in verse. He preferred demonstration to detailed explanation. For example, rather than provide a critical analysis of his contemporaries' poems, he would sometimes rewrite them in his own preferred manner – in effect, translations from Russian into Russian.[12]

In November 1748 the Academy of Sciences published Sumarokov's 'Two Epistles, the First about the Russian Language, the Second about Versification'.[13] The first Epistle consisted of 142 lines of verse, the second was much longer, at 422 lines. The tone was satirical. In places this makes the text somewhat esoteric for a modern reader, who needs footnotes to identify the targets of the author's barbed comments, but the gist is accessible. Literature, for Sumarokov, followed a defined range of forms and model authors. It was shaped by the Classicist canon of genres, each with its appropriate style. In the second Epistle he touches on pastoral poetry, the ode, the epic, tragedy, comedy (plus comic heroic poetry, in which 'high words' describe 'low deeds'), satire, fable, epistle, eclogues, the sonnet, the ballad, the rondo and songs. As for the model authors: Sumarokov shows off his formal virtuosity by listing, in the course of just nine lines, thirty-four names – mainly the ancients, but including Rousseau, Milton, Shakespeare (*Shekespir*, scanned as three syllables) and Pope – in a way that fits them all into his version of Alexandrine metre: iambic hexameters with a caesura after the third foot of each line, in rhyming couplets whose rhyme schemes alternated between the 'masculine' (ending in the stressed syllable of an iambic foot) and the 'feminine' (with the addition of an unstressed syllable after the sixth foot). Indeed, Sumarokov's authorial stance was based on a consistent contrast between his own skill and talent and the mediocrity and ignorance of others. Poetry is hard work, but mere proficiency produces 'fabricated nonsense' (*sopletennyi vzdor*) dressed up as verse.[14]

Behind the flippancy there was a linguistic and aesthetic agenda. Sumarokov's starting point is the assertion that Russian is a worthy and appropriate vessel for fine literature, but that its potential has not been realized. 'Two Epistles' opens and closes with this theme. Near the start of the first Epistle Sumarokov declares, 'We need a language such as there was among the Greeks and among the Romans . . . Our language has enough words in it,/ But not enough writers using it'; and 'Our language is sweet, pure, sumptuous and rich.' The second Epistle ends with the plain claim that 'Our splendid language is capable of anything.'[15]

Sumarokov's notion of 'our' language – or, specifically, of Russian as a vehicle for literature – has four features. First, he echoes the vocabulary of early Trediakovskii in demanding *speech-like simplicity*. Sumarokov rejects high-flown rhetoric that confuses obscurity with profundity, and he criticizes those who 'perceive a writer's incomprehensible style as beauty'. We should write as simply as we speak (*Kak prosto govorim, tak prosto iz"iasnenno*).[16] However, simplicity should not equate to artlessness. Speech itself must be cultivated. It should 'include rhetorical ornament that is not customary in simple words'.

Second, and developing this point, Sumarokov introduces (also like Trediakovskii) an aesthetic criterion: taste. He condemns a writer who 'possessing coarse taste, offers society his idle labours as if sweet fruits'. Taste, in this metaphorical sense, was a relative neologism in Russia, an emanation of equivalent metaphorical usage in French (that is, a Gallicism). As we shall see in the following chapter, 'taste' (*vkus*) was to become a totemic criterion in literary and linguistic discussion in the latter part of the century.[17]

Third, Sumarokov rejects the binary opposition of Slavonic and Russian. They are not separate languages. His argument is not linguistic as such but rests on what Sumarokov reckons to be the requirements of Russian itself. He acknowledges that Slavonic can be difficult and hence can fall foul of the requirement for 'simplicity'; but he nevertheless insists, 'It is the same language [as Russian]. If it were to be a different language – as you believe, merely because you don't understand it – then what is left for Russian?' In other words, Russian needs Slavonic. Russian is capacious *because* it includes Slavonic. Take out Slavonic, and the claims for Russian become hollow. Sumarokov is happy to exclude archaism ('If usage has eliminated *ashche*, or *tochiiu*,/ Who forces you to bring them back into the language?'),[18] but he does not equate Slavonism as such with obsolescence.

Fourth, Sumarokov stresses the vital importance of grammar. Language does not do the job by itself. It must be studied systematically. Grammatical correctness is a necessary condition and cannot be taken for granted. Labour, talent and taste are not sufficient in themselves. In places Sumarokov appears to be speaking to fellow *literati*, but there are hints that he is also targeting a younger audience of students, as he urges them to apply themselves to the basics: 'No

9 Christian-Albert Wortmann, *Mikhail Lomonosov*, 1757, engraving

one can earn praise with his writings unless he knows the grammatical properties and rules; nor can he become a writer or a poet if he does not know how to put words together correctly.'

These were ideas in the air. The themes in Sumarokov's 'Two Epistles' – genre and linguistic register, cultivated speech, taste, Slavonic and Russian as parts of an integral literary language rather than in binary opposition, the importance of grammar, the huge intrinsic but unrealized resources and potential of the Russian language – were also developed by others, not least by the third member of our representative triad of mid-century writers: Mikhail Lomonosov (illus. 9).

Lomonosov was a formidable polymath. The breadth and depth of his academic and literary accomplishments would be impressive in any context, let alone for one who grew up in a remote northern Russian village until the age of nineteen and had no formal institutional education. By the age of 34 he was professor of chemistry, also producing pioneering work on physics, astronomy, geography and geology. Outside the natural sciences, he published on history, on rhetoric, on style and genre, not to mention grammar. He was an accomplished author of, in particular, odes. He was also co-founder of Russia's first proper university (in Moscow). Here we look at his prescriptions for Russian as a language for literature. His *Russian Grammar* will be considered in the next section.

Lomonosov's best-known pronouncements on literary language appeared in his essay 'Foreword on the Usefulness of Church Books in the Russian Language', published in 1758.[19] Sumarokov had already asserted that Church Slavonic and Russian should not be split, that Slavonic was necessary for literary Russian. Lomonosov fleshed out the assertion with argument and analysis. His essay, though brief, attempted two tasks: first, to give shape and solidity to the view that Slavonic and Russian should be treated as overlapping zones in an integral linguistic system; and second, to provide a structured guide to what this might look like in practice, in the writing of literature.

Lomonosov begins his 'Foreword' by arguing that, for historical reasons, Russian was peculiarly enriched by its relationship to Church Slavonic. Since the core scriptural and devotional texts consisted mainly of translations, contact with Greek was embedded in Russia's linguistic heritage. Lomonosov contrasts this with, for example, Polish – the language of a land where the devotional tongue had always been foreign (Latin); or even with German, which, like Church Slavonic, had absorbed the riches of the ancient tongues through translation of the scriptures – but only from the Reformation (that is, much later than Church Slavonic). For Lomonosov the Church Slavonic legacy also had important sociolinguistic and political consequences: it helped to ensure the relative unity of language across the vast Russophone spaces of the empire, not divided by the presence of a priestly caste separated from the masses by its use of a foreign sacred tongue.

With its historical advantages established, Lomonosov maps the linguistic resources of literary Russian onto a structure that he presents as consisting of three 'types' of word. The first type consists of words that are common both to the ancient Slavonic texts and to current usage. The second type consists of words of Church Slavonic origin that are rare in general use but are well understood by educated people. The third category includes common Russian words that are absent from the Church Slavonic tradition. Although Lomonosov represents this as a three-part structure, his schema can equally be described as consisting of five sections, for he mentions – but excludes – two further categories, one at either end of the spectrum: obsolete Slavonic words that are no longer in use, and indecent Russian colloquialisms.

Onto this picture of a single spectrum of language with overlapping zones Lomonosov maps his prescriptions for proper literary usage. Careful use of the respective registers of language 'gives rise to three styles: high, middle, and low': 'High style' consists of 'Slavenorussian (*slavenorossiiskie*) locutions: words common to both, and not obsolete. This is the appropriate style for heroic poetry, odes, oratory in prose about important matters . . . Through this style the Russian language is superior to many contemporary European languages, in using the language of church books.'[20] 'Middle style' consists mainly of Russian words but can include the judicious use of some Church Slavonic words (though not enough as to sound pompous) and of some 'low' words (though not enough as to 'descend into vulgarity'). This would be the normal style for plays, for familiar epistles in verse, for satires, elegies and eclogues. In prose it is suitable for 'descriptions of memorable events and of noble teachings'. 'Low style' excludes Church Slavonic words and is suitable for comedies, entertaining epigrams, songs, familiar letters in prose and descriptions of ordinary events.

Lomonosov did not invent the designation 'Slavenorussian'.[21] Derived from an older designation of learned language in Ruthenia (*slovianorus'ska/slovianoros'ska mova*), it appears to be first attested in Russia in the early 1690s, in the preface to the various editions of Karion Istomin's primer, where, in effect, it designates Russian Church Slavonic.[22] In Lomonosov it is used to emphasize the distinctive richness of the shared resources of two related traditions, as asserted also (though without using the term) by Sumarokov and others. His 'Foreword' is too brief to be reckoned a theory. There is no explanation, no definition of terms, no anticipation of counter-argument. It is a succinct distillation. His main point, amplifying the assertion in Sumarokov's 'Two Epistles', is that the Church Slavonic linguistic heritage is vital if Russian itself is to fulfil its potential and achieve appropriate status as a language of literature. To reject Church Slavonic would be an act of catastrophic self-denial. Lomonosov's criteria are historical, social and aesthetic, not just etymological. He explicitly rejects trying to incorporate the totality of Church Slavonic, and embraces only those elements that it shares with vernacular Russian or that a contemporary educated person could reasonably be expected to know – just as he explicitly rejects including the totality of resources available in vernacular Russian, for a language of culture should not be vulgar.

Lomonosov's argument for 'Slavenorussian' rests on a massive oversimplification of the historic relations between Church Slavonic and East Slavonic registers. In the late seventeenth and early eighteenth centuries the contrast between Russian and Slavonic was still represented partly as morphological, to do with grammatical forms and syntactic structures. In Lomonosov's system, and for his contemporaries in the middle decades of the century, the contrast was treated mainly as lexical, to do with individual words and categories of word. A writer of high-style verses in the late seventeenth century, such as Simeon Polotskii, would use the full range of morphological past tenses: imperfects and aorists with full conjugations that differentiated first-, second- and third-person singular and plural, not to mention special forms for the dual. In 1716, when Fedor Polikarpov declared that, in his translation of Varenius's book on geography, he had striven to preserve the Latinate grammar of the original, he meant, in part, the use of traditionally conjugated verbs, which could be mapped onto Church Slavonic. When instructed to turn his Slavonic into the 'simple' Russian language, a significant part of the revision involved converting these traditional tenses into the simple past that is familiar from Russian today.[23] By mid-century, none of the major protagonists would have advocated the preservation of the old conjugations. That battle was over. Now, by contrast, Slavon*isms* tended to be identified lexically rather than grammatically. The relationship between Russian and Church Slavonic was represented not in terms the structures of language, but in terms of registers of vocabulary.

Just as one has to ask what each author meant by the Russian language or by Slavonisms, so one has to ask what they meant by literature. Literature was not an abstract or generalized concept. Lomonosov had in mind a particular literary system: specifically, the Classicist system based on a hierarchy of genres. It is no coincidence that his notion of what language should be maps so neatly onto his notion of what literature should be. He constructs a hierarchy of the resources of language that suits the hierarchical aesthetics of the genres of Classicism. In other words, his solution was entirely within its time. This was its strength and its weakness. For Lomonosov, as for Sumarokov and Trediakovskii, Classicism was the apex of European literary culture, and odes and epics were at the apex of the Classicist structure of genre. It matched a world in which the literary hierarchy reflected and reinforced the societal hierarchy. At the pinnacle, as the overarching patron and inspiration, was the empress and her court; hence the highest of Lomonosov's 'high-style' literary genres, demanding the most elevated language, were precisely those that addressed or glorified the empress and the glorious deeds of those who served her.

Lomonosov's scheme of genre-based literary language was a snug fit for its time; but it was also fragile. In the first place, it was existentially vulnerable to cultural change. If Classicism were to fall or be pushed from its pedestal, Lomonosov's scheme might find itself instantly obsolete and irrelevant. Second, Lomonosov's conception of a literary language for Russia was perilously self-contained. It admitted only the spectrum of 'Russian' and Church Slavonic, with no scope, in theory, for the assimilation of resources from elsewhere (except by translation). Lomonosov was not against the use of foreign languages and imported words in their proper contexts such as technology and scholarship. Latin and German were, after all, habitual languages of the Academy of Sciences. But his exclusion of the foreign from his account of a language fit for literature was deliberate. He explained it as an essential form of linguistic protectionism:

> Through the assiduous and careful use of our kindred Slavonic language, together with Russian, with their shared roots, we ward off the strange and barbarous absurdities that come to us from foreign languages . . . These improprieties now creep in unnoticed, through our inattentiveness to church books, and they distort the innate beauty of our own language, subjecting it to constant change and pushing it towards decline.[24]

This kind of hostility to foreign linguistic incursions into cultured Russian has resonated loudly through the nineteenth, twentieth and indeed twenty-first centuries. We will hear of it again in later chapters. It has been a battle continually fought, in a war never won. Overall, Lomonosov's system, though nicely suited to its age, was too brittle to withstand changes in fashion, let alone a shift in the social ecology of culture. Within a generation, his vision of a literary language shaped to fit the contours of a Classicist socio-literary hierarchy, backed by a prescriptive Slavenorussian purism, was comprehensively undermined. In future, the notion of a Slavenorussian language could only maintain traction across the polemical divides if it ceased to be regarded as exclusive. In a short critical essay of 1825, for example, Aleksandr Pushkin claimed that 'the Slavenorussian [here

'Slavianorussian'] language has an irrefutable pre-eminence above all European tongues.' Pushkin supported this declaration with a close paraphrase of Lomonosov's explanation of the difference between the development of Slavenorussian and the development of German.[25] However, for Pushkin, Slavenorussian, though a vital part of the language's resources, was not a term for an exclusive system. It was somewhere at the core, but it was in turn enriched (not corrupted) both by the language of the 'simple folk', and by free exploitation of the linguistic resources of others (see Chapter Four).

The Dignity of System: Grammars and Dictionaries

A respectable language of culture needed a grammar: a visible, printed grammar; not just a practical guide for foreigners, but an encapsulation of the language as an object worthy of contemplation, as a discipline, a vehicle for thought, as a guarantor of seriousness, a sign of value. Greek and Latin had millennia of grammatical tradition and were the basis of European grammatical education. Church Slavonic had grammars. Foreigners had grammars. How could Russian be a proper thing, a cultural object for its own users, if it was not represented by and for them in the form of a grammar? These were *not* the kinds of questions that troubled traditionalist bookmen in the first couple of decades of the eighteenth century. For them, Russia was not that kind of a language. In 1718, in the preface his revised translation of the *Geographia generalis* by Bernhardus Varenius, Fedor Polikarpov apologized for the fact that this version had not preserved the rules of grammar.[26] Strictly speaking, Polikarpov's words referred back to the *Latin* grammatical structures of Varenius's original, which he had tried to retain in his Church Slavonic version, but which had been sacrificed with the 'simple Russian' revisions. But the phrase is revealing. Church Slavonic was marked by having grammar, like Latin; 'simple Russian' was not.[27] From Polikarpov's apology for using a register without grammar, to the first printed grammar of Russian in Russia by a Russian, the gap stretched for almost forty years.

Before the mid-eighteenth century, printed grammars of Russian were mainly written by and for foreigners. Although they can be considered in the broader context of early modern European thinking about language,[28] their principal target readers were people for whom the vernacular would be useful for practical purposes. The earliest – Wilhelm Ludolf's *Grammatica russica* of 1696 – was meant to support missionary activity. In the early decades of the eighteenth century, grammars were produced to cater for the needs of the growing numbers of foreign residents in Russia. A short grammar for French learners was published in St Petersburg in 1730,[29] as was a grammar of German intended 'for Russian youth'.[30] A partial grammar of Russian from 1731– written in German, hence for the use of foreigners – survives in a manuscript that remained unpublished until the start of the twenty-first century.[31] A brief account of Russian grammar, which scholars attribute partly to a Russian, Vasilii Adodurov (1709–1780), was published in 1731, but in German as *Anfangs-Gründe der russischen Sprache*; and not as a free-standing work, but as an appendix to a *German–Latin and Russian Lexicon* (illus. 10).[32] Adodurov continued to work on Russian grammar, and he eventually produced a manuscript of a fuller version. However, as if to emphasize the pattern, the only printed version of it was an adaptation into Swedish, published in Stockholm in 1750.

At least from the late 1720s the problem was acknowledged, particularly among a cluster of scholars active at the Academy of Sciences including Adodurov and Trediakovskii. The cause of Russian grammar was advocated by Trediakovskii in his speech at the Academy in 1735 (see above, p. 55), at a session that was co-organized with Adodurov. The first printed grammar of Russian for Russians, by Mikhail Lomonosov, was published by the Academy in 1757 (despite the date '1755' on the title page) (illus. 11), a year before the prescriptions for literary styles in his 'Foreword on the Usefulness of Church Books'. Of these two contributions to the culture of language, the grammar was incomparably more substantial and resilient.

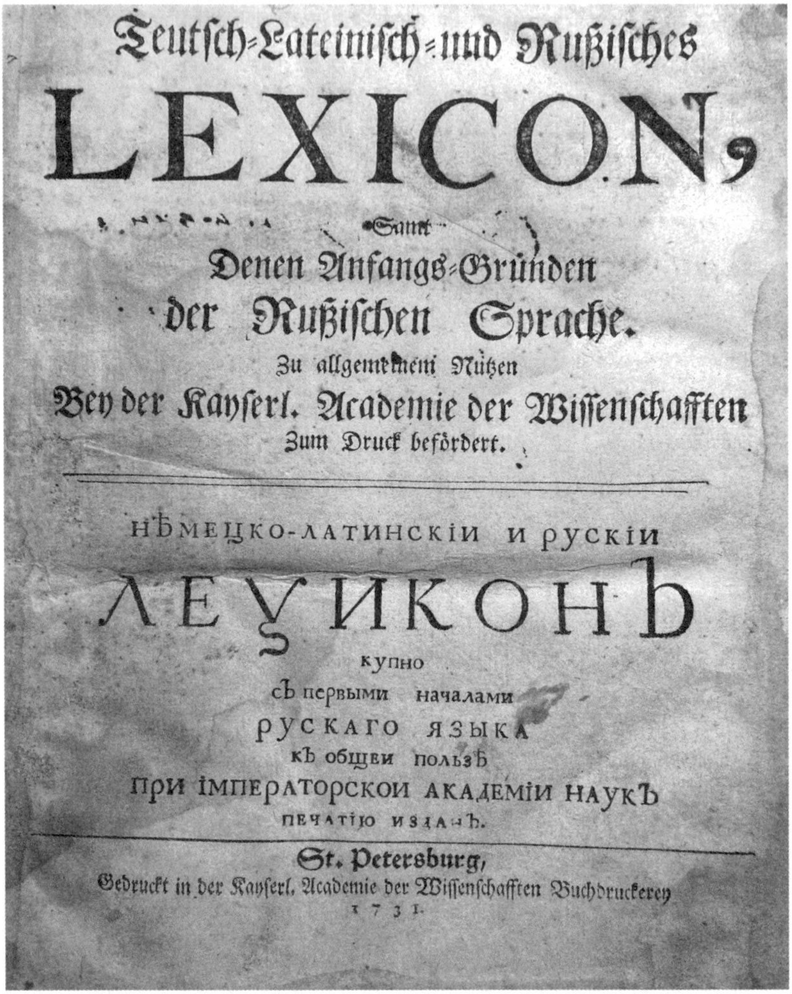
Teutsch-Lateinisch- und Rußisches
LEXICON,
Samt
Denen Anfangs-Gründen
der Rußischen Sprache.
Zu allgemeinem Nutzen
Bey der Kayserl. Academie der Wissenschafften
Zum Druck befördert.

НѢМЕЦКО-ЛАТИНСКІИ И РУСКІИ
ЛЕѮИКОНЪ
купно
съ первыми началами
РУСКАГО ЯЗЫКА
къ общеи пользѣ
при ІМПЕРАТОРСКОИ АКАДЕМІИ НАУКЪ
ПЕЧАТІЮ ИЗДАНЪ.

St. Petersburg,
Gedruckt in der Kayserl. Academie der Wissenschafften Buchdruckerey
1731.

10 *German–Latin and Russian Lexicon* (1731), title page.

Lomonosov was very clear that a grammar for Russians was not just a pedagogical tool or a self-contained exercise in scholarship; it was of fundamental importance in enabling the creation of a culture. His programmatic statements about the significance of the grammar were set out in his preface. First, Lomonosov reaffirmed, in more florid terms than Trediakovskii and Sumarokov, and using a range of conventional panegyric tropes, the claim that the Russian language was as capacious as (or superior to) any other:

The Russian language is superior to many languages not only due to the vastness of the places where it is dominant, but also with respect to its own breadth and amplitude. This will seem improbable to foreigners, and to some native Russians . . . The Holy Roman Emperor Charles v used to say that one should speak Spanish with God, French with one's friends, German with one's enemies, and Italian with women. But if he had been skilled in the Russian language, then of course he would have added that it is fitting to speak in Russian with any of these, for he would have found in it the grandeur of Spanish, the liveliness of French, the sturdiness of German, the tenderness of Italian, and, in addition, the richness and the powerful economy of expression of the Greek and Latin languages.[33]

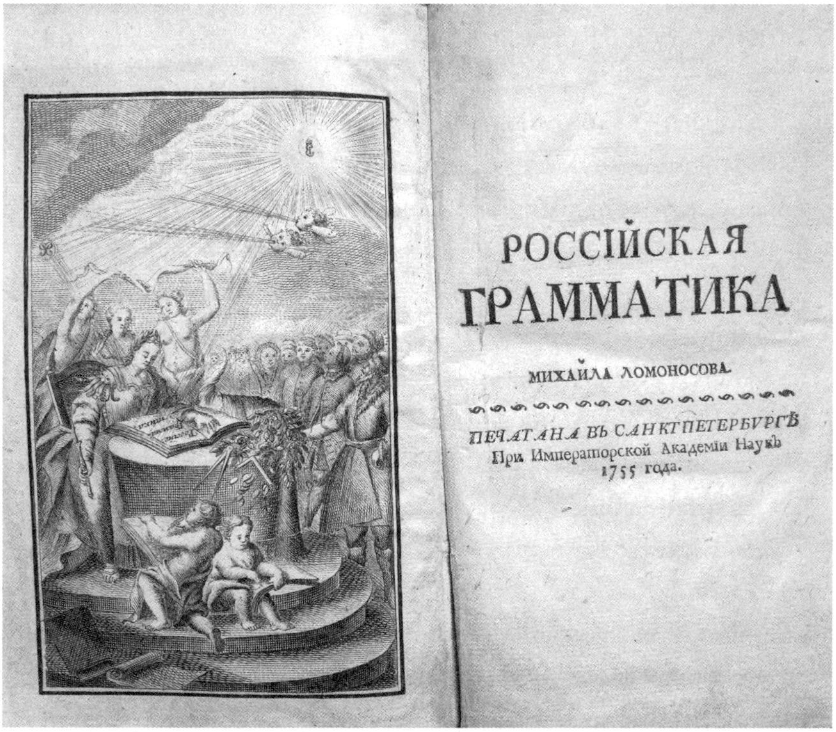

11 Mikhail Lomonosov, *Russian Grammar* (1755 [1757]), frontispiece and title page.

Lomonosov acknowledged that all this related to potential rather than to achievement. Russian was yet to realize itself. In order to become truly what it could and ought to be, Russian needed a grammar. Without it, the status of Russian was peripheral even at the Academy of Sciences. Trediakovskii's address in 1735 was exceptional for being delivered in Russian. Even in the mid-1740s, Lomonosov had to work hard to get permission to lecture in Russian. Many of his scientific publications were in Latin. Grammar would empower Russian, enabling it to fulfil itself as a language of culture:

> Without grammar, rhetoric is blunt, poetry stutters, philosophy is unfounded, history is displeasing, jurisprudence is dubious. And although grammar is derived from common usage of the language, yet through its rules grammar also shows usage itself the way . . . Let the Russian word become ever more perfect in its beauty and its power.[34]

And grammar served empire. Lomonosov's work was dedicated to the infant tsarevich Paul, in the hope that it would enable the Russian language to mature alongside the future emperor, the better to describe the glorious deeds of his ancestors and to glorify the imperial house and the entire fatherland.[35]

Lomonosov's grammar was instantly treated as authoritative. Besides its claimed civilizational significance for Russians themselves, it was also adapted to serve the traditional functions of its genre as a practical tool for foreigners. The Academy of Sciences published a German translation in 1764, and in 1768 an adaptation into French by Jean-Baptiste Charpentier, with the addition of exercises, dialogues and a long list of Russian sayings and proverbs for foreign learners. Lomonosov set the standard for subsequent grammars of Russian. In most essentials its analysis remains compatible with the grammars of the modern language, although in some respects Lomonosov's grammatical concepts and terminology remained tied to classical or Church

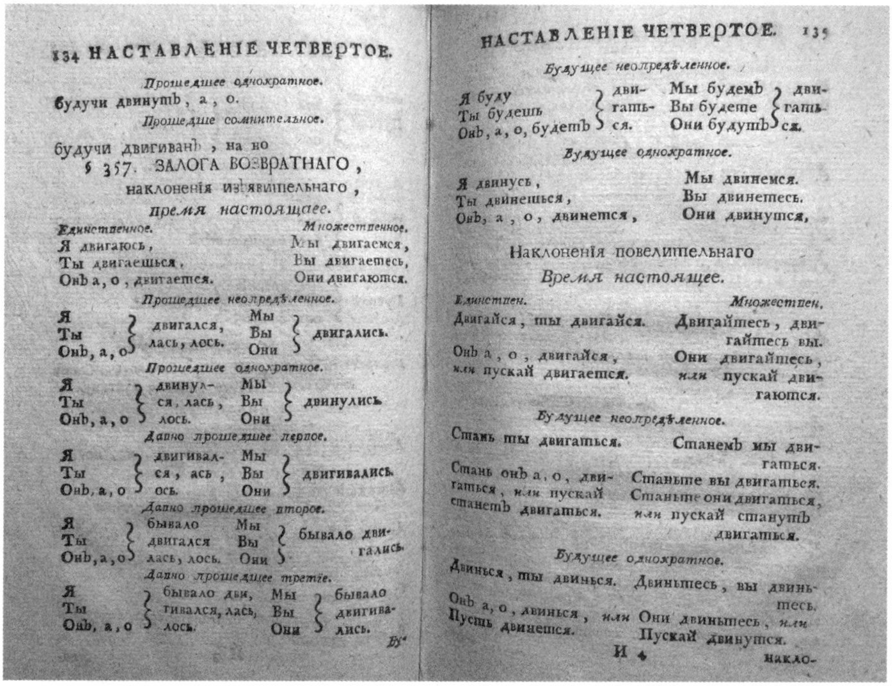

134 НАСТАВЛЕНІЕ ЧЕТВЕРТОЕ.

Прошедшее однократное.

будучи двинутъ, а, о.

Прошедше сомнительное.

будучи двигиванъ, на но

§ 357. ЗАЛОГА ВОЗВРАТНАГО,

наклоненія изъявительнаго,

время настоящее.

Единственное.	*Множественное.*
Я двигаюсь,	Мы двигаемся,
Ты двигаешься,	Вы двигаетесь,
Онъ а, о, двигается.	Они двигаются.

Прошедшее неопредѣленное.

Я, Ты, Онъ, а, о } двигался, лась, лось. Мы, Вы, Они } двигались.

Прошедшее однократное.

Я, Ты, Онъ, а, о } двинулся, лась, лось. Мы, Вы, Они } двинулись.

Давно прошедшее первое.

Я, Ты, Онъ, а, о } двигивался, ась, ось. Мы, Вы, Они } двигивались.

Давно прошедшее второе.

Я, Ты, Онъ, а, о } бывало двигался, лась, лось. Мы, Вы, Они } бывало двигались.

Давно прошедшее третіе.

Я, Ты, Онъ, а, о } бывало двигивался, лась, лось. Мы, Вы, Они } бывало двигивались.

Бу-

НАСТАВЛЕНІЕ ЧЕТВЕРТОЕ. 135

Будущее неопредѣленное.

Я буду, Ты будешь, Онъ, а, о, будетъ } двигаться. Мы будемъ, Вы будете, Они будутъ } двигаться.

Будущее однократное.

Я двинусь,	Мы двинемся.
Ты двинешься,	Вы двинетесь.
Онъ, а, о, двинется,	Они двинутся,

Наклоненія повелительнаго

Время настоящее.

Единствен.	*Множествен.*
Двигайся, ты двигайся.	Двигайтесь, двигайтесь вы.
Онъ а, о, двигайся, *или* пускай двигается.	Они двигайтесь, *или* пускай двигаются.

Будущее неопредѣленное.

Стань ты двигаться.	Станемъ мы двигаться.
Стань онъ а, о, двигаться, *или* пускай станетъ двигаться.	Станьте вы двигаться. Станьте они двигаться, *или* пускай станутъ двигаться.

Будущее однократное.

Двинься, ты двинься.	Двиньтесь, вы двиньтесь.
Онъ а, о, двинься, *или* Пусть двинется.	Они двиньтесь, *или* Пускай двинутся.

И 4 накло-

12 Lomonosov, *Russian Grammar*, on the tenses of reflexive verbs.

Slavonic traditions. For example, in the section on verbal morphology, different types of action in the past are labelled in terms of tense, not aspect, albeit acknowledging distinctive indefinite and semelfactive (single-action) forms (illus. 12).[36] This was typical in early grammatical descriptions of Russian. The re-conceptualization of the verbal system in terms of aspectual pairs (perfective and imperfective) which indicate the type of action rather than the time of action became standard in grammars of Russian only towards the middle of the nineteenth century.[37]

Grammar was a necessary pillar of prestigious systematic description of the language, but it was not sufficient. The second form of systematic description took as its subject not forms but words: a dictionary.

The history of dictionaries in Russia is analogous to the history of grammars. For decades they served either foreign learners of Russian or Russian learners of (or translators from) foreign languages, not Russian users of Russian. The pain of lexicographical labour was noted in Feofan Prokopovich's verse translation (undated but presumably from the early eighteenth century) of a Latin poem by the sixteenth-century scholar Joseph Scaliger, proclaiming that would-be torturers have no need of their conventional methods if they can instead inflict on their victims the agony of compiling dictionaries.[38] In the mid-seventeenth century the Ruthenian scholar and translator Epifanii Slavinetskii, who in 1649 had been brought to Moscow principally for his competence in Greek, worked on a trilingual dictionary of Greek, Latin and Church Slavonic. In 1700 Jan Tessing in Amsterdam printed two trilingual thematic word lists (Latin–Russian–German and Latin–Russian–Dutch) by Ilia Kopievskii (*c.* 1651–1714). They have no title pages, but each tends to be listed under the title of *Nomenklator*, which is how Kopievskii himself referred to one of them.[39] However, the first substantial dictionary to be printed in Russia was Fedor Polikarpov's trilingual (Slavonic, Greek and Latin) lexicon of 1704, a pendant to his trilingual primer, serving mainly students at the Slavo-Graeco-Latin Academy in Moscow. Usually the multilingual dictionaries had foreign headwords. In effect, they were versions of existing foreign dictionaries with Russian definitions added. An exception was the Russian–Dutch lexicon created in 1717 by Iakov Brius (the Russianized version of the name James Bruce, 1669–1735) from a section of his translation of a book on the Dutch language;[40] but foreign headwords were the norm. Such was, for example, the German–Latin–Russian dictionary of 1731 that was modelled on a German–Latin dictionary of 1673; or the polyglot thematic word lists (Russian, Greek, Latin, French, German and English) by Grigorii Poletika (1723?–1784), published in 1763 (illus. 13),[41] which took as its base the 1696 edition of a 'little trilingual dictionary' (*Dictionariolum trilingue*) in English, Greek and Latin by John Ray. Sergei Volchkov published a translation of a German–Latin–French dictionary in two parts in 1755 and 1764.[42]

In 1784 the Moscow University press published a substantial two-volume *New French, Italian, German, Latin and Russian Dictionary*, compiled by Ivan Sots (illus. 14).[43] Thus, plenty of dictionaries were printed during the eighteenth century;[44] but, until almost the very end of the century, all of them were bilingual or multilingual. There was no dictionary of Russian as such.

The earliest examples of Russian–Russian glossaries were small-scale exercises that made no pretence at being serious works of lexicography. On the contrary, they were satirical. Parody preceded reality. From the 1760s onwards, several writers produced brief literary exercises in the genre of satirical dictionaries,[45] humorous games in paradoxical definition: 'Hypocrites: people who know how to live';

[74] [75]

Лѣсной куликъ.	Σκολόπαξ, κος, m.	Scolopax, acis, m.	Becaſſe, f.	Waldſchnepp, m.	A Woodcock.
Дятелъ.	Δρυοκολάπτης, ȣ, m.	Picus, i, Martius, m.	Grimpereau, Pivert, m.	Baumhacker, Holzſpecht, m.	A Wood-pecker.
Крапивишникъ.	Τρωγλοδύτης, ȣ, m.	Paſſer, eris, Troglodytes, m.	Roitelet, m.	Zaunkönig, m.	A Wren.
	X.			X.	
О рыбахъ.	Περὶ Ἰχθύων.	De Piſcibus.	Des Poiſſons.	Von Fiſchen	Of Fishes.
Анжовь.	Εγκρασίχολος, ȣ, m	Encraſicholus, i, m.	Anchois, f.	Sardelle, f.	An Anchovy.
Колюшка, модренецъ.		Pungitius, ii, m.	Cigale, Equille, f.	Stichling, m.	A Banſtickle or Stickle-back.
Севрюга.	Μυςὸς, ȣ̃, m.	Barbus, i, m.	Barbeau, m.	Barbe, f.	A Barbel.
Плотва, плотица.	Λευκίσκος, ȣ, m.	Alburnus, i, m.	Able, m.	Weißfiſch, m.	A Blay or Bleak.
Лещъ.	Ἀβραμὶς, ιδος, f.	Cyprinus, i, latus, m.	Brême, f.	Braſſe, f. Goldfiſch, m.	A Bream.
Ежь морской.	Ἐχῖνος, ȣ, m.	Echinus marinus, m	Heriſſon de mer, m.	See-Igel, Meerigel, m.	A Button-fish.
Коропъ, карпъ.	Κυπρῖνος, ȣ, m.	Cyprinus, i, m.	Carpe, f.	Karpen, m.	A Carp.
Судакъ.	Κέφαλος, άλȣ, m.	Capito, onis, m.	Cabilleau, Chabot, m.	Kabliau, m.	A Chevin or Chub.
Раковина сѣрая.	Κόγχη πτυχώδης, f	Concha, æ, ſtriata f.	Peroncle, m.	Graue Seemuſchel, f.	A Cockle.
Треска.	Ὀνισκος, ȣ, m.	Aſellus, i, m.	Merlus, merluche, m.	Stockfiſch, m.	A Cod-fish.
Угорь морской.	Κόγγρος, ȣ, m.	Congrus, i, m.	Congre, m.	Meeraal, m.	A Conger.
Ракъ.	Καρκῖνος, ȣ, m.	Cancer, cri, m.	Cancre, m.	Krebs, m.	A Crab-fish.
Гнюсь.	Νάρκη, ης, f.	Torpedo, inis, f.	Torpille, f.	Taubfiſch, m.	A Cramp-fish.
Ракъ.	Κάμμαρος, ȣ, m.	Cammarus, i, m.	Ecreviſſe, f. de Riviere.	Krebs, m.	A Cray-fish.
Чернильница.	Σηπία, ας, f.	Sepia, ae, f.	Sêche, f.	Kuttelfiſch, m.	A Cuttle-fish.
Плотица.	Λευκίσκος, ȣ, m.	Leuciſcus, i, m.	Vendoiſe, f.	Häſeling, m.	A Dare or Dace.
Морская собака.	Γαλεὸς, ȣ, m.	Galeus, i, m.	Chien de mer, Requin, m.	Seehund, m.	A Dog-fish.
Тюлень.	Δελφὶν, ῖνος, m.	Delphinus, i, m.	Dauphin, m.	Delphin, m.	A Dolphin.
Кузнецъ.	Χαλκεὺς, έως, m.	Faber, bri, m.	Dorade, f.	Meerſchmid, m.	A Doree, or Dorado
		угорь.			Angui-

13 A page from the *Dictionary in Six Languages* by Grigorii Poletika (1763); note that only the English list is in alphabetical sequence.

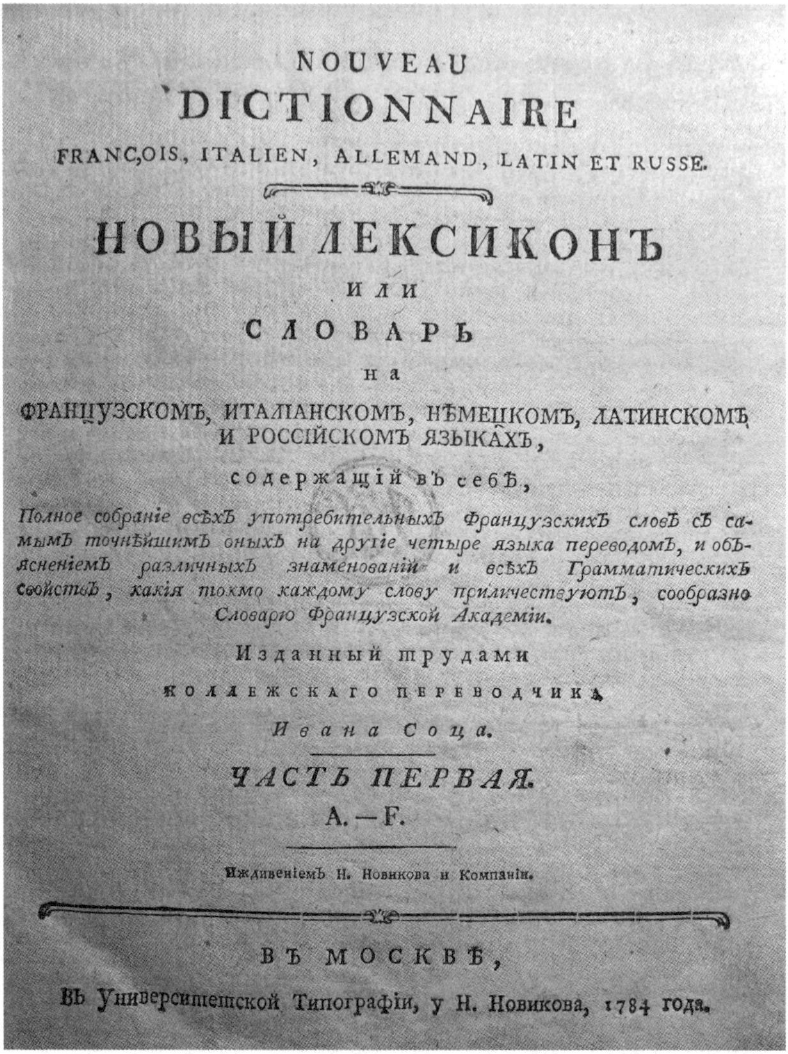

NOUVEAU
DICTIONNAIRE
FRANÇOIS, ITALIEN, ALLEMAND, LATIN ET RUSSE.

НОВЫЙ ЛЕКСИКОНЪ
или
СЛОВАРЬ
на
ФРАНЦУЗСКОМЪ, ИТАЛІАНСКОМЪ, НѢМЕЦКОМЪ, ЛАТИНСКОМЪ И РОССІЙСКОМЪ ЯЗЫКАХЪ,
содержащій въ себѣ,
Полное собраніе всѣхъ употребительныхъ Французскихъ словъ съ самымъ точнѣйшимъ оныхъ на другіе четыре языка переводомъ, и объясненіемъ различныхъ знаменованій и всѣхъ Грамматическихъ свойствъ, какія токмо каждому слову приличествуютъ, сообразно Словарю Французской Академіи.

Изданный трудами
Коллежскаго переводчика
Ивана Соца.

ЧАСТЬ ПЕРВАЯ.
A.—F.

Иждивеніемъ Н. Новикова и Компаніи.

ВЪ МОСКВѢ,
Въ Университетской Типографіи, у Н. Новикова, 1784 года.

14 Ivan Sots, *New French, Italian, German, Latin and Russian Dictionary* (1784), vol. I, title page.

'Regret: *see* Marriage'; 'Oath: a device to convert untruth into truth'; 'Patience: a virtue that is easy to preach to others'.[46] So, by the latter part of the eighteenth century, the idea of a monoglot dictionary had become embedded in the cultural landscape. All that was lacking was the real thing. In 1783 Catherine II (r. 1762–96) founded a new institution especially for the purpose: the Russian Academy (not to be confused with the Academy of Sciences), headed by Princess Ekaterina Dashkova (1743–1810). The *Dictionary of the Russian Academy* (*Slovar' Akademii rossiiskoi*) appeared in six parts from 1789 to 1794, with articles on over 43,000 words. This was Russia's first printed monoglot dictionary.

Despite its unprecedented scale, the *Dictionary of the Russian Academy* was not designed to be comprehensive. There was no virtue in the indiscriminate accumulation of words. The dictionary was selective, prescriptive, normative. The Academy's task was to curate a lexical representation of the Russian language as it ought to be. The obvious first question, therefore, is: *which* language? The title page affirms that this is a dictionary but does not actually name the language. In the introduction, after a brief overview of the variant paths taken by Slavonic and Russian, the answer becomes clear: this is a dictionary of their combination, a dictionary of the Slavenorussian (*slavenorossiiskii*) language – because (and here the editors again echo Lomonosov) 'the abundance, dignity, power and beauty of the language used today depends on the unification of the two [i.e. Slavonic and Russian].'[47]

The compilers took care to define the boundaries, to clarify what was in the dictionary and what was not, and why. Having gathered an unprecedented abundance of materials the Academy 'had to concern itself not about words but about their selection'. Their principal categories of exclusion were:[48]

I Proper names ('of people, lands, seas, towns, rivers, lakes etc.');
II Technical terms ('words and locutions from the arts and the sciences that are not in general use but are known only to scholars and artists; with the exception of Russian natural phenomena that have their own particular names, usually in the common vernacular');
III Obscenities ('all words and expressions that are contrary to decency');

IV Obsolete words ('all ancient words that have fallen out of use'), though with rather fussy categories of exceptions: the editors claimed to retain words that were 'helpful in understanding deeds and rituals of old', or which 'are formed from roots that are still in use;

V Regionalisms, 'except those which, on account of their clarity, power and succinctness can serve to enrich the language' or – significantly – 'which can serve as substitutes for foreign words';

VI 'All foreign words introduced unnecessarily, for which there are Slavonic or Russian equivalents'. The editors declared that, from among foreign words, they would retain only:

A Greek and Hebrew locutions accepted in Holy Scripture, that are known in all languages and are in use both among educated people and among the simple folk and that require no translation;

B Names of institutions of authority, degrees, honours, ranks and functions introduced in recent times; such words are included in the dictionary exactly as prescribed by law;

C Names of scholarly or artistic works.

The examples of usage were taken from sources in 'Slavenorussian: that is, from church books and the best secular writers, which exemplify a high, elegant style'.[49] As if to balance this, the editors also had an eye for popular language, for Russian as such, especially as hallowed in proverbs and folk sayings; but with an important caveat: 'No language, in truth, can equal the Russian language in the abundance of its proverbs and sayings. However, since many of them are low, and some of them are not decent, the Academy has preferred those that are brief and sharply meaningful or manifestly edificatory.'[50]

There were limits beneath which the compilers were not prepared to descend. Obscenities were excluded. One might be tempted to infer from this that obscenities were not, or should not be, in any way relevant to the educated literature of Classicism. One would be wrong. Classicism did have space for the deliberately transgressive, both in theory and in practice. Sumarokov's second 'Epistle' allowed for incongruous combinations either of low themes described in lofty words, or of lofty themes described in low words. This was the 'dual nature' of humorous poems.[51] The most extreme exponent of such incongruity was Ivan Barkov (1732–1768). Barkov was no outsider. His career was spent in the closest proximity with the legislators and systematizers of the Russian language. A capable Latinist, for a decade he was, in effect, Lomonosov's assistant and secretary. He even copied out Lomonosov's grammar. Yet he is known as the author of poems that are often, quite inadequately, called erotic. They were more than erotic. They were deliberately, joyfully obscene, permeated with words that would never sully a normative Academy dictionary: *ebat'* ('fuck'), *pizda* ('cunt') and so on. These were not 'popular' poems in a generally colloquial style. They were, for the most part, constructed as learned odes and other classically canonical forms. The implied readers were fellow elite literati. Such literary caprices can be set in a long European tradition of educated bawdy. Learned men could play clever games with words and themes that were normatively taboo. Naturally, such works could not be printed, but were circulated in handwritten copies. Barkov was by no means the only exponent. A late eighteenth-century manuscript collection, with the general title *A Maiden's Plaything* (*Devich'ia igrushka*), included poems attributed not only to Barkov himself but to several of his esteemed contemporaries.[52]

The existence not just of Barkov's poems, but of a tradition of what have become known as 'barkoviana', underlines the extent to which the *Dictionary of the Russian Academy* represents a fantasy language, even with respect to the Classicist literary pursuits of the very circles within which the dictionary emerged. There is some advantage, of course, in setting norms that are narrower than usage. If all is permitted, there can be no transgression, and what's the fun in that? Obscenities have been continual sources of both delight and indignation in cultures of Russian to the present day (see Chapter Nine).

For all its limitations, the *Dictionary of the Russian Academy* was a monumental achievement. Its articles – not counting preliminaries and word indexes – take up around 3,500 pages, in double columns. The materials on each main word are substantial, with subdivisions on derivatives and with a liberal spread of examples of real usage. Though inevitably revised and superseded, in important respects it set the principles and parameters of Russian normative academic lexicography for the next quarter of a millennium and beyond. The academic tradition resisted inclusive, descriptive lexicography. It was the responsibility of the Academy to reflect and prescribe proper Russian, educated Russian as it had been and as it should be. Their dictionaries were and are of the Russian *literary* language. The preface to the seventeen-volume Soviet academic *Dictionary of the Contemporary Russian Literary Language*, published between 1950 and 1965, announced that 'the present dictionary of the contemporary Russian literary language is explanatory, historical and normative . . . It is based on the normative vocabulary in general use, as represented in the most important literary and political science sources.'[53] The Soviet dictionary contained some 110,000 words, taken mainly from a list of named literary texts starting from the early nineteenth century ('from the time of Pushkin') – that is, it began several decades after the first Academy dictionary ended. Its most recent iteration, the *Large Academy Dictionary of the Russian Language* (*Bol'shoi akademicheskii slovar' russkogo iazyka*), which, at the time of writing, has reached its 28th volume and which promises 150,000 words, likewise states that it is 'the most substantial normative lexicon of the Russian language . . . containing Russian lexicon in general use from the age of Pushkin to our own time . . . As a normative dictionary, the *Large Academy Dictionary* is the guardian of the cultural tradition of the language.'[54]

Thus the eighteenth-century *Dictionary of the Russian Academy* can be seen both as a fulfilment and as an initiation: a monument of its day and for posterity. In relation to the past, it was the final key element in the creation of a systematic formal and practical account of Russian (or Slavenorussian) as a language of education and culture dignified by usage, by study and by its embodiment in works of literature. In relation to the future, it was a monumental statement of lexicographical principle and intent that set the mission and the core agenda for academic dictionaries of Russian to the present day. And, like any monument of linguistic normativity, every fresh iteration was potentially controversial in new ways.

3

True Feeling, Gallicism and the Authority of Taste

The *Dictionary of the Russian Academy*, published between 1789 and 1794, was the culmination of the mid-eighteenth-century project to establish a version of the Russian language that might stand alongside other imperial languages. For the writers and scholars who contributed to this project, and for the empresses and nobles who patronized it, Russian was elevated to its true potential through, on the one hand, the creation of authoritative grammars and dictionaries that encapsulated its structures and resources, and, on the other hand, the practical display of its glories in fine works of literature. This project drew strength from its reliance on a set of firm hierarchical assumptions: a social hierarchy in which culture radiated from, and strove to be an adornment for, the imperial court; a literary hierarchy based on a system of genres; and a linguistic hierarchy that set registers of language as overlapping zones on the Slavenorussian spectrum. Foreign imports, though common in technical and scientific usage, and in polite conversation, had no formal role in these hierarchies and were barely acknowledged except when unavoidable.

Ironically, however, at precisely the time of the *Dictionary*'s publication, many of the core assumptions that had underpinned these achievements were being undermined. All three hierarchies of cultural authority – social, literary and linguistic – were challenged. New fashions wafted in from abroad, new institutions of authority emerged among the Russian elite, nurturing new tastes, new moods, new aesthetic values, new attitudes to language. In the social hierarchy, centres of cultural authority (what might now be called cultural hubs) began to form outside the imperial court, in the salons of noble ladies, among circles of like-minded friends. In the literary hierarchy, the grandiloquence and scale of the ode and the epic lost ground to more subdued and reflective genres such as elegy and pastoral, and even to narrative prose. In the linguistic hierarchy, the strong preference for Slavenorussian exclusivity in literature (if not in conversation) was confronted by a newly inclusive attitude to foreign words and styles – specifically, to Gallicisms. In terms of the conventional sequence of literary movements, these changes can be associated with a transition from Classicism to Sentimentalism (or to Pre-Romanticism). In sociocultural terms they can be linked to the emergence, albeit to a very limited extent, of a private sphere of culture separate from the court and the academic institutions.

It should not be assumed that such devolution of cultural activity and authority was necessarily in *opposition* to the court, or that fine sentiment and aestheticized rusticity were in themselves subversive. On the contrary, they were encouraged and facilitated. In literature, pastoral had impeccable classical provenance, and comic operas with peasant themes were popular at the court of Catherine II from the 1770s.[1] In the 1780s Catherine enacted a series of measure expressly designed to advance institutional and cultural diffusion. For example, in 1785 her Charter for the Nobility protected hereditary property, guaranteed a range of immunities and stipulated a right to representative institutions. A decree of 1783 abolished all restrictions on the private ownership of printing presses: in 1770 there had been around a dozen printing houses in the Russian Empire; by 1790 there were over fifty. The state was knowingly loosening its monopolistic grip on cultural production, planting seeds for the emergence of something that may eventually begin to look like elements of civil society.

In the new modes of culture, grand panegyric on a public stage made way for quiet introspection, for the evocation of true feeling

– sentiment, sensitivity, sensibility.[2] The new aesthetic values assumed that literature should reflect and enhance the refinement of taste, not a fixed structure of genres. Everything, including glory, was transient. New literary models included the novels of Samuel Richardson and Jean-Jacques Rousseau, Laurence Sterne's *The Life and Opinions of Tristram Shandy, Gentleman*, and especially his *A Sentimental Journey through France and Italy*, and Goethe's epistolary novel *The Sorrows of Young Werther*. Instead of rulers on thrones and heroes on battlefields, literature now could equally well be peopled by shepherdesses beside babbling brooks, by the quiet shades of lost friends in rural graveyards.

What were the implications for the culture of the Russian language? The old systems were not designed for the new tasks. The Slavenorussian project served the Classicist literary structures well, but, faced with the aesthetics of Sentimentalism, it was not fit for purpose. This mismatch provoked contrasting responses: for some, the new literary mood required the development of a new style of writing. For others, if literary fashion was incompatible with tradition, then fashion – not tradition – must be resisted. For its proponents, the new style should appeal to the taste of young ladies (or to young ladies of taste). For its opponents, if the language of Russian culture became a mere plaything of transient taste, if it was no longer anchored in the dignity of its Church Slavonic heritage, then it became rootless, arguably even un-Russian. Thus the most rancorous polemics about the new style focused on the question of its openness to foreign imports, on the extent to which they enhanced the language or debased it. This was the first version of what became a recurrent cycle of such debates. On this occasion the object of linguistic dispute was French: the status of Gallicisms.

It may seem odd that an argument about the infiltration of foreign words into the literary language should have broken out so late. Foreign imports as such were not new. There had been occasional splutterings against them, such as Avvakum's invective a hundred years earlier against excessive deference to Greek. Yet, for the most part, it was accepted that the traditionally high-status language of writing – Church Slavonic – had been permeated with direct and indirect Graecisms from its inception, and also that, in the administrative sphere, Russian had assimilated a certain amount of vocabulary of Turkic origin. In the early decades of the eighteenth century, as we have seen, there was a massive influx of new vocabulary from, in particular, German, Dutch, Latin and Polish in newly developing areas of science, technology (including military technology) and education. Among the leading figures in Russian Classicism, both Vasilii Trediakovskii and Mikhail Lomonosov spent several formative years studying abroad (in France and Germany respectively), while Aleksandr Sumarokov's extensive list of prestigious literary models, in his 'Two Epistles', consisted entirely of foreign writers.

However, none of this seems to have had much impact on the mid-eighteenth-century agenda for developing the Russian language itself. Those who worked on establishing Russian as a language of culture fully acknowledged the status of the major ancient and contemporary foreign languages as exemplars. Nevertheless, both Lomonosov's system of literary styles and the *Dictionary of the Russian Academy* resisted foreign words except those that were long assimilated or, like cookies on a modern website, were deemed strictly necessary. Their own purpose was to elevate Russian as a language of equivalent dignity: as a language distinctive in its own resources, not as a language to be dissolved in a flood of foreignness. In their view the peculiar richness of Russian, its potential and its identity, derived from its organic combination with Church Slavonic. Slavenorussian could stand proudly alongside the prestigious tongues of Europe, independent and separate. In his 'Foreword on the Usefulness of Church Books in the Russian Language' Lomonosov had advocated his system of styles partly on the grounds that it helped to 'ward off the strange and barbarous absurdities that come to us from foreign languages' (see above, p. 65). In a particularly grumpy article entitled 'On the Elimination of Foreign Words from the Russian Language', published in 1759 – the year after the publication of Lomonosov's 'Foreword' – Sumarokov declared that the adoption of foreign words (especially when they were imported 'without necessity') constituted 'not the enrichment of a language, but its corruption'.[3] Sumarokov went on to assert that, while in the wider language the battle for purification may already have been lost, it was particularly important to protect the language of print.[4] He also made a sharp distinction between tradition and innovation: the assimilation of words from Greek had been 'praiseworthy', but 'French and German disfigure (*obezobrazhivaiut*) our language'.[5]

Just when Slavenorussian might have seemed to have established its position securely, it was being breached at its very centre. Foreign lexical encirclement and infiltration (through the languages of technology, scholarship and warfare, through the incursion of myriad experts and pedagogues) were already tough to hold at bay; but from the 1750s it became increasing modish, even prestigious, for Russians to speak French even among themselves. The fashion spread from the top, at the court of the Empress Elizabeth. From the court, the use of French as the conversational language of polite society spread to the higher nobility and thence more broadly among sections of the gentry.[6] The hypothetical society ladies, invoked as the implied audience for the new style of Russian writing, might not necessarily even converse routinely in Russian, at any rate in polite company. In such circumstances it was possible to envisage a danger that Russian, having been with such effort cultivated and raised to the level of a civilized tongue, could relapse to become a language spoken mainly to and among the servants.

Or sometimes – God forbid! – French itself might leak into the speech of the wrong type of person. Foreign words were acceptable when used by those who were entitled and competent, but such words should not escape into the mouths of those who were too ignorant and culturally ill-equipped to manipulate them appropriately. In his letter to Trediakovskii in 1736, among many detailed observations and suggestions about language, Vasilii Tatishchev lamented the misuse of foreign words among low-level civil servants who did not realize their own absurdity:

> we know that foreign words are misused by the most self-aggrandizing secretaries and clerks, who do not actually know any [foreign] language, but who consider that such extreme foolishness is actually a sign of their own great intelligence, and who boast of that of which they ought to be ashamed.[7]

Tatishchev went on to assert that such abuse of language in administration should be suppressed by legislation; but he also indicated that it might be combatted by literary means, through comedy and satire. On legislation to limit foreign words when using Russian as a state language, Tatishchev was almost three hundred years ahead of his time (see Chapter Nine). His literary remedy could be put into practice more quickly. The genre-based literature of Classicism did not entirely exclude Gallicisms and French from the language of Russian literature, but from its higher registers and genres. French had a place in comedy: that is, in a context where it was held up to ridicule.

From the 1750s the ignorant, often foppish display of French was a stock theme in Russian comedy.[8] The classic text for this – in the sense that it is the only such play that has come to be regarded as a classic – is *The Brigadier* (*Brigadir*, written in 1769) by Denis Fonvizin (1745–1792). *The Brigadier* is constructed around two families across two generations: on the one side, a military officer (the eponymous brigadier) and his wife, and their son Ivanushka; on the other hand, a civil servant ('counsellor', *sovetnik*) and his wife, and their daughter Sofia. All the main characters in *The Brigadier* are represented through their distinct habits of speech. Ivanushka and the Counsellor's wife are characterized by their shared infatuation with pretentious Gallicisms. Ivanushka has returned from France and peppers his speech with French phrases which, in his mind, display his superior sophistication. In the text, some are written in Latin script ('Hélas!', 'Vous avez raison', 'C'est plus intéressant', 'adieu, ma reine' and so on), others are transliterated (for example, *rezoneman*, *indif-eran*, *bil'edu*), though of course the difference between the two scripts is invisible in performance. He declares that he would ideally like to find a wife with whom he could speak only French. The Counsellor's wife complements this with her own Gallicizing speech habits, which consist partly of adapting imported words to Russian morphological patterns and syntactic structures, and partly of phraseological calques or pseudo-calques (for example, *ia kapabel'na*, *diskiutirovat'*, *sdelai kompaniiu*, *sur'eznaia materiia*). Entranced by such linguistic signals of affinity, Ivanushka and the Counsellor's wife quickly become flirtatious with each other.

However, *The Brigadier* is not only a satire on Gallicism. The Brigadier himself also uses imported words, but in an older military and administrative register that is equally significant as a limiting cultural marker (for example, *artikul*, *bataliia*, *ekzertsitsiia*). The Counsellor's exotic vocabulary is, in turn, appropriately bureaucratic: he speaks of *sekretari*, who write *ekstrakty*. But the Counsellor has another register. When touching upon lofty subjects, he sprinkles his utterances with high-style Slavonisms: sometimes in a show of pious moralism, sometimes in the service of incongruously amorous pursuits. A running joke through all of this is mutual incomprehension: the Brigadier does not understand his son's French (*Son*: *Je m'en moque*. *Brigadier*: What on earth is *manmok*?). His wife, as ignorant of Church Slavonic as she is of French, continually misunderstands the Counsellor's grandiloquent attempts to declare his affection for her. Indeed, it turns out that even Ivanushka, although he declares that he would only want a wife with whom he could speak French, does not properly know French himself. He is a compendium of phrases, not a user of language. Amid all their disagreements, the discordant parties agree fervently on one thing: *none* of them needs grammar, in *any* language.

Thus Fonvizin's play foregrounds not just pretentious Gallicism but linguistic ignorance and incongruity more broadly: a world of the semi-educated, characterized by, on the one hand, its cacophony of ill-assimilated registers of language, and yet, on the other hand, its simultaneous rejection of any need for the systematic cultivation of speech standards. Satire on linguistic pretentiousness was not in itself anti-French. As it happens, Fonvizin's own representation of France, in his *Letters from France* written during a journey in 1777–8,[9] was quite negative: France was noisy, smelly and dishonest (though it did have good roads). But none of this undermined French as a spoken language in Russian high society. The lampooning of poor French was part of a wider linguistic snobbery, the condescension of the well-educated towards the under-educated. Civilized assimilation of French literary and linguistic habits was another matter. Indeed, in Fonvizin's own writings 'the influence of the French language betrays itself in his style, grammar and vocabulary.'[10]

The Sentimentalists, therefore, were not the first to admit some Gallicisms into literature. Their innovation lay in the fact that they welcomed Gallicisms into their new Russian literary norm. Mid-eighteenth-century Slavenorussian had been conceived as a kind of import-free zone, on the premise that the language of Russian culture could only fulfil itself and maintain its proper dignity if it was protected from superfluous foreign elements. The proponents of what came to be labelled the 'new style' turned this premise on its head: Gallicism was to be embraced, not resisted: not to be abhorred as a form of contamination and debasement, but – in direct contradiction to the assertions of, say, Sumarokov in his article on foreign words – to be accepted and exploited as a source of potential linguistic enrichment. Indeed, ideally there was a kind of virtuous circle: the language of literature should be compatible with (and subtly draw on) the speech and taste of polite society; and the speech and taste of polite society would, in turn, be enriched and cultivated by drawing on literature.

By far the most distinguished exponent and proponent of stylistic Gallicism in Russian Sentimentalism was the writer and historian Nikolai Karamzin (1766–1826) (illus. 15). Karamzin did not suggest that all and any Gallicisms should be welcomed uncritically and indiscriminately. His approach was more subtle. Gallicism was not to be flaunted (in the manner of Fonvizin's comic characters). On the contrary, there should be a carefully modulated process of creative assimilation. In Karamzin's celebrated phrase, the trick was to introduce new words and meanings 'so artfully as to deceive readers and conceal from them the unfamiliarity of expression'.[11] Half a century earlier, Mikhail Lomonosov had expressly warned against the 'strange and barbarous absurdities that come to us from foreign languages' and that 'now creep in unnoticed . . .' (see above, p. 65). For Lomonosov, the idea of foreign influences 'creeping in unnoticed' had been an abomination; for Karamzin it was an aspiration.

15 Vasilii Tropinin, *Nikolai Karamzin*, 1818, oil on canvas.

Or rather: by the time that Karamzin wrote this pronouncement (in 1802), it was already an achievement, a literary fact. His article bore the tendentious title 'Why Are there Few Talented Authors in Russia?'. But Karamzin was not some random, opinionated, armchair theorist. In fact, he wrote rather little *about* language. He was a practitioner. His sparse theoretical statements carry weight because he knew what he was talking about. He was by some distance the most successful and influential literary writer in the new manner, whose adherents are often labelled with his name (Karamzinians, Karamzinists). His career as a writer of literature, in the narrowly belletristic sense, was quite brief, lasting barely more than a decade.[12] The 1802 article was written at the end of it. Karamzin's works up to that point were, with one exception, not particularly voluminous, but each was in its way a fresh experiment in genre. Karamzin's first major piece of writing was a literary travelogue, an epistolary account of his journey to Germany, Switzerland, France and England in 1789–90. Published as *Letters of a Russian Traveller*, it was deliberately reminiscent of Laurence Sterne's *A Sentimental Journey through France and Italy*, first published in 1768. A bestseller in French translation almost as soon as it appeared in English, Sterne's work was first translated into Russian in 1789. Karamzin's most iconic Sentimentalist text, first published in 1792, was his short story 'Poor Liza' (*Bednaia Liza*), about a doomed affair between a young nobleman, Erast, and Liza the flower-seller (for 'even peasant girls are capable of loving'). Erast, obliged to stick with his own kind, eventually abandons Liza, who, grief-stricken, drowns herself. Life followed art, and the picturesque pond, by a monastery outside Moscow, soon became a place of sweetly sorrowful pilgrimage for the story's devoted admirers, who would carve their initials on surrounding trees. Karamzin's other short stories included experiments in the Gothic ('The Island of Bornholm', 1793) and in medievalism ('Marfa the Mayoress, or the Subjugation of Novgorod', 1802). From the early 1800s until his death, he devoted himself to an entirely different and vastly more ambitious project. Karamzin's *History of the Russian State* (in twelve volumes, unfinished) was an extensively researched, copiously footnoted yet fluently written academic history that established his reputation as an authoritative historian who was also revered as an exemplary stylist, a kind of Russian equivalent of Edward Gibbon.

Karamzin's status rests mainly on his prose. Like any contemporary man of letters, he also composed verses, but the most respected poet of Russian Sentimentalism (or Pre-Romanticism – the terms overlap) was a slightly younger contemporary, Vasilii Zhukovskii (1783–1852). Zhukovskii announced his arrival – also in 1802 – with his poem 'The Village Graveyard' (*Sel'skoe kladbishche*), a rendition into Russian of Thomas Gray's 'Elegy Written in a Country Churchyard'. This became an instant classic of its kind, introducing the genre of graveyard poetry with its reflections on mortality and loss, its evocations of nostalgia and the sweetness of sorrow. In addition to a steady flow of lyric poems, Zhukovskii also experimented with quasi-medieval and supernatural balladry, mainly, again, through adapting foreign models.

Karamzin's readership quickly extended beyond Russia and Russian. His works, including the *History*, were excerpted and used as models of style for non-native learners of the language.[13] His *Letters of a Russian Traveller* appeared in German in 1799–80. An English version (translated from the German) was published in 1803. Its frontispiece was an engraved portrait of Karamzin (illus. 16), probably the first portrait of a Russian writer to be published in England. An English translation of four of Karamzin's short stories also appeared in 1803 and was reprinted the following year.[14] Eleven volumes of his *History of the Russian State* were published in French shortly after they appeared in Russian, from 1819 to 1826. The preface to the English edition of the short stories asserts that Karamzin's 'peculiarly fascinating manner of relating and describing has established the fame of a genius'.[15]

Why should any of this have been objectionable to those who cared about the culture of the Russian language? The problem lay in

Karamzin's notion that he could slip Gallicisms into the language of literature almost without it being noticed. *He* may have thought that the result sounded natural, and many subsequent readers may have felt likewise; but some of his more vigilant contemporaries were not so easy to lull into linguistic complacency. Upholders of traditional standards were not prepared to have the Gallic wool pulled over their eyes. Mere pleasantness of language was not the point: there were fundamental principles at stake. Then, as in later equivalent polemics, the opponents of foreign linguistic infiltration did not all speak with one voice. Purist extremism was rare. For example, not many would have subscribed to the views of the priest and pedagogue Vasilii Protopopov, who, in a booklet published in 1786, proposed cleansing Russian even of devotional terms derived from Greek, such as *liturgiia*, *evkharistiia*

16 James Hopwood, *Nikolai Karamzin*, 1803, engraving, after an original by Fedor Kiunel [=Friedrich Kühnel].

17 Orest Kiprenskii, *Aleksandr Shishkov*, 1825, oil on canvas.

or *kafedra*.[16] Protopopov was not mainstream. The most vocal, persistent and – for non-literary reasons – influential critic of the new style was Aleksandr Semenovich Shishkov (1754–1841).

In the cultural history of Russian, Aleksandr Shishkov (illus. 17) is a kind of benchmark figure of passionate linguistic conservatism. As a literary author he is negligible. By contrast with Karamzin, Shishkov's vocation was for opinion rather than for practice. Alongside a career first as a naval officer and then as a state functionary (eventually with the rank of admiral), Shishkov fought his linguistic battles on four fronts: first, through the 1800s, as the most verbose and virulent critic of the new style; second, as one of the principal organizers of a literary club for like-minded linguistic traditionalists, the 'Colloquy of Lovers of the Russian Word' (*Beseda liubitelei russkogo slova*, 1811–16); third, from the early 1820s, as a dedicated and effective opponent of attempts to render the Bible from its traditional Church Slavonic into contemporary Russian; and fourth, from 1824 to 1828 – lest we imagine him to be merely a cantankerous onlooker – as minister of education.

Shishkov's extensive polemical tract, *A Discourse on the Old and New Style of the Russian Language*, was first published in 1803, and reissued with supplementary material in 1813.[17] It was a sustained, uncompromising, frontal attack on Gallicism, as signalled in its very first sentence:

> Anyone who loves Russian literature, and has dabbled in it even slightly, and has not been infected by passion for the French language – a passion that is incurable and that deprives one of all reason – such a person, on opening the majority of our contemporary books, will unfortunately discover what a strange style, alien to our understanding and to our ear, is now dominant.[18]

The tone is sustained to the finish:

> It is an irrefutable truth that, for as long as we fail to love our own language, our own customs, our own education, so in many of our arts and sciences we will remain far behind others. One must live by one's own wits, not by the wits of foreigners.[19]

Shishkov scoffs at the claim that French brings *élégance*, unless – he says – one renders *élégance* as 'piffle' (*chepukhá*).[20] But his generalized polemic is backed up with specifics. He correctly identifies various levels of Gallicism, from transliteration through morphological calques to syntactic calques, and presents what he regards as abhorrent examples of each. Among straightforward imports he decries, for example, *morál'nyi, estetícheskii, epókha, stséna, garmóniia, entuziázm, katastrófa*. Among semantic calques he particularly dislikes anything to do with the verb *trógat'* ('to touch') in an emotional rather than physical sense, including the semantic barbarism *trógatel'nyi*, 'touching', infected by the French *touchant*. He mocks calque compounds such as *razvítie* (= *développement*), *perevorót* (= *révolution*), *sosredotóchit'* (= *concentrer*). And he regards with special distaste not only the calque compound *vliiánie* (= *influence*) but its Gallicist construction with the preposition *na* (like the English 'influence *on*') where normal rules of Russian would require the preposition *v* (as in 'influx *into* . . .').[21]

Such lists make strange reading in retrospect. The problem is that, in every one of these examples, the words and constructions that Shishkov cited as barbaric have subsequently become entirely normal, neutral parts of standard Russian. His lists underscore the danger of imagining that correct language can be frozen in time and made to survive only on its previously accumulated resources. The compilers of the *Dictionary of the Russian Academy* fell into the same fallacy in excluding foreign words for which, in their view, Russian equivalents already existed. Equivalence can be an illusion, and semantically analogous forms can develop distinctive nuances. And hindsight can be deceptive. There is rarely an obvious rule that determines which imported forms or meanings will quickly be rejected as temporary fads, and which will eventually be absorbed into the language, either by displacing native equivalents, or by providing a means for semantic differentiation. There has rarely been a time without somebody expressing their indignation about neologisms or imports or vulgarisms that disfigure the language. From a modern perspective, the imported expressions listed as objectionable in Sumarokov's article of 1759 look more mixed than Shishkov's list of 1802. Some of Sumarokov's detested barbarisms have subsequently become normalized (for example, *frúkty* for 'fruit' rather than *plody*, or *sup* for 'soup' instead of *pokhlëbka*), but others have indeed turned out to be transient (for example, *pansív* or *manifík*).[22] Nevertheless, the impression is that Shishkov was railing against an unstoppable incoming tide.

Aleksandr Shishkov is easy to caricature, but he was serious, persistent, in some areas systematic, and on occasion notably effective. He was also by no means a lone voice. In Russia there have been many

Shishkovs (with different names) over the subsequent couple of centuries. And beyond Russia there have been very many who have shared his distaste for what they interpret as foreign contamination of their languages. A distinguished example from England was Dr Samuel Johnson, who, in the preface to his *Dictionary*, expressed concern about the fashion for lazy translation from French, which 'if it be suffered to proceed, will reduce us to babble a dialect of France'.[23] Shishkov's *Discourse* is a great deal more than a few random rants. He presents, by means of diagrams formed of concentric circles, what could plausibly be reckoned a theory of semantic fields. He appends two substantial annotated lists: forty pages of observations on phrases from recent literary works and translations; and, lest it be thought that he is entirely negative and incapable of offering constructive alternatives, over a hundred pages of Russian (that is, Church Slavonic) words that, in his view, were too rarely or inadequately exploited.[24] A significantly expanded version of this list was published in 1825.[25] Shishkov collaborated in revisions of the *Dictionary of the Russian Academy*, and had a long-term project for compiling an etymological dictionary.[26] At the Colloquy of Lovers of the Russian Word he tried also to nurture talent sympathetic to his preferred idiom, rather than merely to complain about his opponents. But perhaps his most telling campaign on language was his last, when he took a stand against the translation of the Bible into contemporary Russian.

In February 1816 Alexander I decreed that the Russian Bible Society (an offshoot of the British and Foreign Bible Society) may publish the New Testament in Russian. By the middle of 1824 the Society had printed and distributed several hundred thousand copies of the Russian New Testament, as well as over 100,000 copies of the Psalter. Its momentum looked unstoppable. Already it was preparing for publication a Russian version of the first eight books of the Old Testament, with the ultimate aim of producing a complete Bible. And suddenly it was over. Until May 1824 the Society's president, Prince Aleksandr Golitsyn (1773–1844), happened also to have been minister of education. In May 1824 he was dismissed from both posts, as president of the Society and as a government minister. The new minister of education was Aleksandr Shishkov. The Society's publishing activities were stopped. In 1826 the new tsar, Nicholas I (r. 1825–55), brought an end to its independent existence.[27]

As in his reaction to the new style two decades previously, Shishkov felt compelled to articulate his objections to the Russian Bible vigorously and extensively.[28] Sometimes he framed his objections in ostensibly philological, quasi-Lomonosovan terms: the idea of 'translating' the Bible from Slavonic to Russian was absurd, because Slavonic and Russian were one; but to render scripture into a lower register (of the Slavenorussian spectrum) was to compromise its dignity. However, even Shishkov found it hard to maintain this position consistently. In practice he wrote about the Russian versions not as stylistic transpositions but as translations, with all the dangers involved therein.

Shishkov's opposition to the Russian versions of scripture were underpinned by his conviction that they may be heretical, or may facilitate heresy. In the first place, sticking only to the issue of language, Russian and Slavonic were not just semantically equivalent versions of the same thing. Any transposition or translation has an effect on the meaning. This introduces a risk of error, which in the case of scripture could lead to heresy. Second, at the social level, Shishkov was fundamentally unsympathetic to the main mission of Bible Societies, to make the scriptures accessible to all in their own languages. If *anybody* is allowed to read the scriptures for themselves, without learned or priestly intermediaries, who knows what erroneous understandings might result? And third, Shishkov was suspicious of the fact that the Bible Society movement had its origins abroad, in non-Orthodox lands: surely this was part of a mission to undermine Russia's true faith.

Shishkov's brand of traditionalism was in important respects deeply untraditional. For centuries Russian eulogies of Orthodoxy had praised the fact that the Faith had been made available to them in their own tongue, and not through a learned intermediary such as Latin. Shishkov now defended Church Slavonic precisely for its inaccessibility to those who were not specifically trained in its interpretation. Having previously tried to draw a line between Russian (or Slavenorussian) and the influence of French, he now tried to draw a firmer line between Russian and Slavonic: Lomonosov might have advocated the usefulness of 'church books' for Russian, but Shishkov made it clear that Russian should not be used for church books. In the previous century, the writers whom Shishkov had earlier held up as role models, Sumarokov and Lomonosov (along with Trediakovskii, about whom he was less enthusiastic), had experimented – even competitively – in producing verse renditions of psalms. Still earlier, in 1680, the authoritatively Orthodox Simeon Polotskii (who had penned the main defence of official Orthodoxy against the 'Old Believer' schismatics) printed his own complete transposition of the Psalter into verse – in Church Slavonic, but obviously not as in the Bible; now, for Shishkov, any transposition was potentially heretical. If previously Shishkov had railed against Gallicism as a foreign contagion, now apparently even the use of Russian itself – in the wrong context – was a foreign conspiracy.

In his own time, Aleksandr Shishkov won some battles but lost his war. The Russian literary language was not constrained by Shishkovian principles. In a longer perspective, however, the spirit of Shishkov survived. The argument between Shishkovians and Karamzinians became, in a sense, archetypal. It can be seen as a template for a recurrent theme in subsequent disputes about what Russian should be: specifically, about whether foreign linguistic imports and influences should be regarded as opportunities for cultural enrichment or as threats to cultural identity; and about whether language contacts should be embraced, resisted or controlled (see Chapter Nine).

4
The Authority of the Writer

In the story of Russian as it ought to be, each new solution addresses the limitations of the existing system, and each turns out to be limited in new ways. For Peter I the priority was to outflank the ecclesiastical near-monopoly, both in the interests of effective administrative communication and in order to develop secular learning and technical skills. His notion of 'simple' Russian took as its basis the idiom of his own administration and was entirely open to an abundance of foreign lexical imports for these purposes. Language was honed to its administrative and educational functions. The mid-eighteenth-century scholars and writers, who broadly subscribed to the assumptions and aesthetics of Classicism, brought a vision of order both to the study of language (leading to grammars and dictionaries) and to the prescribed registers of its usage. They associated the development of a worthy language with the development of a worthy literature, and, in Mikhail Lomonosov's scheme, each literary genre had its appropriate register on the linguistic scale. Language was determined by genre; genre was signalled by language. The 'new style' of the late eighteenth century, associated with the broader cultural trends of Sentimentalism, undermined the social and linguistic hierarchies of Classicism, reorienting literature to different social spaces and different aesthetic priorities. Language was determined socially, by a notion of contextual taste in polite society.

Karamzinian Russian was crafted partly in response to what were perceived as the limitations of Classicism in accommodating new cultural impulses. But it, too, turned out to be fatally limited: not because of the Gallicisms that Aleksandr Shishkov and others so detested, but precisely because of its orientation towards a particular notion of taste, a particular mode of feeling and imagery, a particular kind of evocation. Classicist registers of language varied according to genre; Sentimentalism really knew only one register. There was a stylistic sameness about it. Karamzinian verse was much like Karamzinian prose. The new style was attuned to salon-based Sentimentalist taste, but salon-based Sentimentalist taste was not eternal. Classicism and Sentimentalism were founded on different types of historicism. Classicist historicism tended to treat literature as a continual reimagining and re-embodiment of past models and forms. Sentimentalist historicism was more open to acknowledging change, the authority of the present. Its strength was therefore also its weakness. The new style of the late eighteenth century was contingent. Tastes changed. In the early nineteenth century, in Russia as in Europe more widely, sentiment yielded to passion in the advance of Romanticism. And Romanticism produced a source of cultural (including linguistic) authority that in previous generations might have been regarded as, at best, monstrously presumptuous, or, at worst, blatantly heretical: the creative individual.

The contrast in attitudes to linguistic authority is nicely captured in a pithy exchange, in 1821, between Aleksandr Shishkov and the poet Aleksandr Bestuzhev (1797–1837). 'Writers', declared Shishkov, 'are the creators of their compositions, not of the language.' 'Writers', retorted Bestuzhev, 'are the creators of the language.'[1] These formulations are, of course, aphoristically over-schematized. Bestuzhev's assertion should not be taken literally. He was not claiming that writers should actually invent new languages, nor was he suggesting anything like the later avant-garde experiments at the boundaries of language, sense and non-sense (on which, see Chapter Six). The forms and structures of the language of the Romantics conformed to a kind of Russian that Lomonosov would have recognized. Nor was it particularly radical to assert that the potential of literature – and hence of language – could only be fulfilled by good writers. This had been clear both to Classicists and to Sentimentalists, especially in the statements of those who were themselves mainly practitioners rather than theorists. 'Our language has enough words in it,/ But not enough writers using it,' complained Aleksandr Sumarokov in 1748.[2] Just over half a century later, in 1802, Karamzin likewise lamented the dearth of good writing, in his article 'Why Are there Few Talented Authors in Russia?'. All could agree that, if the repository of good and prestigious Russian was to be literature, then self-evidently it needed writers who were up to the task. Nevertheless, the exchange between Bestuzhev and Shishkov captures a significant shift of perspective on the structure of literary and linguistic authority. For the advocates both of Classicism and of Sentimentalism, good writers were needed in order to perform well the roles that were prescribed for them. Under Romanticism, the writer prescribes the role.

The elevation of the authority of the writer implied a rejection not only of the authority of inherited norms but of normativity itself. For much of the previous century the main participants in the movement to develop Russian as a language of culture had been concerned with what such a language *should be* in general, for others as well as for themselves. The Romanticist attitude was individualistic: the language of a literary work should be determined by its creator; writers could take control over the tools of their craft. Such an approach validates choice – or, in a more Romanticist idiom, freedom: the emancipation of the writer from the hegemony either of historically determined genre or of socially determined taste. A writer's voice was his own. In theory this was a striking reversal. In practice, what did it mean? It did not mean that every individual Romantic writer produced an individual style of language. Declarations of freedom could themselves become formulaic, predictable, indicators of belonging rather than of emancipation. Romanticism had its own verbal and stylistic clichés, its own norms. Gently picturesque meadows and glades gave way to wild crags and tossing seas; gravestones in cemeteries – reminders of transience and mortality – gave way to blood-caked corpses on fields of battle; sweet sorrow turned to black despair; decorously modulated sentiment gave way to transgressive excess – to passion, or to irony that could shade into corrosive cynicism; edificatory and reflective travelogues through conventionally civilized spaces gave way to reckless and dangerous adventures at or beyond the fringes of civilization, paradoxically both escaping authority and affirming empire. In Russia as elsewhere in Europe, the venerated presiding genius of Romanticism was Byron. In distant hindsight the cult of Byron can seem almost self-parodic in the extremity of its devotion. 'I aspire to be Byron,' wrote the sixteen-year-old Mikhail Lermontov (1814–1841) in 1830: 'we share one soul, we share our torments;/ O would that we might share one fate.'[3] Two years later the young poet was ready to declare his independence: 'No, I am not Byron, I am another/ Chosen one, as yet unknown,/ Like him, a persecuted wanderer,/ But with a Russian soul.'[4] This kind of performative freedom can look no less restrictive and collective than any other in the sequence of cultural fashions.

However, there was a different kind of performative freedom of language, roughly coterminous with Russia's age of high Romanticism but not constrained by it: a kind of performative freedom that has often been regarded as foundational for the subsequent status and achievements of Russian as a literary language. It is not based on a theory or a movement, but on versatile and virtuosic practice, and it is associated above all with the works of one writer: Aleksandr Sergeevich Pushkin (1799–1837) (illus. 18). Unlike Lomonosov, or Karamzin, or Shishkov, Pushkin advocated no norm.[5] He could slip into and out of the habits of any convention but was constrained by none. It is, perhaps above all, this liberating versatility that led to Pushkin being described as the 'founder' of the modern Russian literary language.[6] If understood literally, the label is nonsensical. Pushkin did not 'found' any language. Yet his prodigious reputation has made

18 Orest Kiprenskii, *Aleksandr Pushkin*, 1827, oil on canvas.

it hard to avoid the impression that Pushkin was the source, the enabler, the inspiration, for much of what followed. Pushkin's reputation has been fostered not merely by pedagogues and demagogues but by scholars and writers, by radicals and traditionalists, by autocrats and dissidents.[7] Since the mid-twentieth century the main multi-volume Academy dictionaries of the literary language have declared that the scope of their coverage as beginning from the age of Pushkin (see Chapter Nine). The phrase 'Pushkin is our everything' (*Pushkin – nashe vsë*), coined in an essay of 1859 by the writer Apollon Grigorev (1822–1864), is still intoned as a kind of ritual affirmation of collective identity in language. And it makes little difference whether the intonation is reverent or ironic, celebratory or supercilious. Pushkin's pervasive presence can be resisted but not easily ignored.

This is not the place either to defend or to dispute Pushkin's posthumous status in Russian representations of the history of the culture of Russian. The aim here is to outline what Pushkin did with language that made him seem distinctive, that came to be perceived as so enabling for others, and that appeared to justify the inversion of linguistic hierarchy such that authority was ceded to the individual writer.

Pushkin's reputation was exceptional in his own lifetime. Indeed, while still at school, at the elite *lycée* next to the imperial palace at Tsarskoe Selo outside St Petersburg, Pushkin was already recognized as a literary prodigy. Ever since the arbiters of culture put the language of literature on a pedestal, they had been frustrated by the paucity of exemplary literature through which that language could fulfil its potential. Pontification was hollow without demonstration. Karamzin's advantage over Shishkov was that, in his own mode, he was a good writer. Pushkin's generation of literati was more diverse and productive than any of its predecessors, especially in poetry, with Pushkin himself acknowledged as the brightest star in the constellation. Moreover, Pushkin's talent was restless, versatile, experimental. Sumarokov had tried his hand at a range of genres; Karamzin's relatively few literary works were all, in a sense, generically distinct, but they were stylistically homogeneous. One could narrate Pushkin's literary biography as a sequence of experiments in form. In each experiment Pushkin focused on honing the appropriate shapes, the registers of language, the structures of implied feeling – and then moving on to something else, a new challenge of language and form.

Pushkin's first book, published in 1820, was a long mock epic, *Ruslan and Liudmila*. It was hugely successful, but he never wrote another. Next, in the early 1820s, while in internal exile in the southern borderlands of the empire, he wrote what are called his 'southern poems', the closest he came to high Romanticism: alienated individuals in exile or captivity in exotic locations – the Caucasus among hostile tribesmen (*The Prisoner of the Caucasus*), a Tatar palace in the Crimea (*The Fountain of Bakhchisarai*), Gipsy encampments in Bessarabia (*The Gypsies*). He wrote one long historical narrative poem (*Poltava*, 1823), one historical verse tragedy in quasi-Shakespearian mode (*Boris Godunov*, 1825); a cluster of verse playlets, all written over the course of a few months in 1830 (*Little Tragedies*), a group of short stories (*Tales of Belkin*, also 1830), a Gothic tale (*The Queen of Spades*) and a quasi-historical novella (*The Captain's Daughter*), not to mention his extraordinary generic hybrid narrative poem *The Bronze Horseman* (1833), with elements ranging from ode through epic to psychological tragedy.

Alongside this relentless experimentation there were two constants in Pushkin's poetic output: his lyric poetry, which was the staple of his writing throughout his career; and, over the course of nearly a decade, his verse novel, *Eugene Onegin*. Pushkin started writing the novel in May 1823, while still in exile in the south. He continued it during his period of banishment to his family's estate at Mikhailovskoe, near Pskov, in 1824–6, and he completed it in the summer of 1831. It was published in instalments (as separate booklets) between 1825 and 1832, and as a complete book in 1833. At the start, Pushkin purports only to have a vague idea of how the work will progress: 'here', he says in his preface to the first printing of the first chapter, 'is the beginning of a large poem which will probably never be completed'.[8] At the end he makes an elaborate show of abandoning his work arbitrarily, as if in mid-plot, although in fact it is carefully shaped to end exactly thus.[9] The mode of writing which he devised specifically for *Eugene Onegin* – a fourteen-line stanza with a distinctive pattern of rhyme, along with an authorial stance that continually hovers between flippancy and engagement, between distance and involvement – was set at the start and was sustained with absolute consistency to the end. Indeed, the form and manner were so deeply embedded, so inextricably enmeshed in the work for which they were devised, that they barely figured again in Russian literature except in deliberate homage to, or parody of, Pushkin's verse novel. This association of form with work extends into English, where Vikram Seth's 1986 novel *Golden Gate* is written in the 'Onegin stanza', explicitly in homage to Pushkin.

Pushkin's effervescent *Eugene Onegin* – not to be confused with Tchaikovsky's solemn opera that borrows the title, the basic elements of the plot and some of the words, but is quite different in spirit – can objectively be described as his masterpiece: not necessarily in the broad sense of being acknowledged as his greatest work (though, for many, it is precisely that), but in the older and more precise sense of being the artefact in which he most thoroughly and overtly demonstrates his mastery of his craft. Pushkin constantly foregrounds his own manipulation of stylistic levels and devices. Language is not merely a medium for expression but a principal theme. *Eugene Onegin* is a sustained display of linguistic virtuosity.

At the simplest level: each of the principal characters in *Eugene Onegin* moves in their own aura of conventional vocabulary and imagery. This is how they are created, this is how they see themselves and others, this is how they understand or misunderstand each other. The sisters Tatiana and Olga are formed from different sets of Sentimentalist or Pre-Romanticist verbal association. Olga is a collection of unreflective rosy-posy, pretty-maid clichés of light and flighty affection. Tatiana is moodier, by implication deeper, and more towards the Zhukovskian end of the spectrum, associated with the moon, with dreams and nocturnal balladry rather than light pastoral. The young Vladimir Lenskii, steeped in airy German Romanticism, is killed in a duel by the more Byronically sceptical Onegin, the eponymous (anti-)hero. And then there is the figure of the author; or rather, multiple figures: from a participant and acquaintance of the protagonists, to their affectionate, indulgent but capriciously controlling creator, liable at any time to deflate the bubbles of their literariness with a disruptive dose of ostensibly plain prose – a deliberately virtuosic trick, of course, since in fact Pushkin never actually breaks the tight structures of his own poetic Onegin stanza – except when demonstratively stepping outside the implied narratorial voice: when citing his protagonists' letters to each other.

In itself there is nothing new in linguistic characterization, or in associated mutual misapprehensions. As we saw, Fonvizin had used a similar device over half a century earlier in *The Brigadier*. But an analogy with Fonvizin would be skin-deep. Pushkin's *Eugene Onegin*, though often humorous, is not a comedy. In Fonvizin's play, stock language is a device that belittles, contains, distances, satirizes. In Pushkin's verse novel the literary sensibilities evoked through the respective auras of language and imagery *may* be distanced, may be viewed with amusement or scepticism, but they are also fully validated. When within a convention, Pushkin makes it authentic, real, a device for empathy rather than for separation; until he switches register, whereby stylistic device is unmasked as stylistic device. There is no settled neutral reality. Everything is foregrounded as a register of language, but no register is allowed to stand unchallenged by another. Pushkin mocks Classicism by inserting a prologue almost as an afterthought, more than three quarters of the way through the book; yet the shaping is in its way as disciplined and symmetrical as anything in Classicism. He apologizes to Shishkov for his Gallicisms ('Sorry, but I don't know how to translate this . . .').[10] His heroine, Tatiana, his 'true ideal', in fact wrote in French because she 'knew Russian badly'; but the narrator retains a soft spot for Gallicism anyway ('like the sins of youth'), while declaring that he really does 'not like Russian speech without any grammatical mistakes'.[11] Despite the superficial similarity, this is a long way from the agreement, among Fonvizin's protagonists, that they do not like grammar.

Such open, ludic jibes are merely the surface. For a sense of the deeper resonances of Pushkin's manipulation of convention, just one example will have to suffice. *Eugene Onegin* has a very simple plot. The moonstruck provincial, Tatiana Larina, confesses to her nanny that she has fallen in love with the weary sophisticate Onegin. He condescendingly rejects her. He flirts with her younger sister, Olga, and kills his friend Lenskii in the resultant duel, after which he has to flee. Tatiana meanwhile wanders into Onegin's abandoned house and browses through his books, 'reading' Onegin through the marks he made in the margins – that is, through her reading of the signs of his reading of books. This is a revelation to her, a new literary sensibility (predominantly Byronic). She apparently realizes that what had seemed original and individual in him may be merely derivative, generic. Is he in fact just a 'complete lexicon of modish words'? A 'parody'?[12] Some years later, on returning to St Petersburg, Onegin sees Tatiana, now a lady in high society. He, in turn, falls in love with her. She, apparently rising above her past naiveté, rejects him. But the terms are paradoxical: she sees through him yet she professes still to love him. And she muses on what might have been: she would happily abandon her high-society life, with its glittery superficiality, for a shelf of books, for a wild garden and for the modest dwelling where they first met, and the humble, shaded graveyard where her poor nanny rests . . .[13] That is, she lapses into a pure Sentimentalist idyll of bittersweet nostalgia for a past that never really was.

Tatiana exits, leaving Onegin enveloped in an utterly different (but no less conventional) set of linguistic resonances: he is 'as if struck by thunder', plunged into a 'storm of emotions', interrupted by the 'sudden clanking of spurs' as Tatiana's husband appears. Gentle, Sentimentalist elegy is shattered by the harsh sounds and violent imagery of Romantic melodrama. And then, just as suddenly, they vanish. Enter the author, who chooses to abandon them – forever. Time to lapse into prosaic language, and into prosaic sentence structures that appear to disrupt the expected rhythms of the verse (while remaining, of course, strictly metrical); time to stop. 'Hurrah! Long overdue?'[14]

Pushkin did not found a literary language, but he transformed the approach to expressive potential in the combinations of inherited resources. He did not abandon the disciplines of Classicism, or the sweetness of true feeling (whether in its rusticity or in its Gallicisms), or indeed the clichés of high Romanticism, outmoded and limited though they all may have been. But nor was he restricted by or confined to any of them. Part of his display, in *Eugene Onegin*, was to show that he could operate effectively, affectively, in any idiom he chose. Linguistic and generic convention serve him, not the other way around. He sweeps up all the registers and debates around what cultured Russian ought to be – and shows that his Russian can be any or all or none of them. The authority of the individual was not in the creation of a language but in the assertion – backed up by sustained virtuosic demonstration – of the writer's right to manipulate the resources of language as he pleased.

Pushkin's contemporary, the critic Vissarion Belinskii (1811–1848), praised *Eugene Onegin* for the capaciousness and granularity of its social vision. He called it 'an encyclopaedia of Russian life'.[15] In the next generation the critic and novelist Nikolai Chernyshevskii (1828–1889) interpreted Pushkin's significance in precisely the opposite way. In a series of essays from 1855–6 entitled *Studies in the Gogol Period of Russian Literature*, Chernyshevskii argued that Pushkin had liberated Russian literature not because of what he said but because of what he enabled others subsequently to say: Pushkin provided the tools, the forms, the language. With the language of Pushkin, a literature of content became possible.[16] A century later Vladimir Nabokov published an extensive commentary on the novel, which he described as 'first of all and above all a phenomenon of style'.[17] Language is at all times in the foreground. It makes the heroes. In a sense, it *is* the hero.

None of this is quite sufficient to explain the place of Pushkin in traditional representations of the culture of the Russian language. His brilliance as a writer is a necessary condition but not a sufficient condition. Pushkin was acknowledged as pre-eminent in his time, but that is as nothing by comparison with his posthumous veneration.

It is sometimes said that Pushkin in Russian culture is equivalent to Shakespeare in English culture. The analogy is misleading. Pushkin is far more important. This is not a value judgement. There is no point in trying to argue that one or the other was a better writer; but Pushkin has become embedded in linguistic identity in a different way. It has helped, to some extent, that Pushkin's language is, for most modern readers, more accessible. Russian of the 1820s and '30s raises fewer linguistic barriers than English of the turn of the seventeenth century. Pushkin's generic versatility has also been important. From folk tale and fairy tale through to historical drama or miniature tragedy, not to mention the constant stream of lyrics, there is a Pushkin for all ages, from early childhood to mature adulthood. For generations of Russians, induction into the cult of Pushkin began almost from infancy. They grew up with his words and his image, grew into a familiarity with Pushkin that could, in effect, fuse with a sense of identity. Pushkin could be studied, of course, but the sense of essential affinity was beyond critical challenge. Historically, socially, politically, Pushkin could be contextualized but not alienated. From the Kremlin to the camps, Pushkin was undeniable. And the Pushkin cult was continually reinforced through all the paraphernalia of public identity-building: monuments, anniversary celebrations, writing competitions, rhetorical eulogies, films, images on chocolate boxes. Pushkin was also zealously instrumentalized as a tool of russification among non-Russian peoples of the empire.

The aphorism about writers creating language was Aleksandr Bestuzhev's, not Pushkin's, but Pushkin came to epitomize its realization in practice. This was not the creation of a literary language as such but the emancipation of the writer from the assumed authority of any one set of aesthetic and stylistic norms. This may indeed sound like the culmination of a journey; and in histories of the Russian language it has often been treated as such. But Pushkin's range, too, was of its time. He was no anarchist of language. He manipulated norms but did not abandon them, and he himself had a powerful sense of form. Even while in awe of his virtuosity and flexibility, his successors could still find new reasons for frustration, new boundaries of language that needed to be crossed.

5

The Authority of the People

By the 1830s the problem of the language of culture (the literary language) might appear to have been solved. Norms were established and institutionalized; correct forms were systematized in grammars, which by now had long ceased to be just for foreigners and scholars but had migrated into education; words were gathered and defined in dictionaries; and writers had sufficiently tested and explored the potential of those norms to serve their purposes expressively and flexibly. But it is never enough. Norms continually draw attention to their own artificiality. Every solution becomes a problem with the next shift in the dominant cultural paradigm. The hierarchical, genre-based norms of Classicism had been undermined by the salon taste of Sentimentalism, which in turn had been challenged by the Romanticist focus on the individual and the writer's right to self-expression. But, for some, Romanticist self-centredness was amoral, lonely, superfluous to wider society, even a kind of malaise. In terms of literary movements, the search for language beyond the norms is associated with the rise, in various guises, of types of Realism.

Change in the culture of language was a symptom of societal change. Literate education expanded, in part to feed the rapidly growing urban bureaucracy. The notion of the 'people' became a more significant and contentious category in philosophical and social thought, in state ideology and in arguments among the intelligentsia about history and identity, about justice and the social order, about the nature and fate of Russia. From the abstract to the empirical: learned institutions, such as the old Academy of Sciences and the new Russian Geographical Society (founded in 1845), began to make it their business to explore the human geography of the empire. In the sphere of social legislation, all of this fed the kinds of concerns that formed the background to the abolition of serfdom in 1861.

Even by the second quarter of the nineteenth century, the curators of the Russian literary language took very little account of the speech habits of the vast majority of the population. This was deliberate. Those who had sought to establish the dignity of Russian as a language of culture tended to filter out such unmediated utterances. In literature the educated spoke to the educated; or in ways in which the educated felt they should be seen to be speaking, regardless of the fact that their own private conversations could be quite pithy.[1] Even the uneducated had to sound linguistically decorous if they were to be taken seriously. Karamzin's poor Liza was a peasant girl who was capable not only of loving but, seemingly, of expressing her sentiments with the linguistic sensibility of polite society. In Lomonosov's vision of a stylistic hierarchy, colloquialism (but not vulgarity) was permissible only in the low genres such as comedy. Fonvizin's uneducated speakers are parodies who clumsily mimic the idioms of their betters. Where were the authentic voices of the uneducated? Where was the writing that reflected and gave status to the real language of the Russian people in all its diversity? That was not the purpose of literature. Part of the mission of the language of culture was to elevate the level of popular speech, not to be contaminated and dragged down by it.

Over the middle decades of the nineteenth century there was yet another shift in literary values and priorities: a broadening of social perspective, a rebalancing of emphasis in the direction of wider social depiction and exploration. While many writers continued to be preoccupied with representing their own kind, others began, in a more focused and systematic way, to redirect their gaze outwards and to open themselves and their works to *non*-educated, *non*-standardized language: or, in neat but misleading shorthand, the language of the people. Again there were consequences for the ecology of forms and genres. Poetry fell off its pedestal, as did the transcendent figure of the poet. The genres of Realism were predominantly in prose: the short story and the novel. With regard to language – insofar as it is possible to generalize at all about the many, many varieties of Realism – the Realist aesthetic involved another radical adjustment of approach. In the crudest terms: while previous literary fashions had tended to value the display of artifice, Realism tended to value its concealment. Rather than flaunting its performative devices, it masked them. Realism crafted an illusion of authenticity. And when the social horizons of literature expanded into the recesses of the city or into actual villages across the country rather than into sentimentally idyllic rusticity, then, in the context of a Realist aesthetic, that posed a new challenge for language.[2] The challenge went beyond style, beyond literature. For some, it exposed a major gap in knowledge: how could one create an illusion of authentic language without knowing what that authentic language actually was? Before it could be adequately represented, the language of the people needed to be heard, recorded, studied. This chapter explores the mid-nineteenth-century anxiety about authentic language – language beyond literary norms – in three contexts: in literature about peasants, in lexicography and on city streets.

Writing the People

Nikolai Gogol's (1809–1852) earliest collection of stories, *Evenings on a Farm Near Dikanka*, was published in two volumes in 1831–2. The tales – fantastical, farcical, often with strong elements of the supernatural, ostensibly chaotic – are set in a Ukrainian village. They are presented through a double narrative frame. The outer narrative is that of the ostensible editor or publisher of the collection, a Ukrainian beekeeper by the name of Rudyi Panko. The 'evenings' of the title are the occasions when the villagers gather to tell stories. The prefaces to the collections are in Panko's voice, but several of the stories are told by others, hence in a variety of individualized voices. At both levels, therefore, the narratives are in character, as if spoken – an early example of a technique that in the Russian critical tradition is known as *skaz*.

Rudyi Panko is aware of his own audience: they sit in distant St Petersburg, a long way away both geographically and culturally ('You won't find anything like this in your St Petersburg'). And he is conscious of narrative style. One of the Dikanka storytellers, for example, is 'quite the young gentleman (*panich*)', whose manner was 'so fancy, so clever, like in printed books'; sometimes, listening to him, try as you might, you couldn't understand a thing: 'where did he dig up such words?'[3] The sense of lexical alienation worked both ways. Rudyi Panko well understands that, just as he sometimes finds bookish words incomprehensible, so his book-trained St Petersburg readers might have difficulty with some of his own and his informants' local Dikanka locutions. In each of the two volumes his preface is followed by a glossary of 'words in this book that not everyone might understand'. In later editions the two lists were amalgamated into one.

While working on the Dikanka stories, Gogol actively sought inspiration in a kind of local authenticity. He even wrote to his mother and others in Ukraine, asking them to send examples of local anecdotes and legends. But there is no pretence that the outcome is documentary. The village is Ukrainian, but the language is not. The narratives are spiced – occasionally permeated – with Ukrainian*isms*. Occasionally, Gogol (or Rudyi Panko) does include phrases that are set in italics to mark them as foreign (that is, Ukrainian). For example, while introducing *St John's Eve* Panko sets up yet another story frame. It seems that on one occasion Foma Grigorevich had told the story in the presence of a writer. Rudyi Panko is not complimentary about writers: 'they come, they ask, they steal all kinds of stuff, and then publish books';[4] rather like Gogol himself, indeed. Anyway, once the pretentious young gentleman turned up with a book and showed Foma Grigorevich an extract which turned out to be a story that had been told by Foma Grigorevich himself, who was duly outraged: 'Spit on the head of whoever printed this! *Breshe, suchyi moskal'*. Did I really say that? *Shcho-to vzhe, iak u kogo chort ma klepki v golovi.*'[5] Whereupon Foma Grigorevich reclaims the story by telling it his own way. His colloquial Ukrainian abuse of the plagiarizing *moskal'* (Muscovite; Russian) is untranslated; but the language of the story that he then tells is Russian.

The linguistic dynamics are not straightforward. Gogol plays on at least two axes of contrast. On the one hand, he highlights the distinction between the regional and the metropolitan, the language of the village versus the language of the city: that is, in this instance, Ukrainian (or, in the terminology of the day, Little-Russian) versus standard Russian. On the other hand, he plays on the distinction between the spoken and the written, between orality and bookishness, between (by implication) authentic storytelling and literary appropriation. These are all key contentious issues in the culture of language. Nevertheless, for all the potential seriousness of the issues, Gogol's mode is comic. And because this is comedy, the use of non-standard speech can be read as traditional rather than radical. Even Lomonosov's system of styles had allowed for vulgar colloquialism in comedy. Comic representation of uneducated speech features in drama from the eighteenth century, as, for example, in the device of egregiously incorrect spelling in a one-act play by Aleksei Kopiev, published in 1794, whose title might be rendered approximately as *Woss Ours Ain't Needed* (illus. 19).[6] For the metropolitan reader, Gogol's early stories were distanced by manner as well as by subject: not a challenge to a linguistic standard, not an expansion of ethnographic or ethnolinguistic horizons, but a parade of funny village folk for the delight and amusement of the educated reader in St Petersburg. Gogol's later style of first-person narration could be more challenging. His idiosyncratic rhythms and lexicon, a kind of poetics of digression

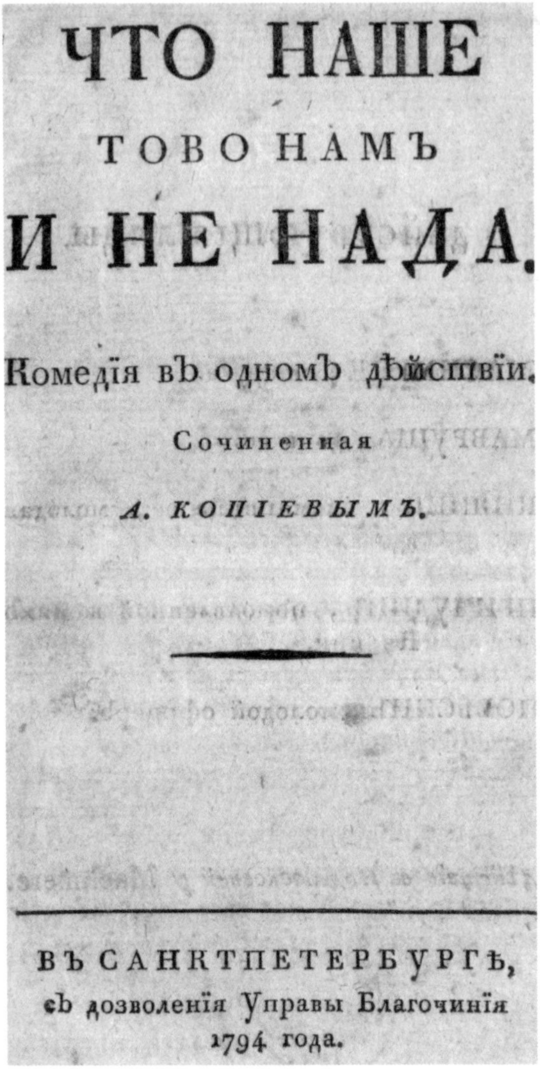

ЧТО НАШЕ

ТОВО НАМЪ

И НЕ НАДА.

Комедія въ одномъ дѣйствіи.

Сочиненная

А. КОПІЕВЫМЪ.

ВЪ САНКТПЕТЕРБУРГѢ,
съ дозволенія Управы Благочинія
1794 года.

19 A. Kopiev, *Woss Ours Ain't Needed* (1794), title page, in ostentatiously non-standard Russian.

and quirkiness, were more nuanced, more subversively humane than Lomonosov might have envisaged, but in the early 1840s they could still be read as vulgar. An early newspaper reviewer of his novel *Dead Souls* (1842) complained that even the narrator's own language was 'incorrect and utterly barbaric'.[7] The reviewer made no allowance for the fact that the first-person narrative style may also be a form of characterization.

Regular attempts to bridge the gap of comedic distancing emerged somewhat later, from the middle of the 1840s.[8] In the first instance they were associated with the kind of writing that came to be labelled (at first disparagingly, then neutrally) the Natural School. The typical genre of the Natural School was the short story, or the 'physiological' sketch. The focus of early physiological writing was urban. The first collection of stories to be labelled as such was *The Physiology of Petersburg*, assembled and introduced by the critic Vissarion Belinskii and published in 1845. As the name implies, physiological writing presented itself as objective, investigating the human anatomy of the city. Such an approach might now be reckoned more ethnographic or anthropological than medical, but the point of the metaphor was clear. From its urban beginnings, physiological writing quickly shifted its gaze outwards into the countryside. The earliest example of rural physiological writing is generally reckoned to be *The Village*, a story by Dmitrii Grigorovich (1822–1900), which was first published in 1846. This was closely followed, in January 1847, by *Khor and Kalinych*, which is best known for its inclusion as the opening story in the 1852 collection *A Huntsman's Sketches*, by Ivan Turgenev (1818–1883).

The two contemporaries present very different pictures of rural Russia. Grigorovich's village is a place of poverty and callousness. Turgenev's narrator – the eponymous 'huntsman' – is struck by the peasants' dignity, good sense and self-reliance. They also have different modes of linguistic representation. Grigorovich was a collector of colloquialisms and regionalisms, with which he sprinkled his peasants' dialogues. Some critics praised his accuracy and honesty, others objected to his negative image of the Russian peasant.[9] That dispute could be reckoned political. On the linguistic level, Grigorovich's direct use of peasant language was a risk. His metropolitan readers were not used to treating uneducated speech seriously, and some did indeed – by generic habit – deride the language as comic.[10] Even in the context of the Natural School in the mid-1840s, it would be a mistake to imagine that peasant language was automatically regarded as a dignified register.

In an essay published in 1845, reviewing a rather pedantic booklet about grammar, Belinskii himself wrote, 'Why do we speak of the language of literature, and not of the language of the people? For the simplest of reasons: the mass of the people lags behind educated society, and for society the people's language has become too impoverished and unsatisfactory.'[11] Belinskii's comment acknowledges that popular language should be taken seriously, but it falls far short of treating popular language as in any sense authoritative. Peasant speech was a legitimate object of interest, but in no way a model. The question was: how to appropriate peasant speech into the literary language, not the reverse? There were no rules. Gabriella Safran presents the quest for solutions as not merely individual but individualistic, a game of competitive listening to peasant voices, a kind of 'competition for nativeness'.[12]

Turgenev was more cautious than Grigorovich, and by implication less dogmatic than Belinskii. His narrator regularly comments on aspects of peasant speech such as intonation, but he is careful not to alienate or demean his peasants linguistically. Most may be illiterate, but their speech has dignity. Khor – an entrepreneurial serf who could buy his freedom but nevertheless prefers the habitual security of his serfdom – speaks in pithy truisms. There are no signs of literate habits such as complex sentences with subordinate clauses, but nor is there an agglomeration of non-literary rustic regionalisms to tax his interlocutor (or the implied reader). Perhaps Khor speaks comprehensibly because he is conversing with the aristocratic huntsman, but there is no sense of strain. His voice is presented as natural, without affectation. Moreover, Turgenev's narrator also conveys peasant speech that cannot be contextually constrained: he has a habit of eavesdropping unobserved, as when he overhears a sad dialogue between the peasant girl Akulina and the pretentious lackey Viktor, who has aspirations above his current station: apart from a few tell-tale diminutives, Akulina's diction, though limited, is formally correct. If Karamzin had taken delight in the fact that even peasant-girls could fall in love, in Turgenev even peasant girls can speak relatively proper Russian.

Turgenev's mode of evoking peasant individuality without linguistic alienation was more comfortable for many of his readers. Nevertheless, Grigorovich's more direct method had its principled followers. Among them was Nikolai Uspenskii (1837–1889), whose village tales were published from the late 1850s. Uspenskii often plunges straight into unmediated peasant dialogues that can be quite challenging in retrospect, and which many contemporary critics felt were too raw and rebarbative to be praised unequivocally as literature; but their linguistic challenge served other purposes. In a well-known review published in 1861 – the year of the abolition of serfdom – the radical critic Nikolai Chernyshevskii was explicit on both counts. In Chernyshevskii's view, Uspenskii could be puzzling because his stories seemed like mere fragments, unworked scraps of conversations, without even lip service to style. But their value, and their author's talent, should not be measured in terms of literary polish. Almost the opposite: Nikolai Uspenskii 'writes the truth about the peasants, without any adornment'.[13] Chernyshevskii's main argument was about character: Uspenskii did not idealize or demean; his peasants were flawed, human, ordinary, real. This was conveyed through their thoughts and actions, but Uspenskii's primary expressive device was the representation of their language.

Collecting Words

Progressive critics such as Belinskii and Chernyshevskii called on writers to represent the language of the people, by which they generally meant the language of peasants. The idea of the language of the people was an attractive illusion. There was, and is, no such thing. The people did not and do not all speak in the same way. In the modern, urbanized world there are many distinct social variants of non-normative Russian. In the mid-nineteenth century the social categories might have been conceived as relatively uncomplicated: the educated elite and the small (but growing) urban underclass were massively outnumbered by the overwhelming majority of the population that consisted of illiterate peasants. However, the country was vast, villages could be isolated and peasant travel was actively discouraged. It would have been odd if all of those who were lumped together under a single social label (the common people, the peasantry) spoke in the same way. Alongside the calls for appropriating peasant speech into the writings of the educated came an interest in the linguistic autonomy and diversity of the peasant population itself.

How wide or deep were the regional differences? Classic Russian dialectology distinguishes three levels of magnification, so to speak: the *góvor*, the *dialékt* and the *naréchie*.[14] In this scheme, a *góvor* might cover just a few settlements which share some features of their speech. A *dialékt* is characterized by systemic features that are shared by several *góvory*. A *naréchie* is characterized by the systemic features shared by several *dialékty*. In English, all three levels are often referred to as dialects (although a *góvor* might also be called a sub-dialect). So, a dialect map of Russia can be quite simple, or highly nuanced, depending on the degree of granularity.[15] At the level of the *dialékt* – let alone the *góvor* – the picture is complex. However, at the level of *naréchie*, the geography of Russian is usually divided into just three enormous zones: the southern dialect zone, the northern dialect zone and a mixed zone between the two. Moscow is in the mixed zone. The main distinctions between the northern and southern zones are in their pronunciations. For example, northerners typically use a hard 'g', while in the south the pronunciation of 'g' is softer and longer (technically, a voiced velar fricative). Perhaps most characteristic is the difference in the treatment of unstressed vowels. Northern pronunciation of *golová* (head), for example, gives each 'o' its full value. This is known as *ókan'e*. Southern pronunciation, by contrast, is characterized by *ákan'e*: the pre-stressed vowel, although written as 'o', is pronounced as 'a' (and the pre-pre-stressed vowel is reduced). In the case of the articulation of 'g', Contemporary Standard Russian follows the northern practice (that is, a hard 'g'), while in the case of unstressed vowels, Contemporary Standard Russian is closer to the southern practice (*akan'e*).

The middle decades of the nineteenth century were also the formative years of Russian historical philology. Then, too, it was commonplace to speak of the emergence of three *naréchiia* of Russian. However, these were conceptualized in a way that was indicative of the age: the three *narechiia* of the Russian language were labelled Great-Russian, Ukrainian (or Little-Russian) and Belorussian.[16] Russian linguists have long shifted away from treating Ukrainian and Belarusian as dialects of Russian, though the notion lingers in some politically charged rhetoric.

The division into just three broad zones – northern, southern and mixed – contributes to the impression that Russian has notably few dialects. The impression is accurate if dialect is understood to be defined principally by pronunciation, by accent. In this there is a striking contrast between Russia and, say, England (let alone with the United Kingdom as a whole). In England, even in the twenty-first century and despite the seemingly overwhelming forces for homogenization (for example, standard education, urbanization, mobility, mass media and so on), major differences in pronunciation persist. Easily identifiable local patterns of speech are separated by remarkably short distances. On a journey from London to Birmingham to Liverpool, then across to Leeds, or Bradford, then north to Newcastle or Sunderland, each stop is an encounter with quite distinct sound-systems and rhythms: from Cockney to Brummie to Scouse to Yorkshire to Geordie.

In Russian, the general features that distinguished north from south, or literate from illiterate, were not new even in literature. Kopiev's 1794 comedy mocked the uneducated through its phonetic spelling of speech that showed strong *ákan'e*. Words, however, were trickier to capture, or to know in their diversity. Non-standard (non-normative) and regional vocabulary only began to be explored in a focused way in the mid-nineteenth century. Literature is selective insofar as it includes that which happens to interest writers; lexicography is systematic (even if not comprehensive). If a short story is a snapshot, a dictionary is, or attempts to be, a panorama. While writers went on forays beyond the received norms, lexicographers had grander visions of expanding the boundaries of recorded language. In the late eighteenth century, the *Dictionary of the Russian Academy* had been – had proudly declared itself to be – normative. Interest in collecting non-normative phenomena such as folk sayings dates from at least the mid-eighteenth century,[17] but remained outside mainstream lexicography and outside the culture of print. Two major projects embody the mid-nineteenth-century challenge to that convention. They were the first large-scale attempts at descriptive rather than prescriptive compilations of the words of Russian; and, although they both perhaps emerge from a common impulse, they were utterly unlike one another. One was the *Attempt at a Great-Russian Regional Dictionary*, first published by the Academy of Sciences in 1852 and with a supplement in 1856. The second was the four-volume *Explanatory Dictionary of the Living Great-Russian Language* by Vladimir Dal (1801–1872), published between 1863 and 1866.[18]

The *Attempt at a Great-Russian Regional Dictionary* was the kind of collective, collaborative project for which scholars might these days apply for a very large grant. It was initiated by the Academy of Sciences in 1845, seven years before its main results were published. Its principal editor, Aleksandr Vostokov (1781–1864), was perhaps the most distinguished academic linguist of his era in Russia and is still known as one of the founders of historical and comparative Slavonic linguistics. He produced both a grammar and a dictionary of Church Slavonic. He was the author of a popular abbreviated grammar of Russian, first published in 1831 and reissued frequently. For the purposes of the *Attempt at a Great-Russian Regional Dictionary*, the Academy recruited a network of informants. In each of 31 administrative provinces (*gubernii*) the principal provider of lexicographical materials was the region's Director of Schools. The sources gathered by each Director of Schools are listed in the dictionary's preface.[19] In a few cases the Directors of Schools could provide local vocabularies that had already been printed (for example, from the Vologda and Tver regions). Mostly, however, the Directors of Schools subcontracted the lexicographical groundwork to local teachers. The preface lists about one hundred such contributors, who gathered words themselves in their respective towns or districts.

In its conceptualization and realization, the *Attempt at a Great-Russian Regional Dictionary* is both transparent and ambiguous. On the one hand, it seems like a comprehensive and inclusive project, a gathering of words from across the expanses of Russia, from the far north to the steppes, from west of Moscow to eastern Siberia and beyond, including even some materials from the Russian colonies in North America (provided previously by a linguistically curious naval officer).[20] It is worth noting that, despite the vast scope, the editors were quite strict in their conception of the 'Great-Russian' language area: no lexical materials were sought from the Ukrainian or Belarusian regions of the empire. Another decision of the editors was to present the dictionary in the form of a single word list, regardless of where each word had been recorded. The entry for each word states where it was gathered, but there are no separate regional lists. It would be very difficult, on the basis of this dictionary, to construct a map of regional expressions. Although the framework and methods of the project appear to be scrupulously ethnographic, the effect is to represent the vocabulary of the regions collectively, as a whole, by implied contrast with the standard language of the capitals. On one interpretation, therefore, at least at the level of vocabulary, the *Attempt at a Great-Russian Regional Dictionary* could be said to anticipate by around 150 years a trend in linguistics that treated peasant language as a whole, as an integral social dialect irrespective of region.[21] On another interpretation, the dictionary could be said to represent everywhere and nowhere: it becomes a lexicon of a generalized, collective 'other', not of any variety of real spoken language.

Not that the editors described it as such. They promoted it as a pathway to self-discovery and self-fulfilment. The dictionary turns our minds towards 'the patriarchal ways of our villagers and brings us closer to them'. More than that, by expanding lexicographical space, we can overcome time: 'listening closely to the language of the people we discover treasures that have survived for centuries. In peasant huts, where our songs and folk tales and proverbs have been preserved, many precious words have been kept safe from all-corrosive Time.'[22]

Vladimir Dal's *Explanatory Dictionary of the Living Great-Russian Language* reflects the same mid-century urge to seek beyond the metropolitan educated norms of language, the same lexicographical curiosity. However, it is quite different in its vision, its methods, its scale, its results and its understanding of what makes or should make the Russian language. This was no collective research project, but the obsession of an extraordinarily driven individual. The regional dictionary was a work of lexicographical ethnography, dealing *only* with non-normative local vocabulary. Dal's project was more ambitious and radical: to combine his newly assembled colloquialisms and regionalisms *with* received normative vocabulary so as to form a new, integrated, total representation of an expanded 'living Great-Russian language'.

Vladimir Dal (illus. 20) is an unlikely lexicographer. His first career was as a doctor, eventually a military surgeon, who also became well connected in St Petersburg literary circles. In 1837 he conducted the post-mortem on Aleksandr Pushkin following the latter's fatal duel. Dal was the first in a line of distinguished Russian writers who were also doctors (of whom the best known are Anton Chekhov and Mikhail Bulgakov). He dabbled in writing from at least the early 1830s, but recognition and prominent publications came later, in the mid-1840s. In 1845 Dal became one of the founding members of the Russian Geographical Society (from 1850 the Imperial Russian Geographical Society), which itself was an important institutional product of the wider interest in systematic exploration.[23]

Vladimir Dal, like his younger contemporary, Dmitrii Grigorovich, cannot be reckoned a household name among Anglophone nonspecialists in Russian literature, so it is important to stress that, in

20 Vasilii Perov, *Vladimir Dal*, 1872, oil on canvas.

the mid-1840s, both Dal and Grigorovich were at the heart of the St Petersburg literary world, key figures in early Russian Realism, especially among the writers associated with the Natural School. In 1845, when Vissarion Belinskii put together the seminal collection of stories with the collective title *The Physiology of Petersburg*, among his six contributors were Dal (writing under the pseudonym of V. Luganskii) and Grigorovich. In the following year, among the literary offerings published in various issues of the monthly 'thick journal' *Notes of the Fatherland* (*Otechestvennye zapiski*), were two of the earliest stories by Fedor Dostoevskii (including his classic *The Double*), an instalment of Aleksandr Herzen's novel *Who Is to Blame?* (also pseudonymous), a play by Turgenev, plus a novella (in two instalments) by Dal/Luganskii; and Grigorovich's story *The Village*.[24]

The timing was not coincidental. The 'physiological' preoccupations of the Natural School made Dal a man for the moment – and not merely because he happened to be a doctor. Dal was a collector of words and phrases all his adult life. His peripatetic military service served him well. Wherever he went, there, too, went his ever-growing baggage of index cards; thousands and thousands of them. Collecting is never complete, but eventually, as he entered his seventh decade, he decided that it was time to publish. Besides the four-volume dictionary of words, Dal also produced a massive, thousand-page assemblage of over 30,000 folk sayings, *Proverbs of the Russian People*, arranged according to his own thematic classification.[25] On a smaller scale was Dal's collection of obscene folk sayings, which remained unpublished until the very end of the twentieth century (see Chapter Nine).

Dal was a more complex lexicographer than Vostokov in his Academy project. The *Attempt at a Great-Russian Regional Dictionary* was just a word list of regional forms with brief translations into standard Russian, an occasional example, and an indication of the region. Dal organized his dictionary into 'nests': substantial entries covering words that are related, regardless of region, and with quite copious explanations and specimens of usage. For example, for the main headword *blud*, Dal first explains that there are two clusters of meanings: in popular usage the word relates to 'deviation from the straight path, both in a literal and a metaphorical sense', while in 'church or bookish' usage it denotes 'illicit cohabitation out of wedlock'. The extensive entry then goes on to explain a range of derivatives: *bluzhdát'*, *bludít'*; *bludít'sia*; *bluzhdánie* or *bluzhdénie*; *blúdnyi*; *bludník*, *bludnítsa*; *bludniá*, *blúden'*, *blúdni*; *bludiága*, *bludiáshka*; *bludlívyi*; *bludlívost'*; *bludílishche*; *bludodéi*; *bludiáchii*.[26] By contrast, the *Attempt at a Great-Russian Regional Dictionary* has no entry for *blud* itself or for any of the derivatives that its editors judged to exist in the standard language; but it has *separate* entries for *bludník* and for *bludnítsa* (noting that both were recorded in the Tikhvin dialect of the Novgorod region); for *bludniá* (also from the Tikhvin dialect) and separately for the differently stressed version *blúdnia* (from the Nizhnyi Novgorod and Tambov regions) and for *bludiáshka*, from Tver.[27]

Vostokov, through his widely dispersed network of informants, presented the richness of words that were nevertheless 'other' for the metropolitan reader; their otherness was the principal criterion for their inclusion. Dal deliberately transcended otherness in his new holistic vision of the living Great-Russian language. Not everybody understood this. In its generally complimentary response to the start of the publication of Dal's dictionary, the Ethnographic Section of the Russian Geographical Society nevertheless remarked that, in the case of non-standard vocabulary, it would have been desirable to include an indication of the source: where and from whom was the compiler informed of the word? Dal responded that over the course of four decades he had collected around 80,000 words that had not been recorded in any dictionary; that in some cases he had felt it appropriate to note the region, but to identify informants all the time would have been impracticable and would have missed the point: this was the living Great-Russian language; Russian as a whole, not a bunch of ethnographically circumscribed regionalisms.[28]

The point had already been made more colourfully in a speech that Dal delivered in April 1862 at the Society of Lovers of Russian Letters. Here, like Vostokov, he presented his work in spatial terms, but in a strikingly different way. Vostokov's vision was horizontal, stressing the vast expanses that had been explored in his word-gathering enterprise. Dal's spatial image was vertical, more personal, more polemical, more writerly:

> Do not imagine that [the additional 80,000 words] consist entirely of indigenous or previously unheard-of regional

expressions. On the contrary: nine tenths of them are simple, everyday words that have until now not made it into our dictionaries precisely because of their simplicity, their artlessness and mundaneness. Dictionaries are put together from books, and books are written by climbing on stilts and high platforms. From the sky we reach for stars, but we do not see what is under our feet.[29]

Language on the Street

In addition to switching planes from the horizontal to the vertical, Dal shifted the mode of sensory input from listening to seeing, from the ear to the eye. His 'seeing' was metaphorical, but others in the age of the Natural School were more literal in their looking. Never mind scouring the extremities of empire and the depths of the countryside: on the streets of the capitals, non-standard Russian could be seen as well as heard. Traditional urban commercial signage had been largely pictorial, but by the 1830s and '40s observers of the urban scene were struck by the abundance of visible verbiage. Presumably the people who displayed such signs counted on a sufficiency of literate viewers for it to be worthwhile. But the literacy of the sign-makers themselves would not always have impressed grammarians such as Lomonosov or even Vostokov. From the mid-1830s the noting of *non-standard* signage became a minor sub-theme in city-writing; usually a cause for condescending amusement. Here the main focus of attention was not vocabulary but orthography, not dialect words but untrained spelling – and, to some extent, clumsy usage.[30]

The first substantial work devoted specifically to Moscow street signs was published in 1836 under the pseudonym of Fedor Distribuendi. Distribuendi distinguished three types of sign: 'elegant' (in which the wording was often in French), 'ordinary' and 'curious'. His 'curious' signs tended to offend the author's sense of harmonious design, but their makers' pretentiousness was also betrayed by their verbal clumsiness: they undermined their own message by their inability to spell properly. Distribuendi gives an example: *Evgenei Medvedev. Voennoi i portekuliarnoi por"t"nnoi* ('Evgenii Medvedev: military and private tailor'),[31] where the spelling of almost every word is in violation of bookish norms: 'Medvedev' is written using the letter *iat'* (ѣ) in the first syllable rather than the second; the first two vowels of *portekuliarnoi* should be 'a' and 'i', not 'o' and 'e'; and the word for a tailor (*portnoi*) has been expanded with two(!) intrusive 'hard signs', plus an additional 'n'.

Yet any reader would know what it meant. The language of the sign was non-literary but functionally adequate. The theme was taken up in more detail a decade later in *The Physiology of Petersburg*. The story 'Petersburg Recesses' (*Peterburgskie ugly*) by Nikolai Nekrasov (1821–1878) opens with a less conspicuous but more verbose kind of announcement: not a brightly painted trade sign, but a simple handwritten note attached to a gateway leading into a somewhat insalubrious courtyard. In Russian the note reads: *At daetsa vnaimy ugal, na vtorom dvare, vpadvale, a o tsene sprasit' kvarternai khoziaike Akuliny Fedotovne.*[32] Translation here is a problem. An English rendition can be either literate or literal, not both. A literate rendition might read 'Basement apartment for rent, in the second courtyard. Questions about the price should be addressed to the supervisor, Akulina Fedotovna.' But this version misrepresents the point, for the notice is not literate according to educated norms, or at any rate its spellings are patently non-standard. Unstressed vowels are mostly rendered as they are pronounced, not as they are supposed to be written. A prepositional prefix is written as a separate word (*at daetsa* should be *otdaetsia*), while, conversely, a separate preposition is elided with the following word (*vpadvale* should be *v podvale*). And so on. Again, the sign may be amusing, but it is functional: the narrator understands it correctly and walks into the courtyard. And there he is faced with another mass of signs, pointers to the various services offered in a dense hive of workshops. The signs are clear enough, though almost every one of them is linguistically just slightly off-key. Another story in the collection, 'The Petersburg Side' (*Peterburgskaia storona*) by Evgenii Grebenka (1812–1848), also cites a sign where the division between preposition and noun is almost invariably wrong (*v khod vzavedenie* instead of *vkhod v zavedenie*).[33]

In 1848 a brief anonymous article on Petersburg signs appeared in the weekly magazine *Illiustratsiia*.[34] The author, who designated himself simply as 'T', similarly relishes some of the non-standard spellings. However, he also suggests that perhaps the golden age of quirkiness was waning:

> Now we should say a few words about the inscriptions on the shop signs . . . Any long-term resident will recall oddities such as: V khot, Vkhot v zavedenie, Renskovoi pogreb, Zdes' priugatavliaetsa tobak, Lafka kuptsa Kopustena, Vechnova tsekhu master Ivanov, and the like.

Here, it is striking that 'T' picks out some of the same phrases and habits as were highlighted by Nekrasov and by Grebenka: the separation of prepositional prefixes; irregular *-a-* for *-o-* in unstressed positions; *-tsa* (-ца) for *-tsia* (-тся) in reflexive verbs and so on. Such correspondences between seemingly unrelated texts call into question the notion of the non-standard. Insofar as one can generalize from such a mixture of journalism and fiction, spelling may have been fluid, but the types of fluidity were fairly regular, even predictable. Fluidity according to a pattern, or within identifiable parameters, is itself a kind of norm. Even 'T', in a footnote, points out the paradox whereby initially substandard inscriptional versions could become their own conventions.

Such fragmentary evocations of a subculture within the urban graphosphere are barely comparable to the sustained literary efforts to capture peasant speech, still less to the monumental labours of the lexicographers. Yet they, too, reflect aspects of the mid-century mood of linguistic curiosity and curatorship, whether among writers associated with the Natural School and early Realism, or in the Academy; whether expressed in terms of individual listening or looking, or in a context of organized word-gathering projects. The common factor was a sense that the norm was not enough, a kind of anxiety about the enormous gap between the cultivated standard and the raw expanse and diversity of Russian as it actually was. Not everybody dealt with such anxieties in the same ways. The Realist reflections on non-normative urban signage shifted from mild mockery towards a recognition that non-literary language nevertheless operated according to functional conventions. The Academy's ethnographic othering, albeit in the service of serious linguistic curiosity, was diametrically opposed to Vladimir Dal's imperious vision of an integral, living Great-Russian language that transcended both regional variation and social stratification. All of them pushed the boundaries of the culture of language. Having reached the urban depths and the rural recesses, where was there left for others to go? What limits of language remained untested?

6

Language beyond Language

In the cultural history of language, today's fashion is tomorrow's cliché, today's creative discovery becomes tomorrow's commonplace, today's innovation becomes tomorrow's stale conventionality. Language culture has a history because nothing is ever quite enough. And sometimes language itself seems not quite enough. Language comes to be perceived as a constricting artifice that one should try to push through and beyond. This chapter explores ways in which the linguistic limits of Russian have been tested. It focuses mainly on the late nineteenth and early twentieth centuries (and hence broadly fits the chronological sequence of this book), but some digressions into other times will be necessary.

The Look of Russian: Boundaries of Form

When language becomes encoded through visible signs, it becomes part of visual culture as well as verbal culture. Written letters and words in alphabetic script are not just annotations of speech sounds. They have their own visual semantics. They stand in variable and dynamic relationships both with the implied non-visible words behind them, and with the implied viewer in front of them. Histories of Russian tend to have paid little attention to what the language looked like. They are dominated by analyses of sounds, structures and words. In considering the culture of the language, we need to look at its surfaces. The detailed history of letter forms is a sub-discipline for palaeographers (in relation to the written word) and historians of typography (in relation to the printed word). In this section we focus on two aspects of the history of the look of Russian: visual form as cultural symbol, and visible writing in cultural spaces.

Letters are made objects. Every scribe, every type-caster and typesetter has to be aware of how the surfaces are shaped. Much of the time this is a received craft, a trained practice of replication. Palaeographers are good at spotting variation even in traditional practices of letter-formation. Here we are more concerned with significances of deliberate change, of two kinds. Some innovations are individual acts of creativity, others have been systemic. We start with the latter: with changes to the basic toolkit, changes for everybody, changes that have shifted the visual semantics of lettering in a way that has had lasting cultural resonance. In Russia there have been two such episodes of culturally resonant systemic change in the look of Cyrillic. The first was Peter I's introduction of a civil typeface in the early eighteenth century; the second was the reform of the alphabet at the start of 1918.

The significance of introducing a new typeface can only be understood in the context of the earlier functions of print in Russia. By comparison with western Europe, print came to Moscow late. Although there is evidence that some printed books were imported from the late fifteenth century, no books were printed in Russia itself before the early 1550s. The first Moscow-printed book with a precise date and a known printer was the *Apóstol* (Acts and Epistles from the New Testament), which was produced by Ivan Fedorov in 1564. However, one cannot properly talk of the growth of a Muscovite 'print culture' (let alone a 'print revolution') from the mid-sixteenth century in the same way that it has become habitual to talk of a western European print culture (or print revolution) that rapidly expanded in the second half of the fifteenth century. In the first place, for several decades Muscovite printing activity was sporadic. There was no continuity, let alone growth.[1] For well over a hundred years, most of the time there was only one printing house in Moscow. Second, the *function* of printing remained almost exclusively ecclesiastical, closely aligned to the practical needs of the church. This overlap in function between printed books and ecclesiastical manuscripts was underscored in the visual equivalence between the two. Sixteenth- and seventeenth-century Muscovite typefaces reproduced the Cyrillic letter forms of the style known as *polu-ustav* (usually rendered in English as 'semi-uncial') with thick black lines and lots of conventional abbreviations. In the absence of competition, the quality of typography was generally unremarkable. Inking and spacing were often uneven, as might be the case in a run-of-the-mill handwritten text. Indeed, the resemblance between print and handwriting is close enough for the untrained modern observer occasionally to confuse the two.

In 1708 Peter I introduced his civil type (*grazhdanskii shrift*), a redesigned alphabet for use primarily in printing non-devotional materials. He played an active role in the design. A page of civil type looks lighter in all senses than traditional Muscovite printing. It is more like western 'humanist' letter-forms such as antiqua, rather than the 'black-letter' equivalent of traditional Cyrillic, with thinner, more flowing and curvaceous lines (see illus. 21).[2] The changed look of Russian was more than an aesthetic preference. It was a cultural and political signal. Civil type was an aspect of the wider and deeper project to expand the sphere of the secular and to raise its prominence and prestige, usually taking visual cues from western Europe (see Chapter One). The new look of Cyrillic print signalled a new function. Under Peter the ecclesiastical near-monopoly of the products of the printing press was broken. Civil type was the chosen medium for books on science and technology, for example. And, perhaps more significant (because the distribution was immeasurably wider), it came to be used as the visual projection of the voice of the ruler himself: the typeface for his laws, his regular decrees and edicts and even some of his routinely issued administrative forms. Church and state were differentiated by the design of printed lettering. The

21 'Comparison of old and new letters', undated (early 18th century), comparing letter-forms in traditional Cyrillic and new civil typefaces.

look of the text instantly declared its cultural sphere.[3] Somewhat confusingly, the convention in modern Russophone scholarship is to call the traditional typeface 'Cyrillic' (*kiríllitsa*), by contrast with the new civil type (*grazhdánskii shrift*). Eighteenth-century textbooks for children labelled them according to their functional distinction:

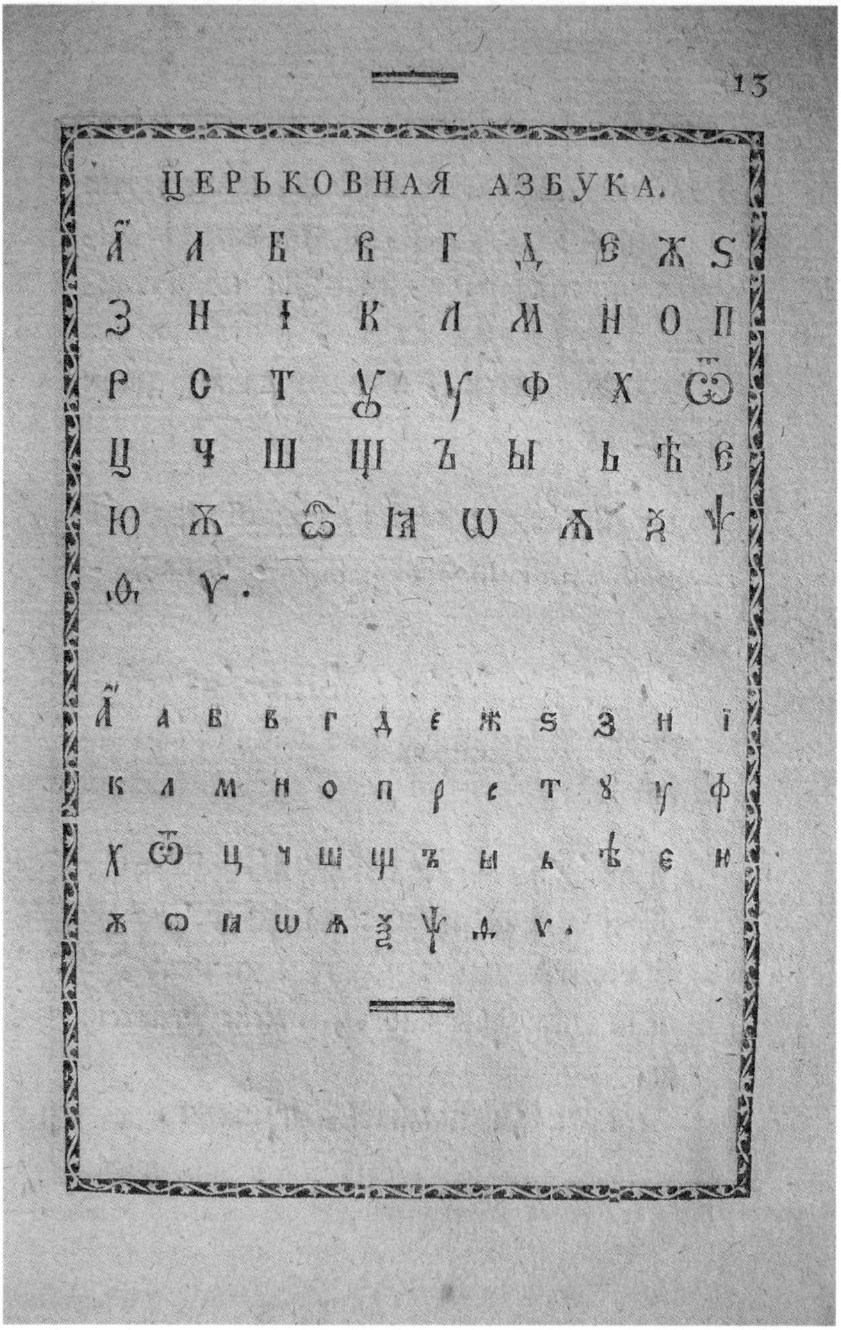

22 Traditional Cyrillic typeface, designated as 'Church alphabet', from a primer for children, *c.* 1781.

the traditional typeface was straightforwardly the 'church alphabet' (illus. 22).[4]

As always, there are more nuances than are visible in the broad generalizations. In the first place, the division of functions was not absolute. Throughout the eighteenth century, some devotional materials were printed in the civil type, and some secular materials were published in the traditional type. Even Peter himself could occasionally recross his own boundaries. For example, the 'manifesto' of 3 February 1718, in which he renounced his son Aleksei as heir, was printed and disseminated in *both* typefaces.[5] Second, one should not confuse the introduction of a new typeface with the introduction of a new alphabet. Handwriting in the chanceries of Moscow had long since developed letter forms that were distinct from ecclesiastical semi-uncial. To that extent, semantic differentiation through the look of the language pre-dates Peter's initiative of 1708. Indeed, some features of the civil typeface were deliberately quite close to chancery handwriting. However, it mattered that this cultural differentiation was now formally enshrined in print. Peter took Russian print culture in a new direction. He established print as the technology of secular authority and he needed his new typeface for the purpose. The civil typeface projected the voice of the state. In distant retrospect it seems peculiar that a mere change in type design could have had such broad cultural and political implications. It was only possible because, in Russia, even a century and a half after its introduction, print culture was still in a kind of infancy: restricted institutionally, thematically and aesthetically, a long way from the diversity of print capitalism as it had developed in western Europe.

Initially devised to distinguish the secular from the devotional, civil type came subsequently to represent a related but not identical change. In language it symbolized Russian as opposed to Church Slavonic. Most of the time this is mere convention. To this day, for example, scholarly editions of early texts, based on Church Slavonic manuscripts, will often use a traditional Church Slavonic typeface.

Occasionally, however, the visual binary proved inflammatory. In Chapter Three we touched on the indignation that was provoked in the early 1820s when the Bible Societies started the mass printing of translations of books of the Bible into Russian. For its opponents (including, prominently, Aleksandr Shishkov), there was a danger of heresy, on two counts: due to the deliberate machinations of the extraneous, non-Orthodox organizations promoting the project (specifically the British and Foreign Bible Society); and due to inadvertent error that is an almost inevitable consequence of making the sacred text accessible to all without intermediaries. Russian-language versions of the scriptures put souls at risk. Moreover, just by glancing at the Bible Society texts, before even beginning to read them, you could tell that something was not right. The transposition into Russian was visual as well as verbal. Despite being religious texts, they were printed in civil type. The did not even *look* properly religious. The contrast was obvious at first glance (illus. 23). Sensitivity to the visual semantics took several more decades to lessen. The first complete Bible in Russian, in the civil type, under the aegis of the Holy Synod, was published in 1877. Since then, though no longer marking a fundamental cultural divide, traditional Cyrillic lettering has acquired fresh visual meanings as an option in graphic design: on the cover of a historical novel set in the Middle Ages, for example, or on a shop sign, or the label of a vodka bottle or a bar of chocolate, or the packaging for a souvenir. It screams 'traditional'; 'old Russian', sometimes 'national', or 'folk'; not unlike, for example, 'Ye Olde Tea Shoppe' in pseudo-Gothic lettering on the sign above a café in a tourist venue in England.

The second moment of semantically significant systemic change in the look of Russian occurred at the start of 1918: the reform of the alphabet. The Petrine innovation had been about the forms of letters. The 1918 reform was not about design but about the repertoire. In the larger context of the history of alphabets, the changes were rather small. Four letters were abolished as redundant: the so-called *iat'* ('ѣ'), which merged with 'e'; the version of 'i' that resembles its Latin-script equivalent, which merged with the 'и' version; and the less common 'ѳ' and 'ѵ', which merged with 'ф' and 'и' respectively. Apart from that, the most noticeable change was in approved conventions for spelling: above all, the abolition of the 'hard sign' ('ъ') at the end of words ending in a 'hard' (non-palatalized) consonant, where it had remained for centuries, though redundant ever since it had ceased to indicate a reduced vowel (see Chapter One).

Such changes may seem quite trivial, relatively routine, commensurate with several other minor adjustments that had taken place over the centuries but to which we have not drawn attention here.

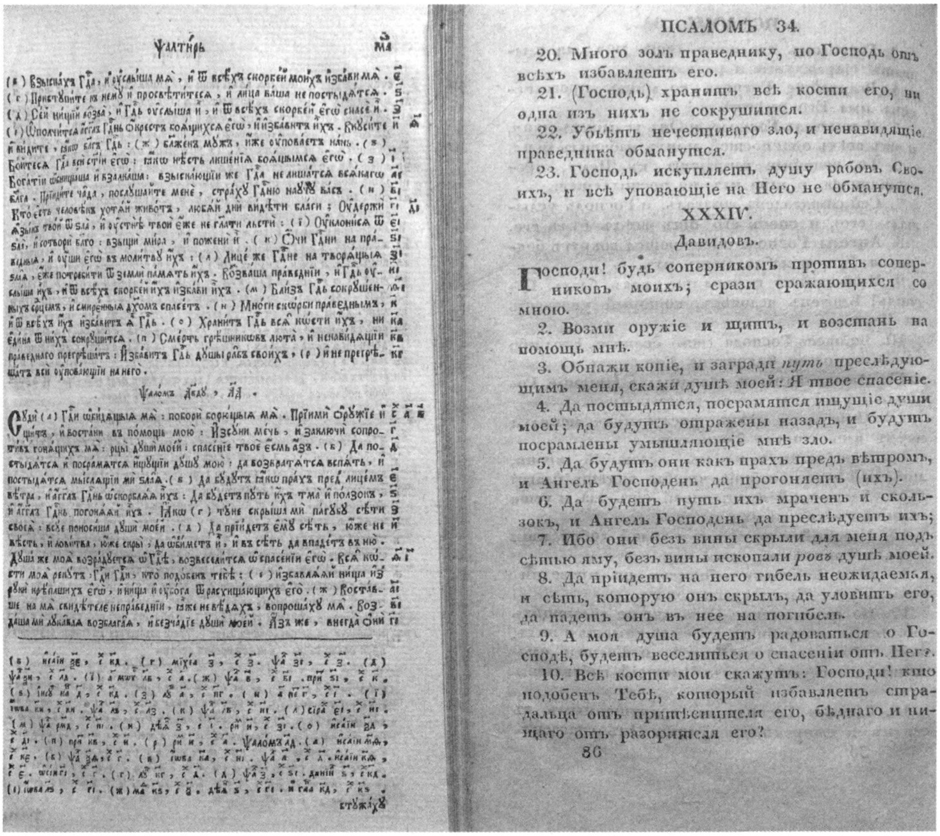

ПСАЛОМЪ 34.

20. Много золъ праведнику, но Господь отъ всѣхъ избавляетъ его.

21. (Господь) хранитъ всѣ кости его, ни одна изъ нихъ не сокрушится.

22. Убьѣтъ нечестиваго зло, и ненавидящіе праведника обманутся.

23. Господь искупляетъ душу рабовъ Своихъ, и всѣ уповающіе на Него не обманутся.

XXXIV.

Давидовъ.

Господи! будь соперникомъ противъ соперниковъ моихъ; сразн сражающихся со мною.

2. Возми оружіе и щитъ, и востань на помощь мнѣ.

3. Обнажи копіе, и загради *путь* преслѣдующимъ меня, скажи душѣ моей: Я твое спасеніе.

4. Да постыдятся, посрамятся ищущіе души моей; да будутъ отражены назадъ, и будутъ посрамлены умышляющіе мнѣ зло.

5. Да будутъ они какъ прахъ предъ вѣтромъ, и Ангелъ Господенъ да прогоняетъ (ихъ).

6. Да будетъ путь ихъ мраченъ и скользокъ, и Ангелъ Господенъ да преслѣдуетъ ихъ;

7. Ибо они безъ вины скрыли для меня подъ сѣтью яму, безъ вины ископали *ровъ* душѣ моей.

8. Да пріидетъ на него гибель неожидаемая, и сѣть, которую онъ скрылъ, да уловитъ его, да падетъ онъ въ нее на погибель.

9. А моя душа будетъ радоваться о Господѣ, будетъ веселиться о спасеніи отъ Него.

10. Всѣ кости мои скажутъ: Господи! кто подобенъ Тебѣ, который избавляетъ страдальца отъ притѣснителя его, бѣднаго и нищаго отъ разорителя его?

86

23 Psalm 34 in Church Slavonic (*Left*, in traditional Cyrillic, 1778) and in Russian (*Right*, in the civil typeface, 1823).

However, in this instance the reform of the repertoire of letters turned out to have cultural resonance, even political resonance, far greater than might have been intended or predicted by those who planned the change. The dates matter. The reforms had been proposed by a commission of the Academy of Sciences in 1912, as a straightforward simplification and modernization. In subsequent years a small number of items were even printed with the adapted repertoire of letters. The intention to institute officially the 'simplification of Russian orthography', as a new approved system, was announced in May 1917, and an edict implementing the change was published on 23 December 1917, to take effect on 1 January 1918.[6] The crucial point is that the reform was decreed by the new Soviet government that had come to power just two months earlier. In very widespread perception, therefore, the reform in the appearance of Russian was and is associated with the Revolution of 1917. Because of when and how it occurred, the rather minor orthographic reform – a slight reduction in the repertoire and contextual use of a small number of letters – has carried a disproportionate semantic load. It became emblematic of a change of epochs. Any reader, just by looking at a page, can instantly associate a specimen of printed (or handwritten) Russian with one of two periods: before the Revolution, or after the Revolution. The pre-reform conventions have become almost universally known collectively as the pre-revolutionary alphabet. It is as if the Bolshevik Revolution changed the face of the Russian language, although the two processes were causally unconnected. Arguably, indeed, the more revolutionary period in the culture of the Russian alphabet began only *after* the reforms of 1918. Fierce debates about the alphabet, along with rival proposals for further reform, continued through the 1920s,[7] but they have left little trace and the general perception of the 1918 reform as the start of a new epoch in the look of Russian remained and remains.

The semantic possibilities of lettering are, of course, by no means exhausted by these two episodes of systematic, top-down reforms enacted by the state. For as long as writing has existed, its potential as a visual medium has stimulated the imagination of scribes and typographers, advertisers and propagandists, journalists and publishers, artists and graphic designers, and many others. In the elite culture of the early modern period, for example, we have already seen expressions of the fascination for diversely decorative lettering (see Chapter One): in the widespread use of the semi-cryptographic style of display lettering known as *viaz'* in everything from manuscript headpieces to embroidered borders, from bronze-cast lettering on church bells to inscriptions round the rims of goblets.[8] Examples of *viaz'*, and a great deal else, figure in the 150 pages of specimen lettering in the manuscript penned by Fedor Basov in 1604. A multiplicity of letter forms characterizes the various versions (handwritten and engraved)

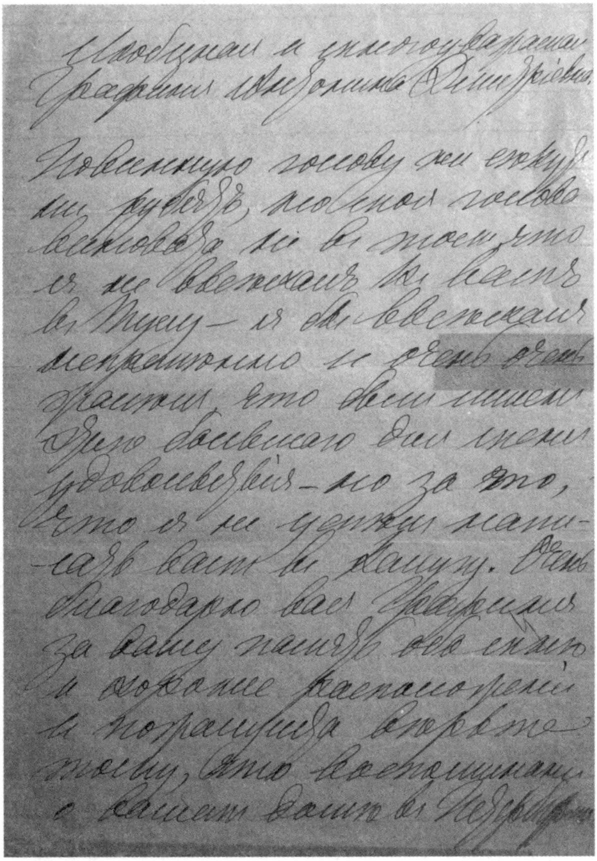

24 Informal handwriting from the 1860s: a note from Tolstoi.

of the primer of Karion Istomin in the 1690s. In the age of competitive publishing, from the late eighteenth century onwards, printers have advertised their services by issuing specimens of their typefaces.[9] At the same time the production of engraved specimen books on penmanship (for use in education) fostered the styles of cursive handwriting broadly typical in Russian bureaucracy and private correspondence since the nineteenth century (illus. 24).[10] Meanwhile, through into the modern age, devotional manuscripts continued to be copied religiously (in all senses) in imitation of their medieval prototypes.

The semantics of typography could be deeper than at first appears. For example, in 1842 the typefaces and settings of the title page of the first edition of Gogol's novel *The Adventures of Chichikov, or Dead Souls* were significantly altered by comparison with those that had

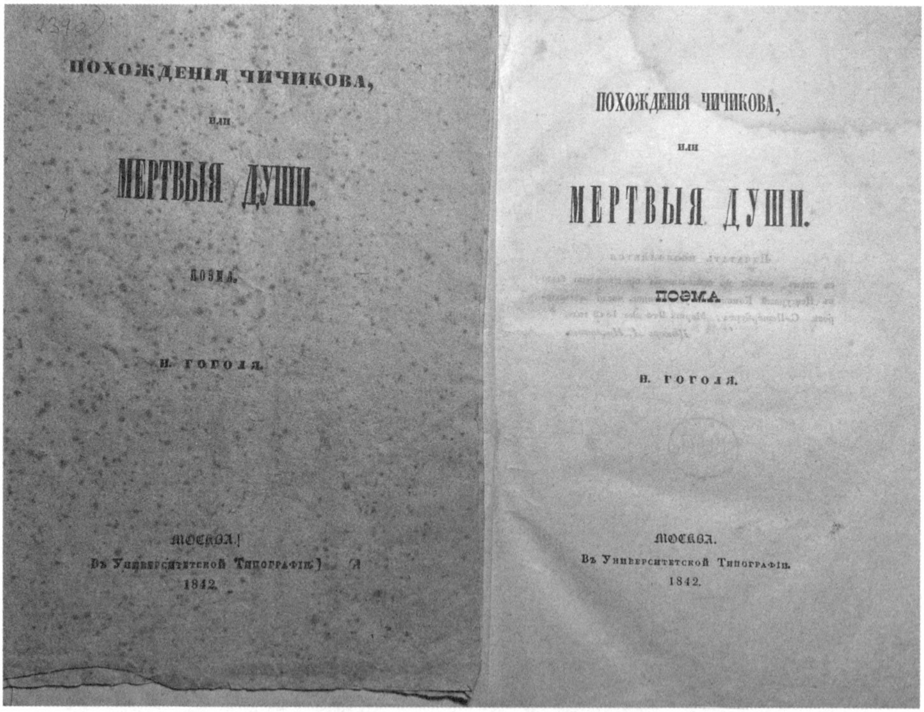
ПОХОЖДЕНІЯ ЧИЧИКОВА,
или
МЕРТВЫЯ ДУШИ.
ПОЭМА.
Н. ГОГОЛЯ.
МОСКВА.
Въ Университетской Типографіи.
1842.

ПОХОЖДЕНІЯ ЧИЧИКОВА,
или
МЕРТВЫЯ ДУШИ.
ПОЭМА
Н. ГОГОЛЯ.
МОСКВА.
Въ Университетской Типографіи.
1842.

25 Nikolai Gogol, *Dead Souls*, 1842: *Left*, title page in proof and *right*, in first edition, showing significant changes in type and proportion.

been used in the proofs (illus. 25): the proportions of the two titles were reversed so that *Dead Souls* became the more prominent on the page (the lettering of the first title became taller and narrower, while that of the second title was far more generously spaced), and the subtitle, *A Poem*, was highlighted by using a broader and more thickly lined font. Visual representation 'said' things about the book, framed it no less eloquently than a verbal preface. For Gogol, the adjustment of type design meant more than mere aesthetic preference. The censor had objected to the title of the novel, *Dead Souls*, on religious grounds, and had insisted that this be merely the subtitle, under the main title *The Adventures of Chichikov*. The proofs were printed with *The Adventures of Chichikov* duly prominent, as blessed by the censor. The typographical adjustment of the title page from the proofs to published book was a surreptitious device to restore, at least partially, the author's intention for the name of the book. Gogol also designed the book's engraved wrapper, which was likewise visually eloquent: *The Adventures of Chichikov* was in small lettering at the top, *Dead Souls* was in medium-sized lettering just below it, but in the centre of the design, in large, bold letters, was his designation of the work as a 'poem' (*POEMA*). Again the manifest intention was to undermine the censor's attempt to package his work merely as a picaresque novel. This is a visual equivalent of what is often called 'Aesopian language' in Russian literature: an indirect way of expressing something that censorship would not allow to be said directly.

All of this is traditional in the culture of manuscripts and printed books. A more fundamental shift in the semantic possibilities of visual language came with a shift in its location from the study to the street, from private reading to public display. The main driver of display lettering through the nineteenth and early twentieth centuries was trade: above all, the proliferation of shop signs that came to characterize the urban public graphosphere. From the 1920s the prominence of commercial signage in public spaces was challenged by the increasingly widespread display of political slogans. From the early 1930s, private shops no longer functioned, and signage on state shops was tightly regulated and far more subdued. The balance was again reversed from the 1990s after the collapse of the USSR.

Until the late eighteenth century commercial signage in the capitals was discouraged and severely restricted. By the middle of the nineteenth century the profusion of shop signs was one of the most notable features of the urban landscape. A cultural phenomenon in itself, it also became a catalyst for, and an object of, cultural reflection. From the mid-nineteenth century, few fictional or factual rambles through St Petersburg or Moscow managed without some observations about shop signs: their design, their language, their aesthetic qualities, their effect on the feel of the city, their sheer density. Letters found their way onto every visible space where it was possible to depict them: horizontally above frontages, sometimes in layers between the storeys of buildings; vertically down the sides; protruding on boards; inset behind windows. By the end of the century such abundant signage was as typical in the provinces as in the capitals. For far more people than any traditional medium of technology up to that point, shop signs brought lettering into daily experience. They transformed the aesthetics of public spaces, the very idea of what a city looked like or ought to look like.

Shop signs have stimulated debates about the culture of language, about the boundaries of Russian, about its relations with non-Russian. In the late eighteenth and early nineteenth centuries French had become common in educated (and even not-so-educated) conversation; but at least this was a vice or a pleasure indulged in private, so to speak. By the mid-nineteenth century, non-Cyrillic, Latin-script lettering was plastered all over the streets, in unavoidable, in-your-face display (illus. 26). The most fashionable language of signs was French. For some, this was a source of delight. Writing from Moscow to his wife in 1832 Aleksandr Pushkin tells her she would be delighted at the return of French shop signs on Kuznetskii Most (French shop signs had been absent in Moscow for several years after Napoleon burnt the city in 1812). Other reactions ranged from the ambivalent to the indignant.[11] Wandering along St Petersburg's Nevskii Prospekt in 1846, for example, Egor Rastorguev was distressed by the linguistic landscape that presented itself to him:

> The peculiar thing, the offensive thing, is that every single sign is in French . . . Oh, our glorious Russian capital! Does your renown really depend on this? . . . Where in Paris could you find even one shop sign in a foreign language? Yet here . . . it is as if St Petersburg is not a Russian city at all . . . Here all the hair stylists turn out to be from Paris, the tailors, shoemakers and bootmakers are from Paris, the dentists and podiatrists are from Paris, the florists and the perfumers are from Paris, the bronze-casters and the clockmakers are from Paris, the upholsterers are from Paris, the lithographers are from Paris. In short: all the artists and craftsmen are from Paris –according to their own shop signs, at any rate.[12]

As in the cultivation of the language more widely, so in public signage, fashions for the foreign have come and gone in waves. Each

26 Nevskii Prospekt in St Petersburg, from a lithograph panorama (1835) after a watercolour by V. Sadovnikov.

27 Saturated signage on a Petersburg shopfront; late imperial period.

time, the cultural messages are read in contradictory and conflicting perspectives. Some observers are thrilled to surf the wave, others are fearful of becoming drenched under it. And, also as in the language more widely, fashions for the foreign in signage have not spread evenly across all urban spaces. Nobody, to my knowledge, has yet attempted

28 Signage on provincial shopping street (the town of Tambov) in the late imperial period.

to map foreignness in public signage across districts, regions and time, but some patterns of differentiation are reasonably clear. In the mid-nineteenth century, Nevskii Prospekt in St Petersburg and Kuznetskii Most in Moscow set trends, but not everybody followed. Photographic evidence from the capitals and across the provinces from the late nineteenth and early twentieth centuries shows an increasingly saturated graphosphere of commercial signage, but often it was predominantly Cyrillic (illus. 27, 28).

The apparently inexorable rise of commercial public writing was abruptly challenged, and then suppressed, by the Bolshevik Revolution and the establishment of the USSR. In public display, the dominance of commerce had to make way for the dominance of politics. The appropriation of public space for political messages was a vital component of the communications strategy of the Soviet government from its very earliest days.[13] Main streets became saturated with posters and placards, banners and billboards and 'wall-newspapers' (*stengazéty*) and murals, some bearing verbal texts alone, others with punchy combinations of text and image. From civil war to public hygiene, from electrification to sovietization, from railway stations to factories, from parades to facades, fixed in place or travelling the country on the slogan-emblazoned agitprop trains, the messages were on show – rhetorical, brash, unmissable.

The political rivalled and overshadowed the commercial but did not immediately displace it. Through the 1920s the two coexisted and interacted in their visual vocabularies. The period of the New Economic Policy (NEP, 1921–8) permitted and encouraged forms of private enterprise. Competitive and aggressive commercial advertising continued through this period, in many respects in its pre-revolutionary modes, but with a strong admixture of Futurist and Constructivist lettering and design. On the main streets every spare surface on and around shop frontages was festooned with lettering.[14] State enterprises were as much part of the competitive dynamic as were private enterprises, and could strive as hard for eye-catching effect. Alongside the fixity of shop signs, mobile forms of display – in particular, the poster – provided fresh opportunities for design and experiment in form. While publishing houses still produced specimens of type design, most of the innovative energy now went into the design of display lettering.[15] An example of the creative focus on letter-design is an album entitled *Fonts and Their Construction* issued in Leningrad in 1927.[16] The album contains 57 alphabets devised by some 50 Leningrad artists and designers, along with the artists' own explanations for their choice of forms. Although some of the alphabets were compatible with letterpress printing, there was a preponderance of fonts intended for open display: from posters in public squares to labels in museums and exhibitions (illus. 29, 30). Real poster-designers revelled in the multiplicity of lettering options: a poster for a company trading in wines could display a mixture of scripts no less striking and capricious in its arrangement than anything embodied in Futurist experimental book production.[17]

The transitional situation of the late 1920s is captured in a booklet of type specimens issued in 1929 from the most official of all sources:

29 Display alphabet specimen, from *Fonts and Their Construction* (Leningrad, 1927).

30 Display typeface specimen, from *Fonts and Their Construction* (Leningrad, 1927).

the publishing house *Pravda* (illus. 31).[18] At first glance there seems to be a somewhat unnerving dissonance between form and content. The page design is reminiscent of early Futurism: fragments of words, fragments of sentences, switches of size within a column and so on. Look more closely and the groups of words coalesce, or semi-coalesce, as fragments of official rhetoric – slogans, citations from Stalin and Lenin.

From the late 1920s, and especially through the 1930s, the balance shifted decisively. The dynamic diversity of commercial signage that had developed over the course of a century was systematically muted and reduced. Monumental displays of Russian became almost the exclusive preserve of politics. Shop signs became austerely functional: no longer competing with each other for attention but serving as plain labels for the contents of each type of shop. In the mid-1930s the state legislated to define the range and style of approved shop signs. Attention-grabbing visual rhetoric was for politics. Shop signs were to be straightforwardly informative: 'bread', 'milk', 'vegetables'.[19]

ОБРАЗЦЫ ШРИФТОВ (РУЧНОЙ) В ЛИН. ЦЕХУ.

Зецессион широкий. Кегль 20. Прописной и строчной (ручной).

ОБИТАТЕЛИ КОТОРОГО С
самого начала порицали нас

Зецессион широкий. Кегль 28. Прописной и строчной (ручной).

ЗА ТО, ЧТО МЫ ВЫ-
делились в особую

Ренесанс. Кегль 20. Прописной и строчной (ручной).

ГРУППУ И ВЫБРАЛИ ПУТЬ
борьбы, а не путь примирения.

Ренесанс. Кегль 28. Прописной и строчной (ручной).

И ВОТ НЕКОТОРЫЕ ИЗ
нас принимаются кри-

Ренесанс. Кегль 36. Прописной и строчной (ручной).

ЧАТЬ: ПОЙДЕМТЕ
в это болото! — А

Герольд узкий жирн. Кегль 28.. Прописной и строчной (ручной).

КОГДА ИХ НАЧИНАЮТ СТЫДИТЬ,
они возражают: какие вы отсталые

Герольд узкий жирн. Кегль 36. Прописной и строчной (ручной).

ЛЮДИ! И КАК ВАМ НЕ СО-
вестно отрицать за нами сво-

РУЧНОЙ ШРИФТ В ЛИНОТИПНОМ ЦЕХЕ.

31 Specimen types from the publisher of *Pravda*, 1929.

As in the mid-nineteenth century, so in the late 1920s and early 1930s, such changes became themes for cultural comment and reflection. They gave rise to a literature of signboard lettering. Signage is a recurrent motif in two satirical novels by Ilia Ilf (1897–1937) and Evgenii Petrov (1902–1942): *The Twelve Chairs* and *The Golden Calf*. The first, published in 1928, plays on the variety and idiosyncrasy of late-NEP signs, while the second, completed in 1931, reflects their demise. In a more lyrical mode, Iurii Olesha (1899–1960) wrote a brief sketch about opening a metaphor shop. An artist painted the sign for him, in deep red lettering against a blue background such that, when viewed from an angle, it looked as if someone in a blue dress was eating cherries. Business was slow. Nobody wanted to buy the high-quality expensive metaphors. The shop closed and the sign was taken down.[20]

For those who oversaw the change from flamboyant to functional shop signs, it was not envisaged as a downgrading, still less as suppression. They were implementing a different vision of the city, a different aesthetics of linguistic display. The socialist consumer mattered. The functionality of shop signs was a rejection of self-promoting flippancy, a calm assurance that the state was providing, an indication of their dignity. In a sense, this was traditional; or at any rate it reflected one strand of traditional attitudes. From the very earliest ruminations on signage in the first half of the nineteenth century, critics and commentators had been divided about the merits or pitfalls of diversity. The 'motliness' or 'variegation' (*pestrotá*) of signage was a recurrent motif in the early literature about public lettering.[21] For some, variegation had been a source of wonder and delight, for others it was a distressing indicator of disorder, even chaos. For the shapers of the mid-Soviet public graphosphere, transparent orderliness was not a retreat from aesthetics but an affirmation. The world was now labelled as it ought to be. Diversity was no virtue, either practically or culturally. The multiplicity of commercial letter designs accumulated by the late 1920s was a relic of capitalist competition; it was 'exceptionally variegated' and needed to be thoughtfully filtered so as to jettison those features that should be deemed 'anti-artistic' (*antikhudózhestennye*).[22]

The very rapid re-commercialization of the streets after the collapse of the USSR again brought Cyrillic into collision with international Latin-script branding – now mostly English rather than French. Just as Nevskii Prospekt in the 1840s was dominated by shop signs in French, or in imitation of French, so, not only in the capitals but in cities throughout Russia, the post-Soviet period saw a proliferation of foreign-language display advertising. Against a background of humdrum, functional, low-key signs in Cyrillic,[23] the visual brashness of non-Cyrillic was deliberately striking. A rather poignant example can be seen in a photograph taken in 2014 in the centre of Moscow, in front of the walls of Kitai-gorod, just a couple of hundred yards from the Kremlin (illus. 32). It shows a monument to Ivan Fedorov, the first named Muscovite printer and hence a key figure in the story of Cyrillic in Russia. In one hand he holds a proof sheet, and with the other he props up the matrix from which – one assumes – the proof

32 Monument to the 16th-century printer Ivan Fedorov, Moscow, March 2014.

33 Western brand names in the luxury shopping mall 'LDT', St Petersburg, June 2024.

has just been printed. The inscription on the pedestal is, of course, in Cyrillic. But that is the only trace of Fedorov's own legacy; and it is barely visible at a distance. He is surrounded by, dwarfed by, almost enveloped in the branded declarations of expensive, Latin-script consumer foreignness selling luxury cars and jewellery. A visitor to LDT (*Leningrádskii dom torgóvli*), an opulent department store in the centre of St Petersburg, even in June 2024 would have walked straight into a graphosphere saturated by Latin-script cosmetics brand advertising (illus. 33). At the other end of the spectrum of cost: a photograph from June 2022 shows a line of fast-food stands in Tsaritsyno park outside Moscow (illus. 34). Here the signs are curiously hybridized: 'Hot dogs' in English, as well as the transliterated *Khot-dog* and *Chíken roll*. A display menu at one stall advertises, among other delicacies, *Big téisti* DOG (illus. 35). Analogous hybrids became common, with Cyrillic and Latin scripts intertwining with each other in the names of shops and brands (for example, АЙСБЕRG, ZАГАР, Студия фоrsмажор) as well as websites and book titles (for example, REALная любовь, Privatизерша, Down Шифтер).[24] It is as well that Aleksandr

34 Fast-food stalls, with signs in a mixture of scripts and languages, Tsaritsyno park, Moscow, June 2022.

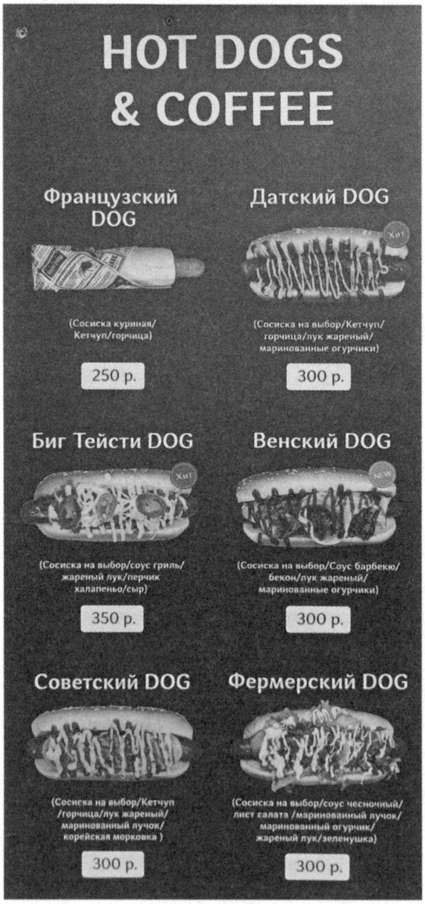

35 Fast-food display menu with hybrid captions, Tsaritsyno park, Moscow, June 2022.

Shishkov no longer walked these paths. Some reaction was perhaps inevitable.

Looking like Russian: Boundaries of Sense

For most of its history in Russia, display lettering has generally aimed to convey an accessible message with maximum impact. Form could change but – with allowance for the occasional cryptographic or Aesopian episode – meaning was meant to be straightforward, striking, manifestly decipherable. To that extent, even experimental lettering maintained one of the core assumptions (or illusions) of a Realist aesthetic: that words mean broadly what they say. However, there has always been an opposite approach, deriving from an awareness of the limitations of language, a belief that words are inadequate bearers of meaning – or bearers of inadequate meanings. In the medieval tradition, devotional and ritual language and practices have often been crafted to evoke worlds beyond words. A classic encapsulation of the problem in the nineteenth century is the aphorism in the poem 'Silentium' by Fedor Tiutchev (1803–1873), written around 1830: there is a deeper truth in silence than in words, because 'A thought, once uttered, is a lie.'[25] At the turn of the twentieth century the Symbolists believed in trying to use language – mainly poetry – to reach 'other worlds'.[26] Nevertheless, through all of this, language was intact. Its boundedness was frustrating, and one could try to use the resources of language to reach beyond it; but the integrity of language as such remained a given. For some, this was not enough. In the early years of the twentieth century – in Russia as in other strands of Modernism – experiments in visible form pushed at the limits of language itself, destabilizing the very idea of meaning.

In 1912 a group of artists and writers prepared to deliver a slap in the face of public taste. This was the title of a collection of works by members of the literary and artistic group Hylaea (*Giléia*), also labelled Cubo-Futurists, or just plain Futurists. The collection included a manifesto, which famously called on the Russian classics

– Pushkin, Dostoevskii, Tolstoi and so on – to be 'thrown from the steamship of modernity'.[27] Its first demands were for the right to verbal innovation, including the right to augment the vocabulary with 'arbitrary words' (*proizvól'nymi slovámi*), and the right to an 'implacable hatred for earlier language'.

From the start, therefore, the Futurist project aimed to undermine conventional language, to defamiliarize expression. Central to this was a defamiliarization not just of what language 'said', but of what it looked like. In Futurist book production, for example, it can be difficult (and pointless) to disentangle the textual from the visual. Futurist books are striking for their bold experiments in design: sometimes through innovative typography, sometimes – by contrast – through engraved (rather than typeset) lettering that imitated rather crude handwriting, like a kind of printed anti-printing.[28] Alternatively, the arrangement of words on the page could be constructed in a way that suggested a guide to intonation or declamation, as in the 'staircase' (*lésenka*) designs that are best known from the poems of Vladimir Maiakovskii (1893–1930). On this level, Futurist attitudes to lettering were compatible with tradition, not so far removed from the pictorial poetry of the Baroque age. However, Baroque concrete poetry, while playing games with expectation, at core confirmed a sense of coherence. It could create pictures and designs and playful patterns from letters and words; but ultimately, once the ludic devices were decoded, the letters 'said' what they were conventionally supposed to say. Futurism could push further. It presented itself as more disruptive. It challenged words as such. Futurist experiment with the visuality of words could detach lettering from any conventional association with meaning. Here, we illustrate the range of disruptive practices on the basis of just three examples: the first is a painting, the second is a booklet and the third is a kind of poem that is deliberately nonsensical if one tries to read it as conventional language.

The painting is *The Cyclist* (*Velosipedíst*), by Natalia Goncharova (1881–1962), produced in 1913 (illus. 36). The cyclist, hunched forward over the handlebars, hurtles through the city. We know it is a city, partly because of the cobblestones and the heavy metal grille on the left of the composition; but mainly because of the shop signs. The lettering is, in a sense, the focus: not the main element of the composition, but *in* focus. Its clarity and stillness contrast with the figure of the cyclist and his bicycle, whose repeated or blurred outlines suggest motion. But the signs are not quite so obedient, not quite so static as the clarity of focus seems to imply. They, too, are subject to disruption. On the right is a picture of a hat, and the letters *SHLIA*, suggesting the word *shliápa* – a hat. But the 'ia' has somehow slipped. It neither follows the preceding letters not starts a new line, as if it has detached itself and floats in its own space. Even more disruptive detachment characterizes the central sign. The word *SILK* (*SHËLK*) is clear; in white against a blue background, it almost dominates. But then come the black letters *NIT*. Puzzling at first, they then

36 Natalia Goncharova, *The Cyclist*, 1913, oil on canvas.

suggest (given the type of shop) *NÍTKI* – threads. But they, too, have slipped, in several ways: there seems to be no reason for the missing ending; they disrupt two-dimensional space by sliding across into the next window, the 'hat' sign; and, most radically, they disrupt three-dimensional space by apparently floating into the foreground, *between* the viewer and the figure of the cyclist. The planes are confused, as if the cyclist has hurtled through a portal to become part of the fabric of the urban graphosphere. Thus, although the visible letter-signs can be deciphered in relation to real language, the effect is not to resolve their meaning but to disrupt their coherence. Though sharply in focus and correctly formed, they participate in the visual slippage that characterizes Goncharova's depiction of motion.

The second example is an extraordinarily innovative booklet: *Tango with Cows: Ferro-Concrete Poems*, by Vasilii Kamenskii (1884–1961), printed in 1914, on yellow wallpaper, shaped as an irregular pentagon, and including illustrations by Vladimir and David Burliuk (1886–1917 and 1882–1967).[29] Kamenskii's production can be described – inadequately – as a collection of poems. That is what is indicated in its subtitle, which also provides an early example of the adjective 'concrete' as applied to poetry. But right from the title page (illus. 37) Kamenskii begins his journey to disruption. Just two elements of the page seem to be anchored in 'normal' printing: Kamenskii's name, in bold, in the lower section, and the place and date of publication at the bottom of the inset label. Above that are five quasi-cryptographic letter-squares. In each of them the letters – of different sizes, some sideways, some upside down – can be followed by different paths, to spell the title, the author's name (again), and at the top, 'FUTURISTS'. So far, so quasi-traditional. The letter-squares demand attention to their form that seems to obstruct habitual reading, but, individually and collectively, they can be decoded as habitual language. In this they are conceptually still compatible with the letter-games of scribes and printers in the seventeenth century.

37 Vasilii Kamenskii, *Tango with Cows* (1914), title page.

But that is just the start. One cannot say that everything in *Tango with Cows* is formally, visually and linguistically challenging, but there is a persistent sense of potential or actual segmentation and disintegration. Somewhat analogous to the shifting of planes in Goncharova's *Cyclist*, the tension in *Tango with Cows* derives in part from the disconcerting coexistence both of a semblance of normality (visual and verbal) and its distortions. Several of the poems are laid out on pages that are divided by thin lines into segments of irregular shape and size. A sense of dominant theme arises from the distribution of dominant words, often in larger type, across the segments. But within each segment sub-clusters go off in their own directions. Some play sound-games by swapping or removing letters, which may or may not result in new recognizable words:

KonstantInopol'

STANTI

STANI

STAI

STA

or: LIKI

KLIKI

ROLIKI

KROLIKI

KOROLIKI

or: UNYLO

NYLO

MYLO

LO

This kind of wordplay, or play on the boundaries between words and non-words, will be familiar to those who, at the end of the twentieth century, came across the children's incantation popularized by Michael Rosen: everybody, verybody, rybody and so on down to a solitary 'y'.

Such formations or deformations, are, at least in principle, pronounceable, even if not easily parsed grammatically or semantically. The verbal and formal recombinative riffs can be led by form, by sound, or by meaning. But Kamenskii can slide off the scale at any point: from that which makes little conventional sense as a word, towards that which makes little conventional sense as a representation of sounds (illus. 38):

СКОЛЬЗЬЬЬ

СЛИЗЬЬЬЬ

ОЛЬЗЬЬЬЬ

The multiplication of 'soft signs' can only speak visually. It has no possible articulation as sound. It is unpronounceable.

Kamenskii produces occasional captions or commentaries. Thus, underneath his 'KonstantInopol'' page of segments, outside the frame of the poem, we read (again in a return to 'normal' typography and grammar) three statements that might be taken to serve as explanatory captions: 'on walls, fences'; '*a creative experiment in ferro-concrete poetry*', and 'poetry is a marriage feast of words' (literally: 'of the matrimonial conjoining of words').

Kamenskii's poems are at an intersection between verbal and visual experiment. Hence most of them cannot be translated as words outside their visual context, any more than one could sensibly detach Goncharova's spatially challenging shop signs from the figure of the

38 Vasilii Kamenskii, *Tango with Cows* (1914), ferro-concrete poem.

cyclist riding both past them and within them. They live in their shapes and configurations. A translation of Kamenskii's 'creative experiment in ferro-concrete poetry' has to start with the look of it, with a facsimile of the words as images on the page.[30] And when presented thus, the translations reveal an additional effect of the original, for at first glance the two do not straightforwardly differentiate themselves as distinct languages and scripts. The visual disruptions extend to the perception of Cyrillic as Cyrillic. By foregrounding the total design and hence the breakdown of linear sequence and familiar verbal structure, the signs initially disengage themselves from the specifics of their host languages. This is a key feature in a comparative interpretation of such Russian Futurist experiments. They were not conducted in isolation. Italian Futurists were producing strikingly similar typographic distortions at much the same time. A glance through an album of Italian Futurist concrete poetry (whether labelled as such or not) immediately reveals conceptual and visual affinities with Kamenskii's ferro-concrete designs.[31] Their linguistic differences seem secondary. Futurist visual rhetoric takes language out of itself. Paradoxically, the intense foregrounding of the materiality of language renders language as such almost immaterial.

Kamenskii destabilizes language but does not cut all ties with it. His ferro-concrete experiments derive their energy in part from a kind of tension between form and the formless, between sense and what appears to be non-sense. For some of his Futurist contemporaries – most notably Aleksei Kruchenykh (1886–1968) and Velimir Khlebnikov (1885–1922), this was still not enough. Frustration with conventional (predictable, rule-bound, grammatical) sense led them to push through it, to ignore it, to create a 'trans-sense' or 'trans-rational' mode (*záum'*). Their texts look like Russian verse: they are written in Cyrillic script, with groups of letters forming what appear to be words, and with groups of words arranged in what look like poetic lines, which in turn may be grouped as stanzas. However, these are not words that would have been found either in dictionaries or in speech.

In the balance of conventional linguistic elements, sound becomes dominant. *Zaum'* posits and explores a kind of essential semantics of sound. Poetry becomes sound; represented on the page like natural language but no longer constricted by it, not frozen into meanings, free to explore its own resonances, to catch echoes of meanings beyond meaning; 'Thought and speech cannot keep up with the emotions of someone in a state of inspiration, therefore the artist is free to express himself not only in the common language, but also in a personal one.'[32] This is a kind of logical extension (or, depending on one's point of view, a *reductio ad absurdum*) of the Romantic assertion, a century earlier, that the writer creates the language (see Chapter Four).

A classic example of early *zaum'* is Kruchenykh's '*dyr bul shchyl*'. As the author explains when introducing it, this is one of three poems 'written in its own language, distinct from others. Its words do not have a defined meaning.'

дыр бул щыл
  убеш щур
   скум
  вы со бу
   р л эз[33]

The Russian Futurists were not the first people to stretch the language of sound beyond the norms of recognized words. *Zaum'* can be seen as an intellectual kind of magical incantation. Many cultures have used sound-based incantation as a portal to the conventionally unknown or inexpressible. Liturgies and rituals are obvious examples, not to mention 'speaking in tongues'. An Anglophone reader might immediately think of analogies with Lewis Carroll. Carroll's nonsense verses are somewhat less earnestly mystical or philosophical, and are closer to hybrid versions of *zaum'* than to its maximalist extremes, but they are technically comparable, as, for example, in the opening stanza of 'Jabberwocky':

'Twas brillig, and the slithy toves
    Did gyre and gimble in the wabe:
All mimsy were the borogoves,
    And the mome raths outgrabe.

Here, however, the nonsense elements are purely lexical. Carroll maintains the appearance of normal syntax and fairly consistent indications of parts of speech: 'brillig' and 'slithy' must be adjectives, 'gyre' and 'gimble' are verbs and so on. And, after this first stanza, Carroll's poem continues in more conventional mode, with a much sparser sprinkling of neologisms. Kruchenykh's '*dyr bul shchyl*' is not thus anchored.

So, to what extent can one describe 'trans-sense' *zaum'* poetry as Russian? Trans-sense was a spectrum of practices. Hybrid versions, like Kamenskii's ferro-concrete poems, are to varying degrees rooted in that from which they depart. They play on being both Russian and not Russian. Khlebnikov developed elaborate theories of the universal semantics of sounds, and likewise wrote poems in a kind of hybrid *zaum'* – dense with acoustically expressive neologisms while retaining links with a recognizably Russian syntax.[34] However, with regard to his fully trans-sense compositions, Kruchenykh was unequivocal: they were written 'in their own language'. They were linked to Russian through their context (they were introduced in and surrounded by texts in Russian), they looked like Russian (being in Cyrillic script), and their implied sounds were reminiscent of Russian, but they were explicitly and deliberately *not* Russian. *Zaum'* tried to take the Russian language beyond itself such that it became an indeterminate other.

If it were not for what followed, the early pictorial and typographic innovations of Futurist books would probably have merited a place in the history of the culture of Russian as forms of experimentation among a rather elite avant-garde. However, their audiences and impacts were massively boosted by the Bolshevik Revolution of 1917. Futurism, and its development in Constructivism, were already revolutionary. They were already intensely focused on creating new ways of displaying and looking at words and projecting language. They had already accumulated experience, momentum and energy. For rhetorical Futurism – visual and verbal – the Revolution was a megaphone with unprecedented capacity to amplify. Its stage was the whole country: not just bookshops and studios, but windows, streets, public buildings, squares, even trains. Its media were not just booklets for connoisseurs and fellow artists, but placards, posters, hoardings for the masses. Goncharova's cyclist in 1912 hurtled past and through the urban shop signs; post-revolutionary Futurists and Constructivists could contribute to the shaping of a new, monumental urban graphosphere.

7

Sovietspeak

The revolutionary cycle in the culture of language began a few years before the Bolshevik Revolution of 1917, and continued to be played out for at least a dozen years after it. As we saw in the previous chapter, by 1917 writers, artist and critics were already engaged in projects of radical defamiliarization, of trying to make words and the images of words work in new ways, of destabilizing norms and experimenting with fresh devices and strategies to generate meanings. For those prepared to step up to it, 1917 provided a platform, a rare opportunity to test intellectual, aesthetic and linguistic experiment in the service of transforming the country. And for some, for a while, it may even have seemed that the voices of avant-garde intellectuals could indeed become the voices of the new Russia: that Futur*ism* might actually contribute to creating the future, that Constructiv*ism* might help to construct socialism. Unfortunately for the intellectuals, there was no smooth and uncontested transition from revolutionary word to deed and back again. In language, as in society, revolution was not an instant event but a set of processes, of contradictory phases, of struggles and disputes both within the elites (new and old) and beyond.[1]

Rhetoric as Ideology

Arguments about the Russian language played out not just against a background of social and political upheavals, but as an integral component of them: arguments about what the new language ought to be, about the social sources of linguistic authority, about norms and their transgressions; and, ultimately, about the very function and purpose of the culture of the Russian language under socialism.[2] On the one hand, it could be said that the point of revolution was to defamiliarize, to create something fundamentally new: in social and economic structures and relations, in governance, in thought, in education, in culture, in language. On the other hand, permanent defamiliarization was not a viable objective. The aim of the Soviet government was to achieve a new order, not a new state of permanent disorder. It could equally be said, therefore, that the point of revolutionary defamiliarization was ultimately as a stage towards a new mode of familiarization. But what should the new authoritative discourse look like? What should be its sources, its models? Who should be its arbiters and curators?

Disputes and experiments continued for a decade before being resolved by the most traditional of devices: power. Broadly speaking, the period of polyphonic debate about a new culture of language extended through the Revolution itself, the Civil War (1917–22) and the period of NEP. The emergence and imposition of a unitary mode of approved verbal culture – in most forms of public verbal performance, from political speeches and journalism through to literature – coincided with the period of and just after the First Five-Year Plan (1928–32). In most essentials, the registers and styles that were established in the early 1930s set the templates for the next half century.

The defamiliarization of language from the Revolution through the 1920s was not only a product of revolutionary ideas about language, of what Michael S. Gorham terms a 'utopian mentality towards language culture'.[3] It reflected a range of responses to external changes on many levels: conceptual, institutional, political, social and educational. Front and centre in those years was the question of the language of those in whose name the Revolution was supposed to have been enacted: the people, defined as peasants and workers. As we saw in Chapter Five, writers from the mid-nineteenth century had been keen to register voices of the people. By contrast, the post-revolutionary imperative was that peasants and workers should speak for themselves. It mattered that the Revolution should not merely listen to but provide a platform for – and be articulated in – the real, unmediated voices of peasant or proletarian writers. A few had already become established before the Revolution, such as Maksim Gorkii (1868–1936), but not remotely on a scale envisaged in the post-revolutionary imperative. Authenticity was important, so language did not have to be classically correct. However, a different kind of correctness also mattered: correctness at the level of ideas, and familiarity with the emerging idioms of Soviet life. 'The flood of correspondence from peasants and workers that appeared in newspapers and separate collections over the course of the 1920s revealed a range of collective heteroglossia [that is, a diversity of voices] that reflected stylistically the ambiguous tasks of the new writers.'[4] The question was: to what extent was linguistic authenticity a guarantor of Bolshevik ideology? Or could the two undermine each other? It was not obvious that peasants and workers would innately speak Bolshevik. Sometimes it became obvious that they did not, that there was a gap in language culture to be bridged.

So, the language culture of the first post-revolutionary decade was – depending on one's position and evaluation – diverse or cacophonous. Different registers, reflecting different sources of linguistic and cultural authority, competed or interacted; not entirely unlike the economic and social diversity (or messiness) of the NEP itself. Where, if anywhere, was or should be the norm? On what should the standard utterances and idioms of the new Soviet society be based? From the late 1920s the authorities worked towards finding a solution. Three factors, above all, combined to produce the eventual outcome. The first was education. At the time of the Revolution, Russia was still a country of largely unschooled peasants.

Education was among the highest priorities to facilitate the creation of an urban proletariat and a literate workforce. Education in literacy needs norms, models, standards; and educationalists and teachers tended to be quite conservative in their view of language.[5] The second factor was the similarly conservative cultural orientations of many of the key figures in the Soviet leadership, who did not necessarily share the radical linguistic positions of avant-garde writers. While Futurists had called for Pushkin, Dostoevskii, Tolstoi and their ilk to be thrown overboard from the steamboat of modernity, Lenin had written appreciatively of Tolstoi as a 'mirror of the Russian Revolution'.[6] In the late 1920s and early 1930s Gorkii, then the doyen of Soviet literati, passionately advocated the Leninist position: the norms of Soviet Russian should be rooted in the classic traditions of its great writers. Revolution might have a huge impact on idiom and register and content: new ideas; new technologies; a huge broadening of the social base of literacy; mass urbanization; social changes that challenged, for example, gender assumptions embedded in the standard language (the entry of women into traditionally male professions such as medicine); and so on.[7] But, in the view that became dominant, revolution did not and should not create the language anew. The way forward was to build on the achievements of the past. The third major factor was the decisive sharpening of Communist Party control over culture. Polyphony was not on the party's long-term agenda.

Did this mean that there was to be no revolution in language after all? Yes and no. With regard to purely linguistic norms, the deliberate outcome was evolution rather than revolution. Yet there was, nevertheless, a radical change in one crucial area: not in language as such, but in the functions of its official register. All bureaucracies have their formulae, all systems of ideas have their key formulations, and a great deal of political rhetoric is repetitious and predictable. It is not in itself odd that Soviet official discourse was all of these things. The distinctive feature, however, was its pervasiveness. Soviet ideology was not a niche interest for ideologues and orators. It was a system of explanation that seeped into almost every area of public utterance and, due partly to the spread of radio, into everyday private spaces as well. The device that demonstrated adherence to the correct system of explanation was the use of the correct language, the stock of lexical, phraseological, stylistic and structural devices whose models were explicitly derived from the 'classics' of Marxism–Leninism (plus, until the early 1950s, Stalin).

The dominant public register is sometimes labelled with George Orwell's term, Newspeak,[8] which has been calqued into Russian as *novoiáz*.[9] Here, rather than filter it through the conceptual prism of an English novel, we call it Sovietspeak. Sovietspeak itself had a long history. Rooted in pre-revolutionary political discourse, established as the sole authoritative idiom by the early 1930s, it remained the principal mode of expression for official pronouncements almost until the end of the USSR (even though in its final years it was less securely monopolistic). Sovietspeak was not absolutely immutable over the decades of its pre-eminence. Keen students of political rhetoric find subtle nuances and variations and substrata. Nevertheless, its main features were sufficiently stable to be described here synchronically, with examples from various periods. At the most general level, Sovietspeak was a total explanatory and evaluative framework. At the practical level it was a more or less consistent rhetorical method with generic rules and norms in the structuring of phrase and argument.

Key words and phrases in Sovietspeak were few enough to be familiar, flexible enough to recombine with each other almost whatever the theme.[10] For example, positive action was frequently cast in terms of 'struggle' (*bor'bá*): the struggle *of* (the workers, the Soviet people, all progressive humankind), the struggle *for* (peace, increasing the productivity of labour), the struggle *against* (imperialism, international capital, sabotage, remnants of the past). Just as struggle had its set objects, it also had its set modes: it was 'uncompromising' (*neprimirímaia*), 'constant' (*postoiánnaia*), 'purposeful' (*tseleustremlënnaia*), even 'eternal' (*véchnaia*). 'Labour' (*trud*) was 'selfless', 'self-denying' (*samootvérzhennyi*). The opinion of the Soviet people – or, better still, the entire Soviet people (*ves' sovétskii naród*), consisting of workers, peasants and the 'people's intelligentsia' (*naródnaia intelligéntsiia*) – could be invoked as 'unanimous' (*edinoglásnyi*) without fear of contradiction.

Alongside the set expressions, Sovietspeak also developed its own jargon to reflect social and institutional *realia*. A characteristic device was the prolific creation of acronyms (abbreviations using initial letters) and stump compounds (abbreviations that combine segments of different words).[11] Acronyms and stump compounds have served as the standard designations of hundreds – thousands, even – of Soviet institutions and organizations: from Narkomprós (***Nar**ódnyi **kom**issariát **pro**sveshchéniia* – the People's Commissariat of Enlightenment [that is, education]), founded in 1917, through to Gazpróm (from ***gáz**ovaia **prom**yshlennost'* – gas industry), established under that name in 1989. A dictionary of Russian abbreviations, published in 1977, contains over 15,000 entries, the overwhelming majority of which originated in Soviet usage.[12] Some acronyms and stump compounds are so long and complex that to outsiders they can seem almost self-parodic, such as MNIPIASUKh (***M**oskóvskii **n**aúchno-**i**sslédovatel'skii i **p**roéktnyi **i**nstitút **a**vtomatizírovannykh **s**istém **u**pravléniia v gorodskóm **kh**oziáistve* – the Moscow Research and Planning Institute for Automated Systems of Control in the Urban Economy); or *Glavzagotmiasomolpróm* – ***Gláv**noe upravlénie po **zagot**óvkam syr'iá dlia predpriiátii **mias**nói i **mol**óchnoi **prom**yshlennosti* (the Central Administration for the Preparation of Raw Materials for Organizations in the Meat and Milk Industries).[13] Complex compounds were nevertheless normalized, familiarized in everyday life, not just in political rhetoric but in consumer advertising (illus. 39). They could become so habitual that they almost ceased to be perceived as abbreviations, functioning as ordinary words which in turn could generate their own derivatives. Such, for example, were the stump compound *komsomól* (***Kom**munistícheskii*

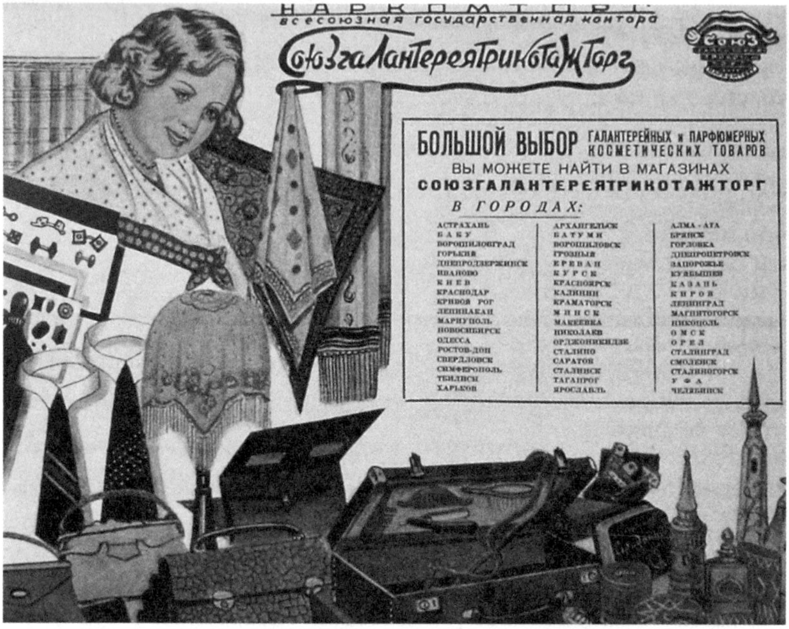

39 Sovietspeak compound words in consumer advertising: Narkomtorg and Soiuzgalantereiatrikotazhtorg, 1938.

soióz molodëzhi – the Communist Youth Union); or *kolkhóz* (***kollektívnoe khoziáistvo*** – collective farm). Acronyms could also become lexicalized. Thus VUZ (*vysshee uchébnoe zavedénie* – 'higher education institution') became the declinable noun *vuz*, producing derivatives such as the adjective *vúzovskii*. Likewise ChK (***chrezvycháinaia komíssiia***, 'Extraordinary Commission' – the first Soviet secret police) became *cheká*, producing derivatives such as *chekíst*, which remained in active use long after the ChK itself had been superseded by differently abbreviated successors, including eventually the KGB. Abbreviations could also be formed from a combination of both methods: part acronym, part stump compound. Vladimir Maiakovskii, along with other poets and artists, produced satirical posters for the windows of ROSTA, the ***Rossíiskoe telegráfnoe agénstvo***. Compounds could be formed by adding an abbreviated prefix, such as *part-* (for *partíinyi*, the adjective denoting the [Communist] party): *partrabótnik*, *partórg*, *partgrúppa*, *partsobránie*, *partdistsiplína*, *partbilét*, *partmínimum* and so on.[14]

Sovietspeak became by far the most widely practised, most thoroughly assimilated official register of Russian in the history of the language. How did it become so pervasive? Three interlinked factors, above all, contributed to its unprecedented ubiquity: mass propaganda, mass education and mass media. Propaganda, education and media were not new phenomena; the new feature was the 'mass' dimension of all of them, individually and combined. Sovietspeak is sometimes labelled a 'totalitarian' language.[15] This is fair to the extent that it was a monopolistic register that was projected outwards from the centre and downwards from the top. But central to the Soviet project was the aim of universal participation: the creation of conscious, active, politically aware citizens who were personally able to read, speak and even write the idiom of power. Universal education

40 'Forward to the Victory of Communism': banner awarded to the Frunzenskii District of Moscow.

– literacy both in the technical sense (in reading and writing) and in the ideological sense (training in the right ideas) – was a prerequisite. As for technologies of dissemination: from the very start, the Soviet authorities assiduously projected their message and their language as never before:[16] in speeches at meetings and rallies, in newspapers, in posters and placards and banners (illus. 40), in film, on propaganda trains that helped to speed the display of words across the land, to help the creation of an ideologically integrated Soviet graphosphere.

All these devices had been available previously, had rulers chosen to exploit them. However, one technology in particular took the distribution of Sovietspeak to a different level: radio. Radio overcame time and space and social division: it 'was instantaneous and immediate. It allowed information from Moscow to be received in Khabarovsk or Baku without delay, and it promised to get through to even the most benighted listener.'[17] In some ways the growth of radio as a principal medium for the dissemination and socialization of Sovietspeak mirrors the ascent of the idiom itself. Regular broadcasting started in 1924. However, through the early 1930s, although its importance was not in dispute, there was no clear consensus on its most effective use, on the tone of presentation, on the extent to which it should be a direct or a mediated platform for the country's leaders, on how best to fill its schedules and shape its wider cultural mission.[18] In the pre-war years, while the government focused its investment on developing a wired network, Soviet radio was still a semi-public medium, amplified in clubs and halls and in the workplace. In the post-war USSR, wired connection became common in new construction, and radio delivered public words directly into tens of millions of homes. At the same time, the reach (and diversification) of radio was enhanced by the spread of wireless sets.[19]

Although the focus here is on the ideologically marked register, one should not imagine that radio fed its listeners a diet of undiluted Sovietspeak. Its mission and repertoire were broader, as was the approach to language culture in Soviet mass education. Just as the USSR's early leaders insisted that the language of the new Russia should be rooted in, as it were, oldspeak (in the literary language honed by the Russian classics), so, in the early years of Soviet radio, listeners, too, tended towards a linguistic conservatism that affirmed the norms of their recently (in many cases) acquired literacy.[20] The culture of Sovietspeak as a mass-participatory, ideologically marked mode was unprecedentedly pervasive, but Russian language usage in the USSR – even in public, broadcast media – was not reducible to pure Sovietspeak. Radio played a powerful role, alongside mass education, in fostering what came to be known as the 'culture of speech' (*kul'túra réchi*). For example, a programme entitled *In the World of Words* (*V míre slov*) in which experts responded to listeners' questions about language, was broadcast regularly, twice a month, from 1962 until after the fall of the USSR (it survived until 1996). Some of the regular questions and answers migrated into print, with the aim of further bolstering the 'culture of speech' across media. An anthology of questions and answers from the radio programme was published in 1982, marking twenty years of the broadcast. The book was aimed at the widest possible readership, with a print run of 300,000. Reflecting its radio source, it dealt with bread-and-butter questions of norms and variations, neologisms, idiomatic expressions and (a favourite in Russian) stress. The substance was reassuringly conservative; but it still had to be framed in Sovietspeak, for, as was asserted in the introduction, 'The culture of our native speech is . . . an essential task for the builders of the new, communist society.'[21] And, as was resoundingly affirmed in the conclusion, as lovers of the Russian language, listeners to the radio programme were united by their 'love for their native words and for their native country, by their interest in its heroic past, its glorious present and its bright future.'[22] The assertion of a link between love of words and love of country was a *leitmotif* that went back at least two centuries, to Mikhail Lomonosov's justification for producing a Russian grammar (see Chapter Two).

High-level fluency in Sovietspeak required training and experience. Besides its characteristic vocabulary, it had, like any register or genre, its characteristic syntax, its formal devices, its traditions of rhetorical expression and structure. Journalists, in particular, could spend years on university degree courses learning how to master Sovietspeak reliably. If there was a hierarchy of authoritative usage, it would show the classic texts of the founding fathers at the top, followed by speeches of current political leaders, and their intermediaries in the party press (which often printed the leaders' set-piece speeches verbatim anyway). One detailed case study of the style and devices of Sovietspeak is based entirely on an analysis of editorials in *Pravda* (the newspaper of the Central Committee of the Communist Party) from the 1920s to the 1950s.[23] Below this, Sovietspeak was pervasive, but not always in equal concentrations. Outside journalism, educational and explicitly ideological publication constituted a huge proportion of Soviet book production. In June 1936 the English magazine *Russia Today* cited figures from the All-Union Book Chamber. Out of a total of just over 450 million books published in the previous year, over 100 million were school textbooks, and nearly 30 million were 'books on the theory of Marx, Engels, Lenin and Stalin'.[24] But that still left a lot of other books. An etiquette developed, which came to be well understood. Many areas of discourse were not in themselves well suited to concentrated Sovietspeak, but its presence had to be adequately registered. Clearly, in an article on grain production in the context of the latest five-year plan one would expect a high level of saturation with Sovietspeak. By contrast, in a lot of academic publication (as in the cited book on the 'culture of speech') it became standard to construct a framework out of elements of Sovietspeak – typically, in a general introduction that would give a theoretical context, reinforced with citations from Marx or Lenin – and then to revert to the academese of the relevant discipline.

Just a small handful of examples can stand for millions of equivalents. Take something particularly obscure, such as the 1948 issue of

Proceedings of the Early Russian Literature Section, published by the Institute for Russian Literature of the Soviet Academy of Sciences. The volume opens with an article on 'Basic Tasks in the Study of Early Russian Literature in Publications from 1917 to 1947'.[25] This exciting survey opens with the statement that 'Soviet literary studies of the past thirty years have travelled an arduous but productive path of liberation from the methodological errors of the past, which distorted a true understanding of the essence of literary development . . .', and it ends, 'Setting aside trivial professional questions [an allusion to Lenin], our duty is to concentrate all our efforts on resolving the fundamental problems of the class-based aesthetic consciousness of early Rus.'[26] Nowhere else in the remaining four hundred pages of the volume is there any return to such focused Sovietspeak. After the general disclaimer, its learned contributors simply explore 'professional questions' in the study of medieval texts.

The second example may strike a modern reader as still more incongruous. The context was far more public, and the stakes were a good deal higher. In July 1963 the literary journal *Novyi mir* (New World) published a short story by Aleksandr Solzhenitsyn (1918–2008), 'For the Good of the Cause' (*Dlia pól'zy déla*). *Novyi mir* was at the epicentre of the 'thaw' in Soviet literature. In November 1962 it had published Solzhenitsyn's prison-camp novella *One Day in the Life of Ivan Denisovich* (*Odín den' Ivána Denísovicha*). The title of 'For the Good of the Cause' was ironic. The story was critical of a decision by Soviet authorities in a provincial town, and it provoked some sharp criticism. In October 1963 *Novyi mir* published responses to such criticism, in the form of letters from Leningrad workers, who defended Solzhenitsyn in pure Sovietspeak: in his critique of the local authorities Solzhenitsyn 'affirms our Soviet, communist sense of justice, the ethical norms of our moral code, the democratic foundations of our life'.[27] As it happens, the preceding piece, in this 'thaw' journal, was a letter from a linguist, in strong support of a project to produce a *Dictionary of the Language of Lenin*, whose completion he describes as 'the international duty of Soviet scholars'.[28] For the outsider and in retrospect, *New World* might seem here to juxtapose two different worlds. But it serves as a reminder that those early works by Solzhenitsyn could only be published because they could be justified *in terms of* Sovietspeak and assimilated into its implied thought-world, not because they challenged it.

The third example is from a collection of stories of the security services. Quotations from almost any page could serve to illustrate the language. Here are just a few:

> In the struggle with enemies we continue the glorious traditions of the ChK and therefore with pride we call ourselves *chekísty*. We actively follow the policies of the party; we do not retreat into the narrow circle of professional interests [see the equivalent phrase in the 1948 medievalists' journal cited above!].
>
> Conducted under the leadership and unwavering control of the party, all the work of the organs of state security proceeds from the interests of the people and the state, with the support of the broad masses of the workers, on the basis of strict observance of constitutional norms, of socialist legitimacy.
>
> Strictly following the directives of the Central Committee of the KPSS [Kommunistícheskaia pártiia Sovétskogo soiúza], *chekísty* vigilantly stand watch over the interests of the Motherland. They will always be merciless towards its enemies . . . Through years of harsh struggle and labour, Soviet people have achieved the very highest authority throughout the world. We are an example and an inspiration for millions of workers on the planet.

This sounds as if it might come from the mid-1930s. In fact it is from a collection of stories of the local KGB in the provincial city of

Voronezh, produced in 1976.[29] The book was clearly reckoned important, and potentially popular, by those who produced it: it had a print run of 50,000 copies.

Rhetoric as Ritual

The letter-writers to *Novyi mir* in 1963, and the provincial *chekisty* telling their stories in 1976, used Sovietspeak as if to represent faithfulness to the traditions of the Bolshevik Revolution of 1917. Manifestly, however, the function of the register was no longer revolutionary. Rather the opposite: it signified conformity, loyalty, traditionality, security. It had become ritualized.[30] A key quality of effective ritual is that its stability is in its own performance – in what it is, rather than in what it says. Ritualized actions and utterances can have a very flexible relationship with belief, on a spectrum running from acceptance of the literal meaning of every word and statement, at one end, to a sense that meaning resides only in the outward show of the verbal act, at the other end. On the one hand, ritualized form can be seen as a method of indoctrination, of ensuring that everybody thinks alike. On the other hand, it may be seen as a device to minimize the role of thought itself. Ideas are messy, ritual is simple. Ritual provides reassurance both for those who prescribe it and for those who adhere to it. Founded in and emerging from analysis, Sovietspeak metamorphosed into performative ritual. That does not mean that it was empty. To dismiss Sovietspeak as 'merely' ritual would be misleading. It had significance in itself; and it could be filled with a great diversity of meanings.[31] Like Christian liturgy, for example, it could represent fervent belief, or conscientious observance, or merely a vague affirmation of community. For some, Sovietspeak explained the world; for others, it was a badge of belonging, a sign of identity, or a form of social insurance (lip service) or a means to career advancement. Ritualized performance provides an assurance of fixity amid uncertainty and change. Performance *is* correctness. Schismatics from the official Muscovite church in the mid-seventeenth century tend to be known in English as 'Old Believers'. In Russian they are more commonly 'Old Ritualists' (*staroobriádstsy* – far more frequent thar *starovéry*). Indeed, the Russian for word 'Orthodoxy' itself, *pravoslávie*, formally denotes correct worship rather than correct belief. Ritual can be superficial, but it can also be fundamental. In the culture of the Russian language the path from Revolution to ritual signals a transition in its basic function: from an emblem of disruption to a guarantor of continuity.

The performative rituality of Sovietspeak helps to explain why the examples above, from different decades and different cultural spheres, sound almost interchangeable. Note, for example, the references to transcending 'narrow professional' interests and concerns. The roots are in Leninism and the insistence that class interests were higher than local professional interests even among workers. In the 1948 academic journal on early Russian literature, the phrase is functionally ambiguous. On the one hand, it may plausibly imply exactly what it says: that, as Soviet medievalists, we do not indulge in antiquarianism for its own sake, but are conscious of our obligation to contribute to the wider and proper understanding of historical processes. On the other hand, it can be read as a ritual framing device of a type that became very common in academic writing: to top-and-tail the book or article in Sovietspeak was necessary and sufficient for its ritual function. The rest of the work could then proceed in its 'professional' idiom. In the 1976 KGB collection the ritualism has gone further. In this context the statement that Voronezh's *chekisty* 'actively follow the policies of the party', and therefore 'do not retreat into the narrow circle of professional interests', looks like a false contrast: surely the professional interests of the security police *are* the interests of the party? Yet, although it is analytically puzzling, it is intonationally and phraseologically reassuring: a purer ritualization that defies analysis.

The Soviet press found formulae with which to transfer ritual performance to the page. For example, from at least the late

1920s through to the 1980s, speeches by party leaders were often reproduced in full in newspapers. But the speeches were not represented simply as texts. They were evoked as performances. So, the flow of words was periodically interrupted with indications of the audience reaction, in brackets and italicized, on an ascending scale from '(*applause*)' through '(*prolonged applause*)', onwards to '(*loud applause*)' or '(*thunderous applause*)' and eventually reaching '(*thunderous applause, turning into a standing ovation*)'. Apart from emphasizing the speech as spectacle, such asides had the secondary and useful function of intonational markers for the well-intentioned reader: showing, in a very long text, a kind of hierarchy of points and phrases to be especially noted and perhaps quoted.

If all this looks a bit predictable and tedious, that was part of the point. Not every moment of ritualized performance demanded hushed concentration and focused response. Often the purpose was to affirm what was known, not to reveal what was unknown. Surprise and a sense of revelation were by no means always desired outcomes. In an article entitled 'Stalin and the Art of Boredom', exploring the musical and literary conventions of Socialist Realism also in terms of a kind of atheistic religious ritual, Marina Frolova-Walker argues that 'tedium was not an unfortunate by-product of Socialist Realism, but a quality which was deliberately cultivated. Rather than attempting to overcome our reaction of indifference or boredom, we should accept it as quite proper for this repertoire, and take it as our starting point.'[32] In the experience of ritual it is but a small step from the entrancing to the soporific. Either way, cerebral attentiveness was not always expected or required.

On an anecdotal level, in a 'narrow professional' sphere: scholars visiting the USSR used to be surprised and mildly irritated by how often, at conferences and seminars, academic presentations would be delivered to the accompaniment of low-level chatter in the audience, and discussion of the papers themselves was not factored into the schedule. The reason was that, quite often, papers were not expected to develop new hypotheses for improvised scrutiny. They were Sovietspeak performances. No knowledge was lost if the attention wandered. This is not a criticism of the participants, merely an observation on the function of the ritual. For an entirely humdrum, random and hence reasonably representative example, we return to the provincial city of Voronezh in the mid-1970s. In March 1975 Voronezh University – or, to give it its full title, 'Voronezh State University, Order of Lenin, named after the Leninist Komsomol' – organized a 'scientific and theoretical conference of Soviet and foreign students' dedicated to the thirtieth anniversary of the victory of the USSR in the Great Fatherland War (illus. 41). A few sample titles of papers give a flavour of the occasion. A fourth-year Soviet student opened the proceeding with a presentation on '[The Communist Party of the Soviet Union] – the Inspirer and Organizer

ВОРОНЕЖСКИЙ ГОРОДСКОЙ СОВЕТ ПО ДЕЛАМ
ИНОСТРАННЫХ УЧАЩИХСЯ
ВОРОНЕЖСКИЙ ОРДЕНА ЛЕНИНА
ГОСУДАРСТВЕННЫЙ УНИВЕРСИТЕТ
ИМЕНИ ЛЕНИНСКОГО КОМСОМОЛА

30 ЛЕТ ПОБЕДЫ СОВЕТСКОГО СОЮЗА
В ВЕЛИКОЙ ОТЕЧЕСТВЕННОЙ ВОЙНЕ

ПРИГЛАСИТЕЛЬНЫЙ БИЛЕТ
И ПРОГРАММА

НАУЧНО-ТЕОРЕТИЧЕСКОЙ КОНФЕРЕНЦИИ
СОВЕТСКИХ И ИНОСТРАННЫХ УЧАЩИХСЯ

г. ВОРОНЕЖ
март 1975 г.

41 Programme for International Student Conference, Voronezh State University, 1975.

of the Soviet People in the Great Fatherland War'. A student from the German Democratic Republic spoke on 'KPG [the Communist Party of Germany] at the Head of the Antifascist Struggle in Germany'. Three papers, by students from Greece, Syria and the USSR, dealt with the role of Soviet youth organizations in the anti-fascist struggle. There was a paper on 'Soviet Patriotism – the Main Source of the Mass Heroism of Soviet Troops in the Great Fatherland War'. The final session included papers on 'The Struggle with Fascism – the International Duty of Soviet Troops'; 'The Unmasking of Bourgeois Falsifiers of the History of the Second World War'; and, wrapping up proceedings, a first-year student of chemistry spoke on 'The Peoples' Struggle for Peace'. Self-evidently, this was not a conference of fresh research or challenging ideas. It was part of an advanced training in performative Sovietspeak. Enthusiasts, careerists or tick-boxers – all are enfolded in the unity of a culture of language. Inquisitive researchers from a different tradition might have been puzzled by the description of the conference as 'scientific' and 'theoretical', but it was not aimed at inquisitive researchers from a different tradition.

At the heart of the tradition of Sovietspeak there is a contradiction. On the one hand, Sovietspeak was a categorical rejection of the experimental (and arguably the more revolutionary) approach that had emphasized the indeterminacy and inadequacy of language, the limits of expression, the desire to take language beyond itself. In principle, Sovietspeak posited the opposite: words mean things; Soviet ideology was founded on a correct analysis of the world; in order to convey this correct meaning, one must use correct words; the absence of correct words implied the absence of correct meaning. On the other hand, the ritualization of Sovietspeak can be seen as undermining its own consistent relationship to meaning. On the surface, ritualization turned official rhetoric from an instrument of change into a symbol of stability. Surfaces mattered: this was the *appearance* of stability. Yet ritualistic language can in practice be more capacious in accommodating change than might appear from the outside, more open in the kinds of meanings that it generates or allows its readers and audiences to experience. Successful ritual is rigid in form, malleable in content. The point of ritualized performance is its own sameness. Performance *is* correctness.

However, precisely because it is ultra-normative, any ritualized language culture – including Sovietspeak – is also ultra-sensitive to formal deviation. Since it depends on an expectation of familiarity, the slightest defamiliarization or variation can be semantically magnified, even if in normal speech the differences might seem trivial. As a device for generating meanings, ritualized language is esoteric. For outsiders the nuances of minor modulation can be difficult to spot and interpret. For insiders their uses are wide-ranging: they can accentuate either inclusivity or exclusivity, creative adaptation or reactive dogmatism. For example, as the goal of achieving communism kept shifting into the future, Soviet publicists were easily able to translate into Sovietspeak their invention of ever more advanced phases of socialism, without any appearance of serious change to the rhetoric. However, *un*sanctioned deviation, even in minutiae, may be seized upon as signifying something far more fundamental than the surface appearance. Control is crucial. The authority of the ritual register is the authority of those who determine it. In the wrong place and the wrong time, a different formulation might be held to be subversive, an act of sabotage, treasonable. Or heretical. In the disputes between the official church and the Old Believer schismatics in the seventeenth century, issues of contention included: should one make the sign of the cross with three fingers or two? Should one say 'alleluia' twice or thrice? Should the name of Jesus be written with one initial 'I' or with two? Should the cross be depicted with eight points or with six (that is, with three cross-bars or with two)? Insist on the wrong answers, and you might be burnt alive.

Wilful deviance was the worst: the deviance of those who ought to have known better. Ignorance was another matter. Native-speaker fluency in Sovietspeak, as in any register of language, was not achieved simply by stringing together a few of the obvious phrases. Mere incompetence in Sovietspeak could become an object of satire more than denunciation. As early as January 1918 the poet Aleksandr Blok (1880–1921), in article entitled 'The Intelligentsia and the Revolution', criticized the self-regarding fastidiousness of his fellow intellectuals who 'mock the illiteracy of declarations or letters that are written in a well-meaning though awkward style'.[33] Michael S. Gorham provides contrasting examples from the mid-1920s: a clumsily cliché-infested letter that aspired to express indignation in high Soviet rhetoric, and a satirical evocation of misapplied officialese in a sketch by Mikhail Zoshchenko (1894–1958).[34] In the high Stalinist period, as ignorance ceased to be an excuse and every deviation tended to be deemed intentional, gentle linguistic satire was squeezed.[35] But it could re-emerge: in journalism through sketches in the satirical magazine *Krokodil*, for example; or in literature, such as the depiction of an inept attempt at epistolary Sovietspeak in a short story from 1974, 'The Peasant Deriabin' (*Muzhík Deriábin*) by Vasilii Shukshin (1929–1974), a writer associated with the so-called 'village' prose in the 1970s.[36] The tradition of treating awkwardness in a prestigious register as comic goes back at least as far as the satire on foppish *faux*-Francophonie in the plays of Denis Fonvizin in the mid-eighteenth century (see Chapter Three). By the mid-1970s, despite the stirring cautionary tales of the vigilance of provincial *chekisty*, oral culture admitted mildly ironic allusions even to central and authoritative Sovietspeak texts, such as the parenthetic indications of applause in the newspaper reports of the leadership's speeches, or the seemingly obligatory formula of expressing gratitude 'personally' (*líchno*) to Leonid Ilich Brezhnev, general secretary of the Communist Party.[37] The flourishing late Soviet subculture of satirical jokes (*anekdóty*) often relied on defamiliarization of Sovietspeak clichés.[38]

Sovietspeak limped on, more by habit than by commitment, until the collapse of the regime that it had sustained and been sustained by. Insider satire on its awkwardness gave way to consequence-free parody of the idiom as a whole – until eventually, sanitized and toothless, it found its niche among the kitsch memorabilia of nostalgia-themed metropolitan eateries.

8

Russian beyond Russia

Aside from its history as a language developed and used principally by and for Russians in Russia, Russian has also been an imperial language and a global language: a tool of administration, integration and assimilation within the empire; and, beyond the empire, a language of an increasingly populous and diverse diaspora, and a vehicle for the projection of soft power. The first section of this chapter outlines some key aspects of the culture of Russian for non-Russians in the empire and the USSR. The second section looks mainly at issues of post-Soviet Russophone culture (or cultures) outside Russia. Just to confuse matters, some areas fall into both sections: first as non-Russian regions of the Russian Empire and the USSR, and then as independent states with Russophone populations after the break-up of the USSR in 1991.

Imperial Russian

The more the empire expanded, the lower became the proportion of its inhabitants whose first language was Russian. Among what were eventually well over a hundred languages spoken in imperial and Soviet space, Russian was always by far the most widespread, but, in the late imperial and Soviet periods, those identifying as native-speaker Russians barely constituted a majority of the population as a whole. In the post-Soviet Russian Federation, around 80 per cent identified as Russian. The most effective means of linguistically

Russifying the state was to lose the empire; or much of it. Before this drastic late twentieth-century rebalancing, however, what were the functions of the Russian language in the empire? And, conversely, what was the impact of empire on the Russian language? The processes can be surveyed in three stages: early imperial, down to approximately the mid-nineteenth century (that is, in broad historical terms, the period of 'long' early modernity), late imperial and Soviet.[1] The early imperial government had little interest in language policy as such, and certainly not beyond the level of social elites. Late imperial policies began to reflect more widely articulated concepts of nation and national culture, alongside the practical issues of an expansion in peasant education and of wider urbanization. Soviet policies and practices reflected two imperatives that were not always simple to reconcile: on the one hand, an ideology of diversity through respect for minority nationalities and cultures; and, on the other hand, an ideology of cultural convergence through the creation of Soviet citizens.

Before around the middle of the nineteenth century Russia's rulers had no consistent language policy, no grand plan for linguistic Russification across the empire. It would have been unrealistic even if contemplated. Imperial governance in the eighteenth century was skin-deep, the link between legislation and implementation was notoriously fragile and the resources for enforcement were limited. The core aims of the empire's rulers, though sometimes dressed out in fine rhetoric, were principally parasitic: to extract value from natural and human resources. If this could be achieved adequately through existing local structural and linguistic means, that was generally acceptable. In any case, the ruling elites showed few signs of being interested in cultures of language – even of the Russian language – beyond themselves. Mass illiteracy was the norm. The multiplicity of spoken vernaculars among the overwhelming majority of the population was merely a demographic fact, not an urgent problem.

Russian was, for the most part, the language of imperial administration – but not exclusively. German remained the official language of administration in Riga for over 150 years after its conquest in 1710. Governors of Riga issued their own documents in German, and Russian decrees issued in St Petersburg and Moscow were sent to Riga for reissue in German translation.[2] After the partitions of Poland in the late eighteenth century, Polish was an acceptable language of administration right through until almost the end of the nineteenth century. As for languages of culture: German and Latin were languages of learning and French became the fashionable language of polite conversation. Even the word of the Lord was deemed fit to be disseminated across the empire in many tongues; indeed, until the late nineteenth century, in almost any tongue *except* Russian (see Chapter Three). According to a report for the British and Foreign Bible Society, by around 1830, in the Russian Empire, it was distributing printed editions of the scriptures, or of parts of the scriptures, in Armenian, Modern Greek, Georgian, Kalmyk, Karelian, Latvian, Moldavian, Mordvinian, German, Persian, Polish, Samogitian, Turkish, Tatar, Cheremisian, Finnish, French, Estonian, Bulgarian and Serbian.[3] An edition of the Quran in Arabic was printed in St Petersburg in 1787 and subsequent editions were issued in Kazan (with a significant Muslim population) from 1801.

The only people to whom such linguistic liberalism did *not* apply were East Slav Orthodox Christians, for whom (until the last quarter of the nineteenth century) the sole appropriate devotional language was deemed to be the Russian version of Church Slavonic. Since at least the early seventeenth century Muscovite churchmen had periodically expressed suspicion of Church Slavonic books imported from Ruthenia, because of the perceived possibility of contamination from its 'Latin' confessional and educational environment. From the late seventeenth century, when the Orthodox ecclesiastical structures in the central and eastern Ukrainian lands were subordinated to Russian jurisdiction, linguistic uniformity became policy there as well. On 5 October 1720 a decree issued by the senate, on behalf of Peter I, explained: some books printed in Kyiv and Chernihiv were clearly inconsistent with Orthodoxy. Moreover, even on title pages, books from the Kyiv Caves press had designated the monastery as being under the jurisdiction of the patriarchate of Constantinople. Such deviations were unacceptable. Henceforth the presses of Kyiv and Chernihiv were to print only approved devotional books in the Russian version of Church Slavonic, for the avoidance of heresy.[4]

The Russian authorities tended not to treat any variety of Ukrainian as a separate language in the way that they regarded German or Tatar as separate languages. In the devotional context, locally distinct Church Slavonic usage in Ukraine was deemed a deviation from Muscovite Church Slavonic. In the administrative context, when Catherine II abolished the Hetmanate in 1781, the language of governance became standard chancery Russian, which thereby rendered redundant the Ruthenian register used in the Hetmanate. Here, linguistic Russification was a direct consequence and instrument of imperial centralization. As for vernacular Ukrainian: until around the middle decades of the nineteenth century it tended to be treated rather indulgently as a quaint regional dialect (or as an agglomeration of regional dialects) rather than as a language in its own right.[5]

In the early modern period, the spread of Russian was mostly by non-regulated means. Partly this was through various forms of language contact, such as the presence of a garrison or the activities of merchants and traders, but the contexts for such contacts were generally somewhat limited.[6] A more active mechanism was self-Russification for social and economic advancement: competence in Russian provided a route to career opportunities for ambitious local elites. Over the middle decades of the nineteenth century the emphasis shifted somewhat. There were several factors that contributed to this, although they were not necessarily related to one another: the emergence and development in Russia (as elsewhere in Europe) of new discourses of nation, nationality and peoples, including a doctrine of Russian nationality; the abolition of serfdom in 1861; an increase in concern for peasant education, including the education of non-Russians; a significant upsurge of urbanization, especially in the western parts of the empire, which tended to create concentrations of Russian-speaking populations; and a major expansion of empire to the southeast, with the incorporation of huge areas of Central Asia.

The first moves toward broadening the role of Russian as an instrument of empire were traditional, aimed at elites and administration. Ruthenian had been abolished as an administrative language in the 1780s. From the second third of the nineteenth century, the administrative functions of both Polish and German were progressively diminished. Even where Polish was retained, administrators were required to obtain a certificate of competence in Russian.[7] More radical, however, were the measures to broaden peasant education. In crude terms, language education policies and practices from the late nineteenth century through into the Soviet period revolved around a simple set of questions: to what extent should basic education be in the local language, or in Russian, or in both? If the answer was 'both', then the implication was – for the first time – a move towards the spread of Russian not just in administration but as the *lingua franca* across imperial space, as a universal second language that should be promoted while simultaneously maintaining and enhancing first-language literacy in the local vernaculars.

In 1897, according to the census of that year, around 70 per cent of Russians over the age of ten had no reading skills in any language. For Ukraine the figure was 80 per cent. Among Baltic Germans the equivalent rate of illiteracy was just 5 per cent.[8] Nevertheless, through the 1860s and '70s, as the movement for more widespread primary education had gathered momentum, the question of education in Russian for non-Russian children generated discussion, rival theories and state regulation. In general, the policy was that non-Russian children in state-sponsored schools should learn Russian. Not everybody agreed on what this should mean in practice: on the place of native languages, for example, and on whether children should study *only* in Russian. The firmest directives related to Ukrainian, where, for some, the question of language was existential rather than merely pedagogical. The hardline position was articulated by Petr Valuev (1815–1890), who was minister of the interior from 1861 to 1868. In July 1863 he instructed the censorship offices that the publication of textbooks – indeed, all books – in the Ukrainian ('Little-Russian') language should be halted, except for works of literature. In this document, known as the 'Valuev circular', the minister asserted that 'most Little-Russians' were indignant at the notion that a Little-Russian language might be taught in schools, since it was their 'well-founded' opinion that 'there was not, is not, and should not be any distinct Little-Russian language. Their dialect, as spoken by the peasantry, is the Russian language itself, corrupted by the influence of Poland.'[9] This is a long way from the amused condescension towards village Ukrainianisms of the first half of the century (see Chapter Five). It was fine for Little-Russian peasants to talk their quaint dialect, but to educate them in it was quite another matter.

A more nuanced approach, especially with regard to education among Muslim and converted Muslim populations in Central Asia, was accepted by Dmitrii Tolstoi (1823–1889), minister of education from 1866 and former procurator of the Holy Synod.[10] Tolstoi was influenced by the ideas and practices advocated by Nikolai Ilminskii (1822–1891). Ilminskii was a versatile linguist and missionary, who taught for a while at the University of Kazan before taking up administrative positions in Orenburg, not far from the modern border with Kazakhstan. A student of Turkic languages of the Tatars and Central Asia (he wrote a grammar of Kyrgyz), he was passionately committed to primary education for non-Russians, principally for converts to Orthodoxy. Russia's massive expansion through Central Asia in the mid-nineteenth century brought about the incorporation into the empire not only of very large numbers of non-Russians, but (of more concern to Ilminskii) of very large numbers of Muslims. Although

Ilminskii initially devised a curriculum based purely on Russian, he came to see this as a pedagogical mistake, and his eventual method began with literacy in the native language. The infiltration of Russian, or of the idea of Russian, was by other means: literacy in the native language was taught using a version of transcription into the Cyrillic script that Ilminskii devised for the purpose. The native language thus *looked like* Russian, and familiarity with Cyrillic could subsequently smooth the way to the study of Russian itself, to which, in Ilminskii's curriculum, pupils would progress in their third year. Ilminskii's mission was to bring non-Russian children to Orthodoxy. The path to Orthodoxy led through the Russian language, but the path to the Russian language could begin with the native language. The method was what Wayne Dowler has described as 'gradualist'.[11]

The expansion of education in the Russian language for non-Russian children stimulated demand for specialized textbooks. For example, in the late 1880s Mikhail Ioakimovich Volper (1851–?), a teacher of Russian from Vilnius, produced a densely illustrated set of three slim volumes entitled *Russian Speech: A Study Guide for Learning the Russian Language in Schools in Which Children Initially do Not Speak Russian*.[12] Volper's teaching aids were bestsellers of their day, both in Russia and abroad. The first volume reached its 61st printing in 1911 (illus. 42). The enterprising author also produced a guide for teachers on how to use the materials, as well as a selection of readings linked to the series, and a practical grammar to be used alongside it – all of which went through multiple editions. His grammatical tables were even published in English translation on both sides of the Atlantic. The editor of the English version states in his preface, 'The compiler of this work is a well-known Russian schoolmaster, and his books . . . are used in practically every school in those provinces in Russia where the language of the native population is non-Russian, and are sold in millions of copies.'[13]

Language policy in the USSR completed the journey, culminating in 'a conscious effort on the part of the Communist leadership

М. Вольперъ.

РУССКАЯ РѢЧЬ.

УЧЕБНОЕ РУКОВОДСТВО,

примѣняемое къ обученію русскому языку въ тѣхъ школахъ, въ которыхъ дѣти при поступленіи не умѣютъ говорить по-русски.

ВЪ ТРЕХЪ ВЫПУСКАХЪ СЪ 600 РИСУНКАМИ ВЪ ТЕКСТѢ.

ВЫПУСКЪ ПЕРВЫЙ.

БУКВАРЬ.

61-е изданіе.

Всѣ три выпуска «Русской Рѣчи» допущены къ употребленію въ низшихъ училищахъ и внесены въ каталогъ, изданный Ученымъ Комитетомъ Министерства Народнаго Просвѣщенія въ 1905-мъ году.

С.-ПЕТЕРБУРГЪ.
Изданіе автора.
1911.

Складъ изданія: С.-Петербургъ, Захарьевская, 9, Книгоиздательство М. М. Гутзаца.

Цѣна 20 коп.

Пособіемъ къ «Русской Рѣчи» служитъ книга того же автора: «Толкователь словъ фразъ и оборотовъ, встрѣчающихся во 2-мъ и 3-мъ выпускахъ «Русской Рѣчи», расположенный по порядку статей въ этихъ книгахъ», въ *двухъ частяхъ: первая часть* служитъ пособіемъ для *учащихъ и учащихся* ко 2-му выпуску «Русской Рѣчи», ц. 20 к., *вторая часть*—къ 3-му выпуску «Русской Рѣчи», ц. 35 к.

42 Mikhail Volper, primer for non-Russian children, 61st printing (1911).

to shape both ethnic identity and national consciousness through language'.[14] In fact, neither the policy nor its implementation were consistent, but its existence and its assumed necessity were embedded in the government's sense of the functions and objectives of the multinational state. 'Multinational' is a key concept here. The human composition of the empire of the tsars had been represented in terms of language and religion: it was multilingual and multiconfessional.

The human composition of the USSR came to be represented in terms of nationalities (*natsionál'nosti*).[15] Language was conceived as one of the defining constituents of nationality, although the relationship between nationality and language was not straightforward: each nationality had its dominant language, but not everybody who defined themselves as a member of a given nationality would necessarily identify the national language as their first language. Moreover, in the early Soviet years, several putative national languages had yet to be codified, or perhaps even recognized in such terms by their largely unlettered speakers.

The principal vehicle was education. Literacy rates were hugely uneven across the different language groups in late imperial Russia: from near zero to over 90 per cent. Averaged over the population as a whole, in 1897 the literacy rate is estimated at just under 25 per cent. By 1939 it was over 80 per cent (nearly 90 per cent in cities).[16] The motivation for bringing letters to the unlettered was partly economic: educated workers would make better workers. But the policy also embodied a vision of the socialist state. And the vision was built on an obvious paradox: on the one hand, nationalities were equal, and national languages and cultures were to be respected, supported, in some cases even created. On the other hand, the overriding goal was to forge an integrated socialist society with a shared sense of Soviet identity, to turn Soviet people or peoples (a plurality) into *the* Soviet people (an entity). An aphoristic expression of how to resolve the paradox was that education should be national in form, Soviet in content. This formula was derived structurally from a phrase in *The Communist Manifesto* of 1848, and was picked up in an essay by Joseph Stalin on 'Marxism and the National Question' in 1936.[17]

What were the implications of Soviet nationalities policy for the cultural history of Russian itself? If we are looking for measures of Russification, then we can find them on at least three levels. First, 'Soviet in content' inevitably meant in many respects Russian in content: that is, very many of the standardized cultural and ideological concepts were first elaborated in Russian. Given the dominance of Russia and Russian in Soviet space, it is hard to disentangle the Soviet from the Russian, even when embedded in education in a non-Russian language. For example, it has been calculated that 'in the 1930s and 1940s some 70–80 percent of all new vocabulary of the languages of the USSR consisted of Russian borrowings.'[18] Sovietspeak, in whatever language, was in fair measure Russianspeak; even when rendered in a non-Russian medium.

Second, let us take literally the question of form: what did national languages look like? Soviet policy switched direction several times on this. Languages of the USSR with traditional writing systems used a wide range of scripts, including Latin, Cyrillic, Arabic, Georgian, Armenian, and Hebrew. In the late 1920s there was briefly a movement to develop Cyrillic for wider use in non-Russian languages. In the 1930s, by contrast, policy switched to developing Latin script as a universal form of encoding language (even using Latin script for Russian was not theoretically excluded). By 1940, policy was to render almost all languages of the USSR, with very few exceptions, in Cyrillic.[19] As prefigured in the pedagogy advocated by Nikolai Ilminskii from the 1860s, from the 1940s most of the major languages of the USSR *looked like* Russian. A visitor passing through large swathes of the Soviet graphosphere might have formed the impression of a visually integrated linguistic landscape. This landscape could extend beyond Soviet borders: also in the 1940s, under Soviet influence, a version of Cyrillic was adapted for Mongolian.

Third, alongside the push for universal literacy in the 'national' languages (that is, the languages of groups defined as nationalities) came the push for universal competency in Russian as a second language. Russian became the *lingua franca* of the educated Soviet citizen. This was enshrined in curricula for primary education, with lessons in Russian for children whose schooling was otherwise conducted in their respective national languages (illus. 43). Policy is by nature 'top-down', but there were also 'bottom-up' incentives: just as it had been under the tsars, but in a vastly broader range of contexts, Russian, like literacy itself, became necessary for career progression, for social mobility and inclusion.

One feature of imperial Russification sits as if outside this narrative of chronological change, since it appears to have been quite consistent from the eighteenth century to the twentieth, and only began to be reversed in some of the post-Soviet states in the twenty-first century. This is the Russification of names. Throughout imperial, Soviet and post-Soviet space it was (and is) common for people to have surnames ending in the Russian-style suffixes *-ov* or *-ova*, and patronymics in *-ovich* or *-ovna*, regardless of their native languages. Why is Ramzan Akhmat**ovich** Kadyr**ov** the name of a president of Chechnya? Why is there a Kazakh writer called Olzhas Suleimen**ov**? Or a Soviet writer of Kyrgyz origin called Chinghiz Torekul**ovich** Aitmat**ov**? The practice was not quite universal: Georgian surnames, for example, tended to

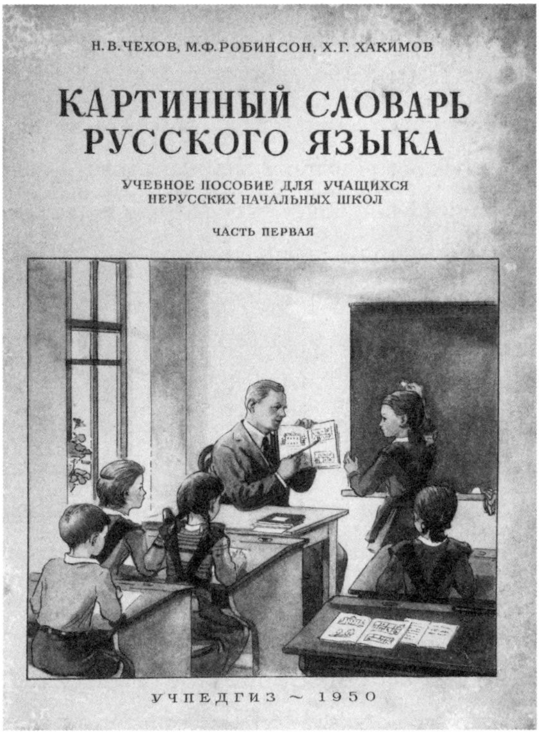

43 Soviet *Picture Dictionary* for non-Russian children, 1950.

retain their Georgian forms. The practice of Russianizing patronymics and family names goes back at least to the eighteenth century.[20] The initial framework was often administrative, for censuses and other documentary purposes, but it became habitual, normalized. Naming is powerful. The result was that a huge proportion of the empire's non-Russian inhabitants formally had names that, while not sounding fully Russian in origin, were co-opted into a Russian onomastic template.

Thus, over a prolonged period, at first haphazardly in disconnected episodes, eventually through conscious policy and practice, the Russian language became an instrument of imperial consolidation. Such, in outline, is the impact of Russian on empire. But what about the reverse, the impact of empire on Russian? To what extent have these extensive and diverse contacts been reflected in the culture of Russian itself?

The simple answer seems to be: at a local level, probably quite a lot, but at the central, rulemaking, level, not very much. Standard Russian – the 'literary' language – reflects centuries of imports from other languages, but, for the most part, the flow of words and expressions has been far more abundant from a relatively small number of prestigious languages *outside* the empire than from the very large quantity of non-Russian languages within it. The pattern of linguistic imports was determined by politics, power and high cultural fashion more than by the mere proximity of and contact with subject peoples. English, French, German or Polish have been more prominently represented in cultured Russian than have any of the indigenous non-Slav languages within the empire. This pattern is also supported by the sequence of imports brought about through contact with Turkic languages. Contemporary Standard Russian includes many elements derived from Turkic. One might initially assume that this is attributable to the presence of substantial numbers of Turkic-speaking peoples *within* the empire. The origin of the Russian Empire itself is often linked to the conquest of Kazan in the mid-sixteenth century, and Russia's last vast expansion came with the incorporation of much of Central Asia (modern Kazakhstan, Uzbekistan, Kyrgyzstan and Turkmenistan) in the nineteenth century. However, although some Turkic expressions did migrate into Russian during the imperial centuries, a substantial proportion of the Turkic elements in the modern language derive from earlier contacts. Part of the Turkic vocabulary is inherited from early Rus of the tenth to thirteenth century, when Turkic peoples (Khazars, Pechenegs, Polovtsians and, to the southeast, Volga Bulgars) were neighbours and rivals of the East Slav polities that bordered on the southern steppe. Another layer of Turkic imports derives from the period from the mid-thirteenth to the late fifteenth century, when Moscow and other Rus principalities were tributaries to the Mongols: that is, from the time when Moscow itself was subject to the administrative and fiscal oversight of somebody else's empire.[21]

In one area, however, there could be a direct route from the language of the colonized into the elite idioms of their colonizers. That was literature. From the early nineteenth century onwards, writers have exploited the resources of non-Russian subjects in creating an aura of what can be called linguistic imperiality. The term 'imperiality' refers to pervasive habits of thought and behaviour and expression embedded in a culture of empire. It is broader than 'imperialism', which tends to be more directly ideological.[22] A typical trope of such imperiality, especially in the age of Romanticism,[23] was the linguistic evocation of the exoticized 'other' on the fringes of empire. The narrative in Aleksandr Pushkin's poem *The Prisoner of the Caucasus* (*Kavkázskii plénnik*, 1822) begins with the location: not in a village or an encampment, but (using local vocabulary for a small settlement) 'In an *aúl* . . .' – and the subsequent text is spiced with local linguistic flavouring: *sáklia* (a hut), *kumys* (fermented mare's milk), and so on. The first few pages of the novel *A Hero of Our Time* (*Gerói náshego vrémeni*, 1840) by Mikhail Lermontov, also set in the Caucasus, are likewise sprinkled with transliterated words and phrases that need glossing for Lermontov's contemporary reader. In the Romantic context this was more than local colour. Linguistic evocation was a mode of appropriation, a conscious absorption of imperial space into Russian self-expression through language.

Global Russophonia

The English language can be somewhat clumsy when dealing with relations between cultural traditions that share a language. Confusingly, although English literature is literature in English, by no means all literature in English is English literature. We have become accustomed to different modifiers, some of which narrow down the locality – American literature, Australian literature – while others are hybrids that may combine language with allusions to locality and/or perceived ethnicity – Anglo-Irish, Anglo-Indian. If we want a catch-all label that detaches language from space, the word is Anglophone, which in turn can be split into categories of World Englishes.[24] The same can be said of cultures in other post-imperial languages: Francophone, Lusophone, Hispanic rather than the ambiguities of French, Portuguese or Spanish. And, by analogy, in the twenty-first century there has been increasing use of the label 'Russophone' as a means of designating and envisioning culture in the Russian language without tying it by implication to a specific territory or state or personal sense of identity. The paradox inherent in such labels is that, although they appear to designate a 'thing', they exist principally in order to accommodate diversity. They are fields that contain many different local ecosystems.

Of these fields, the Russophone is the most recent to be named and explored. Its expansion as an object of study is substantially due to the consequences of the collapse of the USSR. Before 1991 the focus of Russian-language culture was assumed to be geopolitically bounded: broadly speaking, it was what happened in the Russian language within the boundaries of the Russian Empire and the USSR. Interest in the Russian language among non-Russians outside Russia had generally been associated with practical activities such as trade, war, missionary work or diplomacy. Such interest was reflected in the occasional publication of textbooks of Russian, starting with Ludolf's grammar of 1696, printed in Oxford, or the Swedish version of Adodurov's grammar printed in Stockholm in 1750 (see Chapter Two). Following the defeat of Napoleon, and Alexander I's victorious entry into Paris in 1814, G. Harmonière published – at France's Royal Printing House – a dictionary, phrase book and grammar of Russian in 1815, 1816 and 1817 respectively.[25] As for native-speaker Russophones abroad: there had always been pockets of emigration. In the 1560s and '70s Ivan IV ('the Terrible', r. 1533–84) had a furious correspondence with a former servitor, Prince Andrei Kurbskii (1528–1583), who argued with him from the relative safety of the Polish–Lithuanian Commonwealth. In the early seventeenth century a small group of young Russians sent to study in England failed to return home, despite the persistent demands of their government. One of them, after a course at Cambridge, lived out his days as an Anglican priest.[26] However, there is no suggestion that these sporadic early defections planted any seeds of Russian-language culture abroad. In the nineteenth century a traveller through Europe might have found a sprinkling of Russians at spas and resorts, on cultural tours and on pilgrimages or at diplomatic missions; and there were clusters of political exiles, who were the first to engage in regular Russophone publishing, such as Aleksandr Herzen's Free Russian Press, which operated in London between 1853 and 1865. The institutionalized study of Russian in western European university departments likewise picked up some momentum from the mid-nineteenth century. But the substantial presence of Russian outside the empire (and the USSR) was a phenomenon that emerged and took shape in the twentieth century – at both ends of it.

For much of the century the word 'émigré' alluded mainly to people displaced by war, revolution and civil war in the years either side of 1917. 'Émigré literature' or 'émigré writer' became familiar but fairly compact and specific concepts from the 1920s onwards. For most of the Soviet period, foreign travel was severely restricted. The standard identity document was the internal passport.[27] A passport for travel abroad was a rare privilege. Foreign travel was controlled and organized: diplomatic, commercial and military missions; elite sports teams and opera companies; representative delegations to scientific conferences; group tourism to socialist countries. But travel by personal choice was not really on the agenda. From the end of the 1960s an exception was made for Jews. It is estimated that from 1970 to the late 1980s over a quarter of a million Jews emigrated from the Soviet Union, around two-thirds of whom settled in Israel.[28] Israel – with a total population of under 4 million in 1980 – thus became home to the first substantial modern Russophone minority population outside the Russian Empire or the USSR. Language export (that is, the acquisition of Russian by non-Russians from abroad) also played a role in the USSR's diplomatic, economic and educational policies. For example, from the early 1960s to the 1980s tens of thousands of African students were trained at Soviet universities,[29] usually beginning with a language-intensive foundation year. But in magnitude and complexity none of this compares to the Russophone diversity that followed the collapse of the USSR in 1991.

As an immediate consequence of the disintegration of the USSR, tens of millions of native speakers of Russian found that, without even moving from their homes, they had suddenly become members of linguistic minorities in fourteen new independent countries outside the Russian Federation. Soft borders between internal Soviet administrative regions turned into hard borders between sovereign states. Populations that previously might have been subjects of the survey in the first section of the present chapter (on imperial Russian) were shifted instantly into a different category (global Russophone). In Russia itself it became common to label the former Soviet republics the 'near abroad': as if they constituted some kind of intermediate zone, no longer in a political union, yet not fully foreign. Whether

44 Cyprus café, 2012, with signs in Russian.

'near' or otherwise, the result was to create a plurality of international Russophone populations on an unprecedented scale.

Alongside this sedentary mode of Russophone internationalization, the end the Soviet regime opened the gates for individual mobility. Russian-speakers travelled, in very large numbers, across the world, both from Russia itself and from the Russophone populations of the other post-Soviet states: for tourism, for employment, for education at all levels. Russophone service industries sprang up to cater for the needs of visitors and residents. In popular destinations such as Cyprus, cafes and property agents began routinely to advertise their services in Russian (illus. 44). And then there were children. A cross-generational diaspora brings its own range of language options. At one end of the scale, children could be raised in expatriate communities with a strong Russophone identity and with practical support for the language of the country that many continued to regard as the homeland. At the other end of the scale, Russophone parents – whether they regarded their residence abroad as temporary or as permanent – found that they were raising foreigners.

The full-scale Russian invasion of Ukraine in February 2022 produced a new surge in migration for different reasons. From Ukraine, predominantly women and children sought refuge from a war zone. From the Russian Federation, some went abroad in order to avoid the consequences of the internal clampdown on criticism of the government; others left in order to avoid military service. This latest wave of Russophone emigration was particularly active in establishing institutions of Russophone culture such as publishing houses and bookshops,[30] news and information agencies, websites, adult educational networks and classes in Russian for children.

What were the implications for the culture of the Russian language? The study of Russophone culture is a fast-expanding field, polycentric in itself, still exploring its own terms of reference but embracing complexity and diversity.[31] Universities advertise conferences and academic posts in Russophone studies. Research on Russophone language and culture outside Russia has provided data not only from the fourteen non-Russian post-Soviet states, but from, for example, France, Germany, Finland, Canada, several countries of South America, Scotland, the USA, Japan, Sweden, Cyprus, Israel, the Netherlands, Spain and elsewhere.[32] A common observation is that minority diasporic speakers and communities tend to assimilate words, concepts and speech habits from their linguistic surroundings: from obvious *realia* such as the names of local foods or consumer goods or media channels, or transliterated fragments of vocabulary, through to calqued idioms. There are and always have been many varieties of such a process. They can depend on contextual factors such as the size of the minority-language community, the existence of local structures for minority-language cultural and educational support, the extent to which minority-language communities feel themselves to be culturally accepted or assimilated, variations in cross-generational dynamics, attitudes to the majority ('host') language and the degree to which users feel their minority language to be a core element of their personal and communal identities.[33]

There is nothing peculiarly Russian in this. Languages in contact tend to adopt material from each other. Minority languages, in particular, tend to adopt and adapt material from the majority language environment. Purists used to call it 'contamination': a term that implies that it is a kind of deviance, a form of corruption. A less judgemental label is 'code-mixing', at any rate with reference to individual speech practices. If elements of code-mixing become habitual shared practice, they begin to function as their own local norms. Some of those who study the formation of such local speech norms have proposed the concept of 'pluricentrism' as a way of envisaging a kind of structured diversity in global Russophonia.

If, with a training only in Contemporary Standard Russian, you were to embark on a world tour of Russian-speaking communities, and eavesdrop on their conversations, you would hear a great variety of expressions that are likely to be unfamiliar, even incomprehensible, but which are treated as normal in their respective contexts. Normal, but not necessarily normative. One of the most common forms of language cultivation among diaspora communities is pedagogical, and the place where normative choices have to be made is the classroom. What kind of Russian did Russophones outside the Russian Federation want their children to learn? Theorists may stress that effective teaching takes into account the local linguistic context.[34] However, the measure of pedagogical effectiveness is generally assumed to be competence in the dominant norm: that is, in Contemporary Standard Russian (that is, the Russian 'literary' language). Among diaspora communities, just as among the social and local language communities within Russia itself, a diversity of speech habits and even of writing habits can coexist comfortably with a sense of an underlying standard language that is to be taught, of norms that everybody should ideally know. Globally, Russian is spoken in a variety of ways, and Russophone culture has many voices. However, pluricentricity in speech practices – and creative diversity in literary practices – does not equate to pluricentricity of linguistic authority.

A simple comparison with Anglophone normativity clarifies the point. Normative textbooks and courses in distinct varieties of English – American English and British English – have long competed for mass sales in educational markets across the world. Noah Webster's *American Dictionary of the English Language* was first published in 1828. In Russian it is rare for dictionaries and textbooks to embed local habits as language norms.[35] Contemporary ethnographers of Russian find a diversity of speech practices in global Russophonia, just as the early ethnographers of Russian in the mid-nineteenth century found diverse usages across the empire. Russophone cultural practices increasingly reflect and explore this diversity. For the most part, however, the authoritative norms of the culture of the language – the language as cultivated in education and as defined by institutional arbiters of correctness – are assumed to remain unitary. At the start of the second quarter of the twenty-first century the idea that there may be multiple recognized and normatively quasi-autonomous varieties of World Russian, analogous to the varieties of World Englishes, remains more aspirational than empirical.[36] It is, of course, perfectly plausible that more of the different registers of linguistic practice will become formalized, codified, recognized and cultivated as distinctive versions of Russian with their own norms. However, prediction is beyond the remit of the present survey.

Thus, despite the decentring of academic approaches to the post-Soviet Russian language, and despite a flourishing cultural and regional diversity within Russophonia, at the most basic level of linguistic authority, a sense of a central core seems to have held – in general, by and large, for the moment. Global Russophone *culture* is vigorous and varied; global *informal* language usage reflects multiple and heterogeneous interactions with local majority languages, but not (yet) to the extent of generating alternative locally normative variants of Russian, codified and taught as such.

How did the curators of language in the traditional centre – Russia itself – deal with the rise of global Russophonia? How, and with what measure of effectiveness, did Russian institutions and authorities seek to encourage or influence the culture of the language beyond their borders? Russian engagement with Russophonia can be briefly summarized on four levels: informal, academic, quasi-governmental (NGOs) and governmental. Broadly speaking, the more overtly political the intent, the less effective was the outcome.

At the informal level, a striking example of unplanned success through a grass-roots initiative was Total Dictation (*Totál'nyi diktánt*), a project devised in 2004 at the University of Novosibirsk in Siberia. Total Dictation was explicitly non-political, even anti-political. Its rules, published prominently on its website, declared that political, religious and ideological organizations were excluded from being partners or sponsors.[37] Its mission was to promote literacy and correct usage in Russian by means of a coordinated exercise in dictation that was open to anybody who wished to join. At first sight this does not look like an idea with mass appeal, yet Total Dictation became a global phenomenon. In 2024 its centrepiece event attracted around 1.3 million participants in over fifty countries.

Total Dictation activated a shared enthusiasm for the Russian language. Further up the hierarchy of linguistic authority was the portal gramota.ru. Again designed for Russia but with informally achieved global reach, gramota.ru was established in 2000 in partnership with the Russian Academy of Science's Institute of the Russian Language.[38] Gramota.ru itself became a multifaceted organization devoted to the language: a producer of educational tools, a publisher of language courses and dictionaries (online and on paper) and a locus of information about resources. However, at the core of its activities and at the heart of its brand was its online, open-access provision of answers to questions about the Russian language posted by the public. With its institutional partner, gramota.ru positioned itself as the arbiter of correct usage, and it gained very wide acceptance as such, within and beyond Russia. As of June 2024 the site claimed to have over 2 million unique visits per month. In a way, gramota.ru was a kind of twenty-first-century equivalent of the radio programme *In the World of Words* from the 1960s and '70s: engaging with popular curiosity and anxiety about proper usage in the Russian language – but with the greater authority of the Academy, with the greater capacity of a continuously functioning web portal rather than a twice-monthly broadcast, and with the hugely greater global reach of networked technology in the electronic age.

Total Dictation and gramota.ru were Russia-based Internet initiatives that happened to become attractive and useful to wider Russophone communities. On the next step upwards on the scale of institutionalized formality were the state-supported language-based cultural projects that explicitly reached outwards beyond the borders of the Russian Federation. Such projects tended to have two main aims: to consolidate the bonds of the imagined nation beyond its geopolitical boundaries, and/or to use Russian language and culture as instruments of influence (that is, soft power) in non-Russophone communities. Even before the USSR had expired, the Russian authorities began actively to cultivate Russophone populations abroad, promoting the idea of a special bond between language and land. The first Congress of Compatriots (*sootéchestvenniki*) was held in Moscow in 1991. Ironically – but coincidentally – it began on 19 August, the day after the attempted coup against Mikhail Gorbachev. The initiative stalled during the 1990s, and was not revived until the second Congress in October 2006, after which the Congresses took place approximately biennially. When properly nurtured, compatriots should be patriots (though this wordplay does not work in Russian, where a 'patriot' is normally designated not by the somewhat grandiloquently Slavonic form *otéchestvennik* but – perhaps paradoxically – by the imported word *patriót*). Language was assumed to be an extension of nation, and nation was, first and foremost, territorial: speakers of Russian have – or ought to feel that they have – a special bond with the fatherland.

The revival of the Congresses of Compatriots in 2006 was one of a series of more or less coordinated institutional initiatives that were designed to serve related aims. They involved the establishment of two new institutions dedicated to projecting Russian language and culture abroad: Russkii Mir (Russian World), founded in 2007, and Rossotrúdnichestvo, founded in 2008. Rossotrudnichestvo – literally 'Russian Cooperation' – was an agency of the Russian government. Its mission was 'the strengthening of the humanitarian influence of Russia in the world', including 'the strengthening of the position of the Russian language'.[39] From 2021 it became known informally as 'The Russian House' (*Russkii dom*). Rossotrudnichestvo's wide-ranging brief included support for compatriots (including assistance with repatriation), as well as a network of cultural centres, many of which were set up as adjuncts to Russian diplomatic missions.[40] Russkii Mir was established, first and foremost, as a funding body to promote Russian language and culture. Like Rossotrudnichestvo, it set up a network of centres abroad, but the model was different. While Rossotrudnichestvo was explicitly a government agency operating through embassies and consulates, Russkii Mir sought to enter partnerships with foreign cultural and educational institutions. It operated a programme of grants through open application and, most prominently, it funded Russkii Mir centres. For a typical centre, the foreign institution would provide space, while Russkii Mir would provide a library of Russian books, often IT equipment and digital materials, as well as – crucially and most attractively – funds to pay a local director.

In its early years, to many institutions the Russkii Mir package seemed generous and not intrusive. Its application and reporting procedures could be somewhat bureaucratic, but within the normal range for international funding bodies. Importantly the fund demanded no direct role either in the appointment of centre directors or in operations and cultural programming. As was the case with, for example, the analogous network of Confucius Institutes funded from China in a programme that had been initiated in 2004, institutional due-diligence procedures regularly found in favour of proposals for collaboration with Russkii Mir. In Britain, for example, Russkii Mir centres were set up in London at the independent UK charity Pushkin House in 2009, then at the universities of Edinburgh (in 2010, together with a grant of over £200,000), Oxford (2012, at St Antony's College) and Durham (2013). In 2012 the University of Edinburgh awarded an honorary degree to the director of Russkii Mir, Viacheslav Nikonov.

Within a few years, optimism about non-politicized cultural engagement with Russian governmental or government-funded organizations had collapsed. The main catalyst was Russia's active pursuit of territorial ambitions in eastern and southern Ukraine. Among the multiple, overlapping and mutually reinforcing arguments and narratives that were used to justify annexation and invasion was the assertion that the largely Russian-speaking populations of those regions of Ukraine were in fact Russians, and that therefore their land should properly be part of Russia. They were part of the 'Russian world' – the phrase *russkii mir* became ever more strongly associated with an ethno-nationalist claim rather than just with name of a cultural institution. Substantial parts of the Russkii Mir network of centres collapsed. In 2022 Russkii Mir was sanctioned by the European Union (and the University of Edinburgh stripped Viacheslav Nikonov of his honorary degree). Not that any of this was obvious in Russkii Mir's self-presentation. As late as December 2025 its website gave details of over eighty Russkii Mir centres, in forty countries, including several in western Europe (but not the UK).[41] The list was a facade. Much of it was fictitious. Approximately a quarter of the centres had declared their own closure around February 2022. Many more had become defunct without giving reasons. Some of the links were to educational centres that still operated but whose websites appeared to have expunged all references to their previous connection to Russkii Mir. The remaining, functioning Russkii

Mir centres, which displayed the fund's logo on their websites as a partner organization, were located in Azerbaijan, Armenia, Belarus, Bulgaria, Bosnia and Herzegovina, China, Greece, North Macedonia, Moldova, Mongolia, Serbia, Syria, Slovenia, Tanzania and Thailand. Although its principal mission was always to promote Russian language and culture abroad, in late 2025 the site also listed a small number of centres within the 'Russian Federation': in the Donetsk and Lugansk regions – that is, in places that on most international maps would have been defined as Russian-occupied Ukraine.

In global Russophonia, despite widespread and varied local language contacts and interactions, for at least three decades after the collapse of the Soviet Union Contemporary Standard Russian remained broadly acknowledged as the norm, and its curators and adjudicators were institutionally based in Russia itself. The most widely influential Russia-based language initiatives were those which emerged from and in partnership with educational and academic institutions, such as gramota.ru and Total Dictation. In sustaining authority over the norms of cultured Russian, power in language appears to have been most effective without the language of power. As will be apparent in the next chapter, this kind of empirical conclusion was not in keeping with the approach, the policies and the legislative activities of the government of the Russian Federation.

9

Disruptions and Reactions in Post-Soviet Russia

In 1991 the USSR imploded. Through the 1990s and early 2000s networked electronic communication exploded. Either of these processes could in itself have been transformative. Together and more or less concurrently, each amplified the impact of the other. Both reverberated in the culture of the Russian language. Common to both processes were forms of radical defamiliarization, in life and in language. The new world was not made for old linguistic habits and assumptions. In the old world, at least until its final few years, a great deal of publicly disseminated language was deliberately ritualized, formally predictable, familiar by design and function. In the new world, linguistic norms and authority were challenged, undermined seemingly to the point of collapse.[1] This could be experienced passively, as something unsought, undesirable and destructive; and it could be experienced actively, as something creative and enabling. In 2007 the linguist Maksim Krongauz published a short book called *The Russian Language on the Verge of a Nervous Breakdown*.[2] He did not, of course, mean the language itself. Languages do not have nervous systems. Yet his readers will have known what he had in mind: a widespread sense of stress and distress, of linguistic instability and disorientation, of the erosion of boundaries and norms.

However, in the larger context of the language, not all the consequences of change were centrifugal. The demography of the post-Soviet Russian state created a new linguistic landscape. In the last Soviet census of 1989, just over half the total population identified as Russian. The collapse of the USSR meant that the fourteen nominally non-Russian republics became independent states. Although the post-Soviet Russian Federation remained multilingual and multi-ethnic, with some formal characteristics of an empire, it also acquired, suddenly, stronger characteristics of a nation state. According to the 2021 census, just over 80 per cent of its population identified as Russian. Not everything was falling apart for the Russian language. Soviet disintegration produced a context for Russian integration. The cultural, political, ideological and geopolitical implications of this were profound.

In this chapter we will look first at features of this radical defamiliarization, and then at forms of reaction and resistance to it. The main focus of the first section will be on the early post-Soviet period, circa 1991–2010.[3]

Radical Defamiliarization

For some, the end of the USSR brought the beginning of a new freedom; an unlocking of potential; a stimulus to progress; an opening of borders and minds; a smashing of barriers to financial, cultural and personal opportunity. For others it signalled disorientation and humiliation; the collapse of authority, stability and dignity; the disintegration of the social, economic and cultural fabric; instant impoverishment as global competition wiped out jobs and as waves of hyperinflation wiped out savings. On city streets disorganized crime thrived (much worse than organized crime, which tends to favour monopolization and a certain orderliness). The familiar pathways to success and respect became dead ends. The new rules, if they existed at all, were strange and opaque. Money was at the core, as it had never been in Soviet ideology or daily life. And, amid the instability and insecurity, somehow a handful of individuals, in cahoots with power, contrived to emerge with mega-billions.

Much of this came wrapped in fog of unfamiliar words; through technology, commerce, finance or consumer advertising, from fashion houses to fast food chains. Overwhelmingly, the source language was English. Now it was all about the *ímidzh* (or, indeed, about *imidzhméiking*), preferably with the aid of an appropriate *logotíp*.[4] There was a whole new industry of *piár* (whose job it was to *piárit'*). Every successful business needed to hire *sek'iúriti*. In December 1991 the imminent opening of Moscow's first *seks-shop* was announced. Unhappy with your appearance? Try *liposáktsiia*. The urban landscape was transformed by *devélopery*, often using the cheap labour of *gastarbáitery* (English did not have a complete monopoly as the source language). Commercial catering in the USSR had not been a priority (meals were assumed to be provided at the workplace and at home), but now *búrgery* were everywhere – and, pretty soon, *sushi-báry* – where the hard-pressed not-yet executive *ménedzher* (and others involved in *ménedzhment*) could have a reasonably priced *bíznes lanch* (which does not comfortably translate back as 'business lunch'; something closer to a 'meal deal' or a fixed-price menu). And so on. And that is before we even begin to consider the additional deluge of terminology and jargon brought in by the digital revolution itself. Russian had experienced waves of foreign lexical imports in earlier times, but no previous influx had been so pervasive, nothing had seeped into (or flooded) so many areas of life and work across so many segments of society across the entire country.

The cultural opening of the country more or less coincided with the age of the technological revolution. There is no precise starting date for digital transformations in Russia. Various types and levels of networked computing had existed in the Soviet Union long before the Union itself fell apart.[5] Arguably a significant stage-marker in the growth of Russia's connectivity can likewise be set in 1990–91 with the launch of the RELCOM network, but the exponential growth of networked communication should be linked, on the one hand, to the privatizations of the 1990s and the emergence of entrepreneurial providers, and, on the other hand, to the spread of mass access first to personal computers and eventually to mobile devices, beginning from the mid- to late 1990s and continuing rapidly through the early 2000s.

The immediate defamiliarizing feature of networked digital communication – as a general feature, by no means limited to Russia – was its inherent diffuseness. Digital media devolved to the level of the individual the capacity to generate, encode and distribute words almost instantaneously across the globe. They completed the process that had started nearly two centuries earlier with the invention of the electrical telegraph. Digital communication radically altered the sociolinguistic implications of place. Likewise, it seemed to outflank conventional sources of authority, challenging traditional structures of language oversight. Anybody could write almost anything to almost anybody. The technologies decentred language as never before. Linguistic subcultures sprouted everywhere. Some of them flourished and became almost institutionalized; others briefly blossomed and faded. They produced new forms of group etiquette, new linguistic signs of inclusion or exclusion. They could replicate or mutate with unprecedented rapidity. Millions of individuals could suddenly disseminate their own messages worldwide in a millisecond. And by no means all the individuals or groups were mindful of the norms of the Russian literary language. Rather the opposite: decentred linguistic non-normativity became fashionable.

This structural defamiliarization was exacerbated by the fact that modern digital networked mass communication came pre-packaged in an alien tongue: English. In most areas linguistic defences crumbled quickly. For some years, the long-standing, technically precise yet clumsy Russian term *elektrónnaia vychislítel'naia mashína* (electronic calculating machine) held its ground, particularly in its snappier abbreviation *EVM* (*e-ve-ém*), but in popular use it lost out to *komp'iúter*. Early web users either rejoiced in flaunting, or were intimidated by, esoteric barbarisms such as *róuming*, *róuter*, *skáner*, *sérfing*, *sérver*, just as a later generation of tech-consumers had to cope with a continual flow of equivalent imports such as *tachskrín*. The computers and then the mobile systems were imported, global platforms were joined (*feisbúk*, *tvítter*, *iut'iúb* . . .). Mobile network users had *fréndy* (whom it was possible to *fréndit'*) and *follóvery*. Onlinespeak was liberally laced with Anglophone derivatives well after the general switch to Cyrillic lettering. Sometimes the act of importing a word changed its social semantics. Thus a *frend* was not, generically, a friend, still less a *drug* (which would be a standard Russian translation of 'friend'). *Frend* was normally marked as an online term with a specific online meaning. An online *chat* (an activity of, for example, *blógery*) was not a face-to-face chat (an activity of, for example, friends – rather than *fréndy* – around a table). A *displéi* was only a screen – with no relation to, for example, what peacocks do with their tail feathers. The noun *laik*, along with its many morphologically Russianized derivatives (the verbs *láikat'*, *láiknut'*, *laikanút'*, *zaláikat'* and so on) referred only to an online action, with no real danger of being confused with personal feeling of liking someone.[6] Over time the Anglophone flavouring on the Russian Internet became less obtrusive. A lot became morphologically naturalized: people who worked in IT became *aitíshniki*, while an SMS (that is, a text message) was turned into an *eseméska*. At the same time, some transcribed imports were replaced by calques (for example, *follóvery* give way *podpíschiki* – 'subscribers').

The 'foreignness' of early networked language was not limited to imported vocabulary. It was embedded in the system through the use of the Latin alphabet. Before Unicode, there were severe restrictions on rendering Cyrillic. Latin script was the assumed graphic tool of foreign and imported computers and keyboards, whether sending or receiving or displaying. Early digital communication therefore resorted quite extensively to the Latin alphabet in rendering not only foreign words but Russian ones too. Transliteration was unavoidable. Russian in Latin-script computer communication became known as *translit*. Here, too, derivative necessity was creatively appropriated as cultural idiom; *translit* developed its own conventions that played with visual (that is, graphic rather than traditionally orthographic) approximations of Cyrillic letters. Thus, for example, Cyrillic 'р' would conventionally have been rendered through Latin 'r', but in visual *translit* Latin 'r' could stand in for the similar-looking Cyrillic 'г' (*g*), while Latin 'p' was coopted to stand for Cyrillic 'р' (*r*); 'ш' (*sh*) becomes 'w', 'х' (*kh*), not surprisingly, becomes 'x'. Numerals could also serve in this function: '4' stood for 'ч' (*ch*), and '9' for 'я' (*ia*).[7]

Among the oddest – and most earnestly analysed – linguistic inventions of the early Russian blogosphere was a graphic idiom that aimed at defamiliarizing Russian itself, from within, as it were. Its self-designation was a phrase which, if written in standard Russian spelling, would be *iazyk podónkov*, which I render here as 'slimeball language'.[8] A *podónok* is the lowest of the low, the dregs, the pits, a scumbag. However, none of these is properly equivalent, because all of them look like proper English words, whereas the point of slimeball language was precisely the fact that it was *not* rendered in standard spelling; it did *not* look like proper Russian. Slimeball language has an identifiable point of origin and a traceable arc of fashion. It was launched in 1998 on the website fuck.ru. It had two main characteristic features: (i) an abundant use of obscenities, plus some inventive euphemisms for obscenities; and (ii) a radical approach to spelling, and hence to the look of the language.

In standard Russian, by comparison with English, the relationship between speech and spelling is notably regular: look at how the word is written, and you know how it is pronounced. More or less. In order to 'hear' a word on the basis of its orthography, one needs answers to two questions. First, with regard to a vowel: which syllable in the word is stressed? The pronunciation of a graphic sign representing a vowel in a stressed syllable is different from its pronunciation in an unstressed syllable. In unstressed position there is little or no difference in pronunciation between the vowels 'o' and 'a', and between 'e' and 'i'. Second, with regard to a consonant: what is its position either (a) in a combination or cluster of consonants, or (b) in relation to the end of a word? Some 'voiced' consonants (for example, 'v', 'g', 'd') are 'devoiced' or 'aspirated' (that is, they become the same as 'f', 'k' or 't' respectively) at the end of a word, and before other devoiced consonants. The graphic device of slimeball language was as follows: where, because of their position in the word, there is little or no difference in pronunciation between two or more letters – use the 'incorrect' one, the letter that does not correspond to standard spelling. So, in unstressed position, where 'o' or 'e' would be the norm, write 'a' or 'i' instead, and vice versa; and likewise, in the relevant positions where 'g' or 'v' would fit the norm, write 'k' or 'f' instead, and vice versa.

Illustration may be clearer than explanation. In slimeball language, *podónkov* was rendered as *padónkaf* (or *padónkaff* – variations are allowable), *chemodán* (suitcase) became *chimadán*, *krasávchik* (good-looking guy) was *krosávcheg*, an *ávtor* (author) was an *áfftar*, and *potomú chto* (because) could be rendered as *patamú shta*. Naturally, one cannot expect principles to be rigid: once an equivalence between 'f' and 'v' became habitual, so *dévochka* could be rendered as *défach'ko* even though the 'v' is not positionally devoiced. Nevertheless, and despite such mildly perverse deviations, the crucial point is that these forms were meant to be purely graphic. Any spelling was permissible except the conventionally normative spelling, but pronunciation did not change. That was the language's discipline. Slimeball language presented Russian words that did not look like themselves; until one realized that they were.

Slimeball orthography is therefore fully comprehensible once its procedures are grasped. The show of defamiliarization was on the surface. When reading a familiar language, we do not generally move from letter to letter in sequence. We recognize the cluster of letters that form a word. Studies have shown that, for example, if we keep in place the first and last letters of a word, and vary the order of letters between them, we can often read the text without much strain. That is, words are often legible if we use the right letters, even if not necessarily in the right order. Not so with slimeball language. Slimeball language used the wrong letters. Mix up *their* order, and the result *does* initially look like nonsense.[9] But it was not. It was just a visual trick, a game with surfaces. Unlike the trans-sense language of the Futurists, slimeball language was real language dressed up to look as if it was not. It was ostentatiously transgressive while in fact operating its own conventions of normativity. It was a kind of cryptography that became easily de-encrypted through habit. What was the point? Slimeball language was taken up as a counter-cultural project. It generated a critical terminology on the significance of deliberate mistakes, or 'erratives'.[10] It has been called a kind of anti-literacy, or seen as a kind of practical artistic project in experimental orthography (*ortho-art*).[11] This deliberately crafted, initially esoteric and resolutely superficial experiment found an audience of *follóvery*. It became a 'thing', so to speak. Until it did not. The shelf-life of slimeball language was about seven or eight years; not at all bad for a fashion in the fast-moving culture of online idiom. Then it subsided into becoming merely an object of study. Its writerly qualities perhaps mark it as a phenomenon of its time, of the early phases of the Russian blogosphere,[12] before universal connectivity and the radical diffuseness of modern social media.

Paradoxes of Obscenity

In the decentred 1990s, the opportunities for untrammelled non-normativity could be experienced as a sign of the collapse of linguistic identity, or as an opportunity to explore and discover a richer version of it. Thus, for some, criminal jargon on the streets was a sign of lawlessness and a threat to social order. For others, it was a treasury of Russian popular creativity and pithy expressiveness. Boundaries between previously fringe idioms and mainstream colloquialism became permeable on an unprecedented scale. Word-collectors found new fields to explore, and keen audiences for their findings. It was a golden age of non-normative (and non-normal) dictionaries: dictionaries of prison and prison-camp jargon;[13] dictionaries of insults, of gestures or of youth slang; dictionaries of sayings and colloquial expressions, or of folk similes.[14] There were attempts to bring a broad range of sub-normative jargons together into a single volume,[15] or to catch the culture of the moment in an explanatory dictionary of 'current' Russian vocabulary,[16] or to compile an explicitly non-normative academic dictionary of colloquial speech,[17] or to reflect sociolinguistic change in the area of gender lexicography.[18] There were extraordinary original achievements such as a four-volume dictionary based on a 23-year longitudinal study of the language usage of one person in a village near Tomsk.[19] And there were dedicated enthusiasts who delved deep into the unsuspected histories of Russian which, in their findings, spanned multiple millennia: a four-volume, self-published *Etymological Dictionary of the Russian Global Language*, whose author, in nearly 3,000 pages, demonstrated in detail, and a with conviction unlikely to be shared by many readers, how Russian has preserved the roots of the global proto-language,[20] and a study purporting to demonstrate that ancient Etruscan was in fact a dialect of Russian spoken by an early diaspora.[21] Above all, however, there were obscenities, a rising, turbulent tide of them: on the streets, in print where they would never before have been admitted, and online. Obscenities are not just another non-normative or regional or socially circumscribed register. They have deeper and more paradoxical implications for the cultural history of language, enough to merit a section to themselves.

A much-told anecdote runs approximately thus: Vanya goes to Paris. On his return, he tells his wife Manya all about it:

> The Louvre! Manya, okh***tel'no! Kartín do kh*iá, ë* tvoiú mat'! Notre Dame: Ë* tvoiú mat'! Ia okh**el, blia**! Pi**éts! Obosr***sia mózhno! The Eiffel Tower – Nu i kh*íshche, e*éna mat'! . . .' And so on, for at least five minutes, maybe more. Manya looks at him tenderly, even sheds a tear: Oh, Vanya, it's so beautiful! (krasotá-to kakáia).

The asterisked words would widely be categorized as obscenities, words which would fall under the Russian generic label for obscenity: *mat* (see also *máternye slová* – 'obscene words', 'swearwords'; *máternye vyrazhéniia* – 'obscene expressions'). This exchange between Vanya and Manya crystallizes two general points about the way in which *mat* functions. The first point is that obscene language is very often not about obscene things. In origin, most of the asterisked words are sexual, and one is scatological. Yet in context their intended and perceived meanings are neither. On the contrary, they evoke Vanya's delight in the beauties of Paris. Here obscenities describe without being conventionally descriptive. It has been said that they function as a kind of alternative language, a 'shadow-image of the Russian language as a whole'.[22] The second point is that the anecdote is not told with disdain or disapproval. It implies a kind of humorous pride. Among the many, many aspects of Russian exceptionalism, one should include the belief that the Russian language possesses a uniquely rich treasury of obscenities, with opportunities for extensive, virtuoso, improvised, creatively expressive performance. That is, obscenities are both unspeakable (in proper speech) and essential (part of the essence of linguistic Russianness). A 2009 encyclopedic dictionary of key words for the understanding of Russian culture includes an article on *mat*, noting that many reckon it to be 'an inseparable part of the Russian language and of the speech of the Russian people'.[23] The publisher's blurb to a recent Russian book on the subject states that 'the Russian language without obscenities is not quite Russian.'[24]

It is a commonplace, by no means limited to Russian, that obscenity is a quality attributed to forms of expression, not necessarily to what they express. To *have* a shit involves defecation; to *give* (or not to give) a shit does not. Most things that are described as 'fucking brilliant' have little to do with brilliant fucking. Just so, in Vanya's account of Paris, *okh***tel'no* stands for *okhuítel'no*, an adverb ultimately from the noun *khui* – 'prick' – via the verb *okhuét'*; it means 'amazing'. Yet the word still counts as an obscenity. On the page we can sanitize obscenities with asterisks. In speech we can sweeten them by substitution, such as exclaiming 'sugar!' instead of 'shit!' Russian, too, uses culinary euphemisms, such as *blin* (literally 'pancake'), instead of *bliad'* (originally 'whore', but often a generalized expletive, or just an intonational filler); or *khren* (horseradish) instead of *khui*. The language-learner has to understand that *odín khren* – 'one horseradish' – is not part of a recipe. *Khren* stands in for *khui*, and the expression means 'so what?' 'I don't give a toss.'

In themselves such generalities about obscene idiom tell one nothing about the supposedly unique richness of Russian *mat*. Like most claims of exceptionalism, it is rarely based on real comparisons. But we can play with numbers a little. There are perhaps only about half a dozen basic roots that are generally reckoned obscene. The trick, however, lies in the ways in which Russian can expand from this limited base. The mechanisms of Russian word-formation allow it to create very large numbers of derivatives. Two of the pioneers of the linguistic study of Russian obscenities, Felix Dreizin and Tom Priestly, laid out a statistical hypothesis.[25] Looking only at verbs, they started with just eight regular roots. They then surveyed the plain, un-prefixed verbs that can be derived from those roots (for example, *ebát'*, *ebanút'*, *ëbnut'*, *ebáchit'* and so forth; *khuiáchit'*, *khuiárit'* and so on). They then posited the possibility of adding the full range of Russian prefixes; then they incorporated forms with the reflexive suffix *-sia*. They arrived at a total of 1,596 verbs. The same could be done with nouns: first the plain derivatives, such as *khuiniá*, *khuiátina* or *khuëvina*, then the prefixed derivatives; then adjectives and adverbs, such as *khuëvyi/o* or *okhuítel'nyi/o*. The totals multiply exponentially.

If this sounds too much like philological game-playing, we can take a different point of departure: not the multiplicity of derivatives from a single root, but the multiplicity of meanings and idiomatic phrases involving a single word. Perhaps the most remarkable feat of lexicography in this area is the *Big Dictionary of Obscenity* by Aleksei

45 A. Plutser-Sarno's two-volume *Big Dictionary of Obscenities*.

Plutser-Sarno. Two volumes were published, in 2001 and 2005 (illus. 45). Each was devoted to just one word. The first volume dealt with *khui* and the second dealt with *pizdá* (cunt).[26] To be clear: the subject of each volume was only the basic noun, in itself and in idiomatic phrases. The dictionary did not extend to verbs, adjectives or adverbs, or to prefixed forms, or to nominal derivatives. Even with this massive restriction, the core lexical material in each volume filled around two hundred pages. One can barely speculate how many volumes might notionally be required to construct a dictionary that comes close to completeness.

So, on both counts – the number of words, and the number of idiomatic expressions per word – modern studies give credence to the notion of extreme amplitude. Who else could boast such a cornucopia of variegated obscenity? Naturally, for those who ask it, the rhetorical question is sufficient to imply its own answer. Neither Plutser-Sarno nor Dreizin and Priestly explore comparisons.

If we distrust mere statistics, we can turn to writers of fiction. Sergei Dovlatov (1941–1990) tells of a fresh-faced, well-read young sergeant who turns up at a prison camp. Eager to establish credibility, he sprinkles his speech with obscenities. But he makes a mistake, using the word *ebnúlsia*. A linguistically fastidious prisoner picks him up on this: 'You are incorrect. One can say *ëbnulsia*, *ebanúlsia* and *naebnúlsia*. But as for *ebnúlsia* – I'm sorry, but there's no such word in the Russian literary language.'[27] Two points are made at the same time here: the range of linked derivative forms available in *mat*, and the non-randomness, the sense of orderliness for experienced users, who see obscenity as entirely normative in its own terms.[28]

What exactly is being counted? Or, rather, what counts as obscenity? Obscenity is an odd category. In official sources – in legislation, and in quite a lot of academic lexicography – the general label tends to be not *mat*, but *bran'*, *bránnaia léksika*, which might loosely be rendered as 'swearwords', 'abusive language'. This designation for language regarded as taboo in polite society has been traditional for well over two hundred years. A late eighteenth-century alphabet book for children contains a list of moral maxims. No. 34 in the list states that abusive words (*bránnye slová*) 'offend the mouth from which they issue forth, as much as the ears into which they enter'.[29] There is no universal consensus about what exactly is covered by these terms, or by the more colloquial label, *mat*.[30] Even normative lexicographers draw the boundaries in different places. The multi-volume *Large Academy Dictionary*, which declares its principle of 'heightened normativity' (see below), is very broad in its exclusions, but a single-volume dictionary emanating partly from the same institute of the Academy of Sciences is happy to cover what might be reckoned mild obscenities (*zhópa*, *srat'*). In the dictionary's preface the phrase to describe mild obscenity is *bránnaia léksika*.[31] In modern legislation the phrase that covers obscenity is *netsenzúrnaia bran'*: literally, 'abusive words that would not get past the censor' – a curiously circular non-definition which seems to devolve linguistic authority to censors, whose views have themselves been far from consistent over time. A broad consensus on what constitutes *mat* would probably limit its scope to fewer than half a dozen roots. By contrast, in a 2025 government-approved dictionary of Russian as a state language the definition of *netsenzúrnaia bran'* lists fourteen roots.[32]

Obscenity is constructed socially. It is a register of non-normative language, so it is recognized through its (negative) relation to the norm – except, that is, in social contexts where *mat* is itself normal. For example, *mat* has traditionally been highly gendered: acceptable and enjoyed in male banter, but not to be tolerated in front of women and children or in public. In an interview with the popular weekly journal *Arguments and Facts* (*Arguménty i fákty*) in 2014, the film director Aleksandr Sokurov (b. 1951) opined that obscenity (here *skvernoslóvie* – foul language, a Slavonism redolent of moral and religious disapproval) in the theatre or cinema was a symptom of general degradation, but at the same time he declared that '*mat* is male speech, and it is a great shame that we men have surrendered that part of our speech for general usage. It is a shame that women have been allowed to use *mat*. This should be forbidden!'[33] Sokurov's pronouncement may be somewhat tongue-in-cheek in its self-caricatured simplicity, but not to the extent of fully undermining its own position. Any veneer of irony here is wafer-thin. We could almost be back in the late eighteenth century, with Nikolai Karamzin declaring that language must be acceptable to sensitive young ladies in polite society.

For some linguists, *mat* is just one among many varieties of non-normative language. For example, the modestly titled *Fullest Dictionary of Non-Normative Vocabulary*,[34] with some 16,000 words and around 4,000 phrases, combines *mat* with 'criminal, military, naval and other jargon, urban colloquialisms, vulgarisms, taboo vocabulary' (but not rural and regional colloquialisms). Michael S. Gorham links late and post-Soviet educated interest in *mat* with a similar rise in interest in prison-camp jargon.[35] However, in relation to most educated speakers, prison-camp jargon is markedly 'other';

the contemplation of *mat* is introspective. Prison camps are outside everyday society; *mat* is within it. Obscenity is not just a sociolinguistic category; it is a moral category; closer to blasphemy (hence *skvernoslóvie*). It is like sin, and just as contradictory: innate and suppressed, a shameful temptation and a shameless indulgence, an embarrassment and a delight, transgressive yet expressive – expressive *because* transgressive. And sometimes all of these, subtly layered, in the same person. Permissiveness of *mat* is moral self-destruction.[36] Alternatively: permissiveness undermines *mat* itself, and to undermine *mat* is to undermine part of ourselves, part of the defining richness of the Russian language.

These are general features of the culture of *mat*. What, if anything, was specific to the post-Soviet and or electronic age? It is not possible to construct a granular history of Russian *mat*. We are at the mercy of written sources, the overwhelming majority of which, by definition, exclude the unprintable, and, for the most part, the unwritable. It is particularly difficult to establish when or why particular words *became* obscene. For example, in a letter written on birch bark in Novgorod in the mid-twelfth century, the word *pizdá* simply designates the vagina, in relation to fertility in a proposed marriage.[37] There is no indication that the word itself was regarded as indecent or indecorous. By contrast, to call a woman a *bliad'* (whore) was already treated as deeply offensive.[38] The earliest printed Russian obscenities are probably those recorded by the German scholar and geographer Adam Olearius (1603–1671), who travelled to Muscovy twice in the mid-1630s. In his extensive narrative of the journeys, Olearius notes expressions that he transliterates as *bledinsin*, *sukkinsin*, *jabona mat* and *jebutzui mat*, which are easily decoded as *bliádin syn* (son of a whore), *súkin syn* (son of a bitch), *ebéna mat'* (fucked mother) and *ebú tvoiú mat'* (I fuck your mother).[39] According to Olearius, such insults were common.

In Russian writing about language, the existence of obscenity, or at any rate what polite society would regard as indecency, has been recognized as a significant strand of popular verbal culture since the first lexicographers in the eighteenth century. It was acknowledged in the preface to the first volume of the *Dictionary of the Russian Academy*, published in 1789. A subculture of *literary* obscenity has existed also since the eighteenth century, most notoriously in the collection associated with Ivan Barkov and his followers (see Chapter Two). Some writers have flirted with the unsayable by ostentatiously not quite saying it. So, in Aleksandr Pushkin's narrative poem *Tsar Nikita and His Forty Daughters*, written in 1822, the eponymous daughters had everything: they were beautiful, talented, engaging, but they were all born without vaginas.[40] Tsar Nikita sends envoys to search far and wide for the missing parts. One of the envoys finds a witch in a forest. The witch fashions forty vaginas and puts them in a box, to be taken back to the palace. The tsar's servitor is overcome with curiosity and opens the box – whereupon the vaginas flutter away like birds. But all ends well: they return of their own accord, and the tsar and his daughters live happily ever after. Pushkin's poem is transgressive in theme but – ostensibly – not in vocabulary. Pushkin makes a great show of being too fastidious, too respectful and delicate actually to name the missing body part (he has no desire to irritate the 'self-important pious foolish woman, or the excessively fastidious censorship' (lines 25–6)). Except that he does name the parts, sort of. What was the one thing that these maidens lacked? 'Well, nothing really, or very little; a little nothing, a trifle . . .' (lines 20–21). The word translated here as 'trifle' is *bezdélka*. The unstressed 'e' is equivalent to unstressed 'i', so that is can sound like *bizdélka*. Although not instantly obvious visually, the allusion is unavoidable aurally to the knowing listener: *bezdélka* is a sly way of not saying *pizdá*, of transgressing while ostentatiously not transgressing. Here *mat* is an intertext: present in its pointed absence. The device is analogous to Shakespeare's bawdy puns such as Hamlet's to Ophelia: 'Do you think I meant *country* matters?'[41] Even in the age of explicitness, Internet slimeball language likewise produced its own ways of pretending not to say what it was obviously saying, through locutions such as *iukh* (= *khui* backwards) or *nakh* (for *ná khui*).[42]

This is too coy to be classed as *mat*. Many of the 'classic' Russian writers produced obscene verses, relishing the taboo words. However, they did not, by and large, explore the range of *mat* as a flexible idiom. For the most part, they used obscene vocabulary in its literal, sexual meanings. The classically crafted eighteenth-century odes and other poems attributed to Barkov were relentlessly sexual. Mikhail Lermontov's series of 'cadet verses' of 1833–4 do admit the occasional generalized expletive (*ebéna mat'*), but otherwise are pointedly sexual: a young gentleman with literary abilities enjoys the transgressive frisson of composing nicely shaped verses about fucking. An anonymous narrative poem about Luka Mudishchev, an impoverished nobleman with an enormous sexual organ, who is invited to satisfy the demands of a merchant's widow with an enormous sexual appetite, circulated quite widely in manuscript copies before its first printing (abroad) in the late twentieth century.[43] There is very little in this tradition that gives space to *mat* as a broader register of idiomatic expression. At the other end of the spectrum of cultural prestige, mid-nineteenth-century collectors of popular expressions – notably the folklorist Aleksandr Afanasev and the lexicographer Vladimir Dal – gathered sayings and folk tales permeated with pithy vocabulary that was unprintable in its day.[44]

The flow of *mat* into printed literature began in the last quarter of the twentieth century, first as a trickle, in Russophone émigré literature, then – from the 1990s, when it became printable inside Russia – as what was represented as a flood.[45] It can be hard in retrospect to appreciate the power of the taboo on *mat*. Just to talk *about* it could be reckoned uncomfortable. The discomfort was even exportable. In one of the early western European academic studies of *mat*, in a respected international peer-reviewed journal, the authors declared that they had 'decided to publish this article as appropriate for the scope of our journal ("Russian Linguistics in its Manifold Diversity"), the counter-indicating cultural tradition notwithstanding.'[46] This implies that the stigma of *mat* was so powerful that even academic analysis might be thought indecent, and the authors needed to justify their subject. Dictionaries reflected a similar trajectory. The first and perhaps most notorious modern attempt at a dictionary of Russian obscenities was published in London in 1973.[47] In the mid-1990s, the prolific Russian lexicographer Valerii Mokienko published the first version of his *Dictionary of Russian Abusive Vocabulary* abroad, in Berlin.[48] A version appeared in Kaliningrad two years later with very limited circulation, but the substantially updated version (together with Tatiana Nikitina) was published in St Petersburg only in 2003[49] – by which time the path had been cleared, so to speak, by the first volume of the dictionary of Plutser-Sarno.

Because it was suppressed in the USSR, and because of its early association with political dissidence and alternative culture, *mat* tended to be regarded initially as a sign of linguistic liberation and progressiveness, a reassertion not only of emancipated individual identity but even of a kind of innate spirit of linguistic Russianness; except, that is, for those who regarded it as disgusting, degrading, a sign of a loss of any semblance of cultural dignity. However, linguistic snobberies have a way of asserting themselves even among those who ostensibly seek to break them down. For some writers and critics, *mat* became too common, in all senses – cheapened by its crude usage in cheap literature.[50] It seems that there was good *mat* and bad *mat*. Good *mat* was skilfully deployed by good writers. The common language could not be left to common usage. Freedom should not become anarchy. After the early intoxication with an almost vanished censorship, 'abusive words that would not get past the censor' had themselves to be curated by the arbiters of literary taste. The writer Tatiana Tolstaia, blogging from 2007, began by claiming the right to write with mistakes, to violate all grammatical rules, to swear (*materít'sia*), though in practice she herself frequently criticized the non-normative.[51] When Dovlatov's pedantic prisoner pointed out the correct use of *mat* in the 'Russian literary language', he was anticipating the professionals.

This kind of hierarchization is traditional in debates about language. How could it stand up, in the late twentieth and early twenty-first centuries, in the face of the seemingly unstoppable non-traditional force for de-hierarchization that was the electronic revolution?

On one level the Internet was utterly transformative in the extent to which it provided platforms and channels for the diffusion of obscenity, for transcending spatial and social restrictions on its distribution, for the multitude of new performative contexts and opportunities for its display, for rapid cross-regional exchange, for collective inventiveness and so on. Whether blogging, chatting or trolling, obscenity became one of many options, one of the available choices of register, as normalized in a range of online micro- and macro-cultures as it was and had been in oral micro-cultures before electronic media. This does not in itself mean that *mat* was more widely used, but it does mean that obscenities became a very great deal more visible. Pre-digital *mat* was, for the most part, heard but not seen. In digital space, everybody can be an instant self-publisher and global self-distributor. Curated print publication was comprehensively outflanked.

This created a serious dilemma for those who sought to protect the public. To leave obscenity unchecked was outrageous to some; to legislate against it was outrageous to others.[52] On 1 February 2021 a new law came into force that was widely believed to imply a ban on obscenity on the Internet. It was in the form of an amendment, passed on 25 December 2020, to a law on the protection of information. The thrust of the law was that service providers were to be held responsible and accountable for monitoring content in a range of categories including, for example, child pornography, incitement to terrorism and violence, information on the manufacture of drugs and suchlike. Paragraph 1.1 of the amendment to Article 10 of the underlying legislation added a reference to 'materials containing *netsenzúrnaia bran'*'.[53] Meanwhile the protectors of public morality had been thinking about definitions. We have noted the lack of general agreement on what was actually meant by *mat* or by 'swearwords that wouldn't pass the censor'. The state was not blind to the problem. The organization charged with oversight of the media, Roskomnadzor, directly addressed the question of how to define obscenity: 'At the present moment,' it acknowledged, 'there is no single list of words that constitute *netsenzúrnaia bran'*. Nevertheless, specialists agree that the term is applicable to four widely known words beginning with the letters "kh", "p", "e" and "b" [so: *khui*, *pizdá*, *ebát'* and *bliad'*], as well as words and expressions derived from them.'[54] Roskomnadzor also addressed the knotty problem of 'disguised' obscenity through allusion or euphemism. They decided that it was not enough to pretend to be decent just by omitting the occasional letter. Asterisks should offer no protection. Euphemisms could be acceptable, but only if decently distant.

The verdict of the Internet-using masses was expressed immediately and unambiguously. According to data gathered by the media-monitoring company Medialogiia, on 1–2 February 2020, across a representative range of major social networking platforms, there was a massive surge in the number of posts that included obscene words: up by around 30 per cent compared to the equivalent period the previous year.[55] Commentators even in the mainstream media tended to be somewhat condescending. Some of them ironically provided lists of recommended euphemisms and detoxified synonyms. Legislators were quick to backtrack: it was all a misunderstanding, fake news. First, the law imposed a responsibility on providers (to monitor and remove illegal content), not on individuals. Second, the reference to foul language was in the context of possibly slanderous and abusive content, not a blanket ban on obscenity as such.[56] On 23 January 2025 the *Parliament Newspaper* (*Parlámentskaia gazéta*) reported that, over the previous four years, Roskomnadzor had made 750 reports of potential infringements of the obscenity regulation, and had imposed fines to a value of over 450 million roubles (approximately $5.5 million) on various media outlets, but not, at this stage, on individuals online.[57] Nobody was yet attacking a Russian's sacred right to self-expression through *mat*.

Language legislation was not limited to obscenities. These restrictive measures should also be seen in the wider context of reactions to the multiple disruptions of language culture in the late 1990s and early 2000s. In the face of such linguistic anarchy how could order be restored? How could Russian be curated in its new socio-political and technological environment?

Curation, Legislation

How do authorities respond when authority is collapsing? The massive, multifaceted linguistic defamiliarizations of the 1990s induced equally fundamental and multifaceted anxieties, ranging from practical issues of pedagogy to fears about the weakening of Russia's very identity.[58] Anybody might have an opinion, but some institutions had a professional responsibility to curate the language, to maintain both an overview and oversight: an overview of the processes of change, and oversight of standards.

One should distinguish language curation from language nostalgia. Language nostalgia is as old as language change, which some will always perceive as decline. Certainly through the 1990s and beyond there was no shortage of agonized or indignant voices proclaiming the erosion of the former glories of the Russian language. A leader and, to some extent, precursor of late and post-Soviet language nostalgia was the writer and former political prisoner Aleksandr Solzhenitsyn. In addition to many essays on the impoverishment of Russian, Solzhenitsyn compiled a dictionary of what he called the 'expansion' of the Russian language.[59] For him, expansion did not mean the assimilation of new words. Rather the opposite: this was a dictionary of old words that, in Solzhenitsyn's view, would again enrich the language if revived. Solzhenitsyn explained that his dictionary emerged from his deep fascination, over many decades, with the mid-nineteenth-century dictionary of Vladimir Dal, which he used to read slowly, word by word, cover to cover. He ignored the fact that his own endeavour was, in a sense, the opposite of Dal's: Dal had been a compulsive collector of words from real speech, on the basis of which he produced a dictionary of the 'living' language. Indeed, he criticized previous dictionaries precisely on the grounds that they were based on words found in books (see Chapter Five). Solzhenitsyn excavated words from texts of the past, with the aim of making them live again. In fact, Solzhenitsyn's dictionary seems much closer in spirit and execution to Aleksandr Shishkov in the early nineteenth century than to Dal. Like Solzhenitsyn, Shishkov spent years putting together a compendium of words that had, in his view, unjustifiably fallen out of use (see Chapter Three). Like Shishkov, Solzhenitsyn sprinkled his preface with examples of foreign lexical contamination (here from English rather than from French): 'if we admit into the Russian language such intolerable words as *uik-end*, *brífing*, *istéblishment* . . . *ímidzh*, then we might as well say goodbye to our native tongue.'[60]

Nostalgia is common, comforting and usually doomed. The more complex response to change and to perceived linguistic disintegration is to track it, curate it, steer it, filter it into a new normativity. This was the challenge taken up initially by academic institutions, then by the government of the Russian Federation.

A first step was to convert data into a database. Anglophone corpus linguistics began in the 1960s. No corpus is ever complete. Samuel Johnson's comparison of lexicography to 'chasing the sun' (see the Introduction) is not rendered invalid by the development of technologies for mining Big Data. Corpus linguistics takes us to a more distant horizon – whose proximity to the sun is no less illusory. However, both the volume of data and the rate of augmentation are unrecognizably greater than any previous modes of ordering the elements of a language. The *Corpus of Contemporary American English*, for example, records material from 1990 onwards. By 2019 it contained 500 million words. By the end of 2021 it had passed a billion.[61] The *National Corpus of the Russian Language* was initiated in the early 2000s. It depended on a wide range of active partners and collaborators, with leadership from the Russian Academy of Sciences' Institute for the Russian Language, and with support from the tech giant Yandex. As of mid-2025 it consisted of its 'main' corpus and fifteen more specialized corpora, together with a total of over 2 billion 'tokens'.[62] It provided instant open access to an astonishing range of structured data: words, grammatical forms, collocations, statistics on usage, cognate words, specimens of use indexed by year and so on. It had a range of search options for all levels and tastes. It was open about the fact that its inputs tended to reflect the standard language, but it was not intrusively selective (see below). The *National Corpus of the Russian Language* became a resource for anybody interested in exploring Russian, at any level, from professionals to the casually curious. But it was not a dictionary. It allowed the citations to speak for themselves. There were no systematic articles about the words: no definitions, let alone structured presentations of a range of meanings; no pointers to style or register; no clear markers of normativity. People turned to the *National Corpus of the Russian Language* to discover what existed; by contrast, people turned to gramota.ru to discover what was correct. Each query and response to gramota.ru was numbered and logged. By late 2025 there were more than 320,000 of them.

In theory, Russia should have been well prepared to cope with lexical change. The Academy of Sciences, in its role as the guardian and curator of the Russian language, had shown foresight. Already in the 1970s its linguists had recognized that language change was speeding up, and they devised a system for tracking, recording and assessing it, through the Institute for Linguistic Research in St Petersburg, which published an annual record, under the title *New Developments in Russian Vocabulary: Lexical Materials* (*Nóvoe v rússkoi léksike: Slovárnye materiály*).

However, in the Soviet 1970s nobody can have anticipated the sheer scale and velocity of political, social, cultural, technological and linguistic change that would occur within a couple of decades. How did the curators of the Russian language cope?

The series of annual surveys *New Developments in Russian Vocabulary* began with a survey of 1977. Nearly half a century later, at the time of writing (2025), the series still exists. However, such longevity should not be taken to imply continuity. The annual surveys never managed to be quite current. The early issues covering the years from 1977 to 1984 tended to be published with a delay of between three and five years. The last Soviet volume was published in 1989, covering words recorded in 1984. When the USSR collapsed in 1991, the Academy of Sciences publishing house in St Petersburg in effect ceased to operate. Part of its output in the humanities was taken on by the private publishing house Dmitrii Bulanin, which in 1994 produced four issues of *New Developments in Russian Vocabulary*, covering the years 1985 to 1988, and the sequence continued until the volumes for 1993 and 1994 were published in 2008 and 2006 respectively. With over a decade between the year described and the appearance of the relevant volume, the 'new' in the series title became strained beyond plausibility. It stopped. The forces of disruption appeared to be too strong.

That was not the end of the story. Just as the Academy's lexicographers had needed time to adjust to the break-up of the USSR, so they needed time to adjust to the challenges of digital media. Suddenly, in 2018, new volumes started to appear, again published by the Institute itself, beginning with words registered in 2016 (a volume for 2015 followed in a cluster of issues produced in 2020) (illus. 46), after which the sequence resumed its year-by-year regularity as intended. The annual series had skipped twenty years of new words (1995–2014), but these could be retrieved by other means: a ten-year retrospective series, *New Words and Meanings*. Volume I of a compendium of new words from the 1990s appeared in 2009.[63] Volumes II and III followed

46 *New Developments in Russian Vocabulary*: cover designs in the style of word-clouds.

in 2014.[64] Together the three volumes contained around 2,500 pages. The storm had passed, the ship was back on course, order had been restored, the annual updates could resume. The preface to the volume of *New Developments in Russian Vocabulary* for 2015 made a point of restating that it continued the tradition and the structure that had been worked out several decades and a geopolitical and technological epoch earlier.[65]

However, despite the assertion of continuity this had become a different type of enterprise. Above all, the source base, and the methods of analysing it, would have been unrecognizable to the founders of the series. From its inception to the break after the volume for 1994, *New Developments in Russian Vocabulary* was based on printed sources. The first dozen volumes had used what now seems an astonishingly limited set of materials: for each year, just ten periodical publications, over the course of just three or four months. The sources were the daily newspapers *Právda*, *Izvéstiia* and *Komsomól'skaia právda*; the weeklies *Literatúrnaia gazéta*, *Nedélia*, *Krokodíl* and *Ogonëk*; and the monthly journals *Iúnost'*, *Novyi mir* and *Oktiábr'*. In the early 2000s the card index began to be replaced with electronic files. By the time the series resumed, all sources – including those which were also published in hard copy – were mined online.

According to the introduction to the first new issue in 2018, the editors, through such resources as the Russian media database Integrum World Wide, and the national corpus, had access to digitalized materials from over 30,000 federal and regional publications, radio and television channels, websites, libraries and databases.[66]

So the annual distillation had to get a great deal fatter? Strangely, no. As the source base exploded, the published materials in fact contracted. Each volume of the Soviet and immediate post-Soviet series contained around 2,000–3,000 headwords. Each volume of the post-2015 'continuation' contained fewer than a quarter of that number – generally 350–450. How did this happen? The introduction to the 2020 volume (published in 2021) explained: several thousand 'neolexemes' were initially identified, and then deliberately reduced through 'careful selection'.[67] It's all in the algorithm. As the choice became wider, the selection became narrower.

The criteria for selection were not consistently explained. The prominence given to some imported expressions might surprise language users in their countries of origin. So, the volume for 2018 (published in 2020) included articles on the expression *kháili láikli* and derivative forms (the verbs *khaililáikat'* and *khaililáiknut'*, the adjective *khaililáikovskii*). The stimulus was a statement by the British prime minister Theresa May, that in the poisoning in Salisbury of the former spy Sergei Skripal, the involvement of the Russian government was 'highly likely'. As so often, there was a semantic shift in the process of assimilation. *Kháili láikli* did not mean 'highly likely'. Used mainly ironically in journalistic and governmental sources, it was taken as referring to 'unconfirmed information and unproven accusations'. The definition of the verb *khaililáikat'* was 'to make unfounded accusations'.[68] By implication, that which was claimed to be *kháili láikli* was highly likely to be fake news.

There are curious exceptions to the practice of brevity. The volume for 2021 included around 3,000 headwords – overwhelmingly involving items generated by the COVID-19 pandemic.[69] Indeed, the Institute even published a separate *Dictionary of the Russian Language of the Coronavirus Period*, with around 3,500 headwords (illus. 47).[70] A great deal of its vocabulary was international and derived from English, and the dictionary shows the very rapid formation of derivatives and compounds with Russian morphological structures. So, the long entry on *lokdáun* (the change of stress, by comparison with English, is not untypical) is followed by the colloquial verb *lokdáunknut'*, the adjective *lokdáunskii*, not to mention the compound *lokdáun-lait*.[71] But this is nothing by comparison with the morphological and semantic inventiveness around the word COVID itself. Derivatives of *kovíd* occupy more than fifty pages of the dictionary. Some are medical and official, but a great number are ironic and playful: *kovídeo*; *kovídet'*; *kovidiót* (plus *kovidiótka*, *kovidiotísm* and so on). Another fifty pages list and explain derivatives of *koron-*. And then there is *zum* and derivatives (for example, *zúmbi* – someone who spends all their time on Zoom).

The language culture of the pandemic created its own criteria and parameters. Then life got back to normal. After such unaccustomed amplitude, *New Developments in Russian Vocabulary* returned to its habit of hyper-selectivity. The opposite approach – descriptive rather than normative – was taken in the two-volume, 1,000-page and grandiosely named *Linguo-Culturological Dictionary of Borrowings in the Contemporary Russian Language (from 2000 to 2024)*, compiled by T. A. Golikova.[72] With approximately 3,000 headwords, Golikova's dictionary recorded usage (the citations were mostly from the press) but avoided selection or prediction. There was strikingly little overlap between her word lists and those in the Academy's normative updates.

Keeping track of new words, and attempting to exercise prudent oversight over their presentation, was only one part of the Academy of Sciences' larger curatorial task. In the early 2000s, following a resolution by the Academy's Presidium, the Institute for Linguistic Research put together another team for a project that was to be far more weighty in all senses: a new *Big Academy Dictionary of the Russian Language*.

47 *Dictionary of the Russian Language of the Coronavirus Period* (2021), title page.

This was conceived as an authoritative multi-volume work, in a direct line of succession from the original *Dictionary of the Russian Academy* of 1789–94, through the seventeen-volume Soviet *Dictionary of the Modern Russian Literary Language* (1948–65). The declaration of continuity was institutional as well as purely lexicographical. As the preface to the first volume announced, 'The Institute for Linguistic Research at the Russian Academy of Sciences is the direct descendant and legal inheritor of all the traditions, the experience and the achievements of classic Russian (St Petersburg, Leningrad) academic lexicography.'[73]

The 28th volume of the *Big Academy Dictionary* was published in 2024, reaching the end of the letter 'S'. Most of the volumes consist of approximately 650–750 pages.[74] The editorial principles acknowledged change and innovation, as language necessarily assimilates new ideas, technologies, activities and social *realia*. However, in the face of change, the dictionary positioned itself as representing a 'healthy conservatism' (*zdrávyi konservatízm*). It was to be a 'guardian of the tradition of cultured language'. It defined its understanding of the 'norms of the literary language' as 'the relatively stable modes of expression reflecting the regular processes of language development, as established in the best works of literature and as preferred by the educated section of society'. The preface repeatedly stressed that the *Big Academy Dictionary* was normative; indeed, it was 'distinctive for its heightened normativity' (*povyshennaia normatívnost'*).[75]

The editors were aware that there might be a perceived tension between the normative and the historical.[76] They were careful to counter the suspicion that they were reactionary. They accepted the legitimate existence of many kinds of dictionary and database, but at the same time they were clear about their own mission as the compilers of an authoritative dictionary of the literary language. They expressed the hope that the *Big Academy Dictionary*, 'as a normative dictionary, will facilitate the conduct of a purposeful, scientifically well-founded language policy, and will worthily represent the Russian language as a language of international communication.'[77] Far from being retrograde, the editors of the *Big Academy Dictionary* proclaimed normativity as a core obligation of academic lexicography. Far from being at odds with the times, for them 'heightened normativity' was especially necessary in a period of linguistic confusion. How else can disoriented language users know where to find security and reliability, the reassurance of order amid the chaos?

Such attitudes reaffirmed the conventional role of academic institutions in curating the language. However, over the first quarter of the twenty-first century there was a radical shift in the structure of linguistic authority. For the first time in the cultural history of Russian, the state itself took direct control of the process of defining the norms of the language. The academic institutions had always been state-funded and had always been assumed to be serving the needs of the state, but, by and large, they had been trusted to perform their functions responsibly and autonomously, as the designated experts. Through a series of laws and directives enacted between 2005 and 2025, the academic institutions curating the language were converted into subcontractors delegated to produce normative materials according to government specifications.

The device that brought about this change was legislation, on a topic that might initially have seemed rather 'niche': Russian *as a state language*. General legislation on the Russian language was both prohibitive and prescriptive. In prohibitive mode it touched on such topics as obscenities, language deemed to promote 'non-traditional' sexuality, or language that fell foul of increasingly broad notions of 'extremism'.[78] In prescriptive mode it was concerned with norms for the language when used for state purposes. One might have supposed that this would involve, say, the production of internal style guides for civil servants, perhaps including lists of approved terminology for official publications. However, stage by stage the definitions of 'state' usage became more and more extensive and inclusive. Eventually, the declared scope of Russian 'as a state language' was broadened to the extent that, for the practical purpose of defining norms (and in the reference works commissioned by the government for the purpose), it became almost indistinguishable from the notion of the standard ('literary') language as a whole.

On 1 June 2005 Vladimir Putin signed a new law: 'On the State Language of the Russian Federation'. Amendments were passed in 2014 and 2023.[79] A brief preamble declared that the purpose of the law was 'to guarantee the use of the state language of the Russian Federation throughout the territory of the Russian Federation, to guarantee the right of citizens of the Russian Federation to use the state language of the Russian Federation, and for the defence and development of the culture of the language'. Articles 1–3 of the 2005 law listed the areas of usage to which the law was applicable. All of them, in the first version, related to official discourse: from the drafting of laws and international agreements, through to the formulation of road signs. Successive amendments broadened the scope. In 2014 the notion of Russian's use as a state language was expanded so as to cover, for example, 'mass media', as well as public performances of literary works, art, theatrical performances and other stage entertainments: that is, almost any public use of Russian. The legislation on Russian as a state language was also the formal context for the new law on obscenity that came into force in February 2021. The laws were backed up with practical measures – in the first instance, through creating institutions of oversight and control. In August 2020 a Government Commission for the Russian Language was set up.[80] Part of its remit was to create and implement a process for reviewing and approving normative grammars and dictionaries of Russian as a state language.[81]

In the mid-2020s, the sequence reached its logical conclusion. The end product was not to be simply an approved list of existing publications. Instead, the government would take direct control. On 22 April 2024 it announced its intention to commission and run its own new digital resource, which it termed 'the federal state information system *The National Lexical Corpus*'.[82] This was to be fundamentally different from the existing *National Corpus of the Russian Language* in two respects. First, it would be prescriptively curated, focusing not on usage in general but on norms. Second, although the actual work of compiling the corpus would be subcontracted to an academic 'supplier' (*postavshchík*) it was to be commissioned and operated (as its *zakázchik* and *operátor*) by the Ministry for Science and Higher Education.

Finally, on 30 April, the government published its list of normative dictionaries approved for the use of Russian as a state language. There were just four of them. All had been specially commissioned for the purpose. Two of them were, in effect, word lists with a technical purpose: a guide to correct spelling (an orthographic dictionary) and a guide to correct pronunciation (an orthoepic dictionary).[83] For both of these the contracted developer (*razrabótchik*) was the Academy of Sciences' Institute for the Russian Language in Moscow. One was a dictionary of foreign words, contracted to the Academy's Institute for Linguistic Research in St Petersburg.[84] And one – the most fundamental – was a general 'explanatory' dictionary (*tolkóvyi slovár'*), commissioned from St Petersburg State University.[85] Almost simultaneously with the announcement of their approval, all four dictionaries appeared, fully formed.[86] They had clearly been in preparation long before the announcement. They were big. The *Explanatory Dictionary* was in two volumes, and contained around 45,000 lexical entries and their definitions, in double columns across 1,700 pages. The *Orthographic Dictionary* listed over 70,000 spellings. The *Dictionary of Foreign Words* stressed in its introduction that it was 'brief', but it nevertheless contained definitions of around 17,000 words.

If 'Russian as a state language' was represented with such amplitude, what, if any, was now the difference between it and the literary (standard) language in general? The answer seems to be: very little. Successive laws had defined the scope of the state language ever more broadly. The new approved dictionaries were as capacious as any other chunky single-volume or two-volume normative dictionaries of standard Russian. In effect, 'Russian as a state language', initially a somewhat niche concept, had grown to such an extent that it inhabited almost the full body of its host.

Arguably, the main innovation was in the packaging rather than the substance. Each dictionary was prefaced by a declaration of its status as a work commissioned in accordance with the government's laws and the president's instructions. This was a fact, but its declaration also had a somewhat ritualistic air, not so unlike the prefatory formulae of Sovietspeak. In the history of the culture of Russian, the distinctive feature was not the degree of normativity in itself, nor even the idea that the state should have a role in directing the cultural uses of language: in 1718 Peter I had instructed Fedor Polikarpov to 'use the words of the Ambassadorial Chancery'; in 1736 Vasilii Tatishchev had argued that the inappropriate use of foreign words by state employees should be restricted by legislation (see above, p. 85). Laws about language in public display had been promulgated periodically from the eighteenth century to the twentieth. The new feature here was the open, systematic and principled appropriation of formal linguistic authority: the performative enactment of control.

Is this not comparable to the state's control over public language in the USSR? Comparable, perhaps, but not identical. Sovietspeak was a state idiom that was obligatory in official discourse and seeped outwards into the wider standard language. The oddity of the legislation of the first quarter of the twenty-first century, on Russian as a state language, was that – beyond the assertion of patriotism and traditional values[87] – it did not seek to inculcate any particular form of official state rhetoric. It made a show of *controlling* the standard language, without necessarily claiming to *change* it.

Uniformity of packaging was no guarantor of uniformity of content. If anybody were to ask 'what, then, is the list of approved words, which I can consult in order to check my own usage, or to find out what is and is not acceptable?', it would be hard to produce a definitive answer. Even a cursory glance at the four approved dictionaries reveals discrepancies in their word lists. For example, the explanatory dictionary and the dictionary of foreign words had entries for *uikénd* (weekend), but the spelling dictionary and the pronunciation dictionaries did not; the dictionary of foreign words and the spelling dictionary both had entries for *khéppi-end* (happy ending), but the explanatory dictionary and the pronunciation dictionary did not. And so on. Nor was there an entirely consistent relationship between these obligatory norms and actual usage in state contexts. For example, at a press conference in Minsk on 27 June 2025 (just two months after publication of the edict that named these dictionaries as authoritative and approved) President Putin spoke scathingly of western attitudes to Russia and to its economy: 'they take us for ninnies (*durachkí*)'; 'they keep saying our economy is dead, but pretty soon they'll conk out (*sdókhnut*) themselves.'[88] Neither of these derogatory colloquialisms, as used by the state president, appeared in the explanatory dictionary of the language of the state; both of them were in the spelling dictionary; the pronunciation dictionary had a related form of one of them (*dókhnut'*), but not the other. The simultaneous release of approved dictionaries did not, therefore, operate according to a single list of approved words.

In other significant ways, too, content was more flexible than might be implied by the packaging. For example, the legislation touched on the traditionally sensitive question of imported words. The law on language (Article 1.6) stated that there should be no recourse to 'words and expressions that do not conform to the norms of the modern Russian literary language, with the exception of foreign words that have no equivalents in general use in the Russian language'. This was a deliberate echo of the preface to the very first *Dictionary of the Russian Academy* of 1789, whose editors had declared that they would exclude 'all foreign words introduced unnecessarily, for which there are Slavonic or Russian equivalents' (see above, p. 76). Indeed, the editors of the new dictionary of foreign words were particularly keen to emphasize that they operated according to old and hallowed principles. However, despite the show of reassurance for traditionalists, this was no neo-Shishkovist or neo-Slavophile version of a Russian language cleansed of western contamination. In practice the editors excluded only new imports that they judged unlikely to become embedded in usage. They retained huge numbers of words that would have made Aleksandr Shishkov apoplectic with indignation, or that Mikhail Lomonosov might have called 'strange and barbarous absurdities' (above, p. 65). This was 'business as usual' for experienced historical lexicographers. None of the dictionaries avoided foreign imports as a matter of principle. Here the overall approach was perhaps linguistic statism, but not crude linguistic nationalism – although parallel legislation, passed in June 2025, did seek to protect citizens from excessively visible signs of foreignness by imposing restrictions on the use of Latin script in public display.[89]

What had changed, therefore? For the language at large, little or nothing; for the culture of the literary (standard) language, also not much. Neither the lawmakers nor the dictionary-makers claimed to be linguistically innovative in the context of normative lexicography. The new elements were, first, a concept of 'Russian as a state language' that was so broad as to become virtually coterminous with the idea of the literary or standard language; and, second, an unprecedented broadening of the legislative framework for government authority and control of the processes of validating acceptable language usage.

In a wider perspective, these legislative and lexicographical initiatives of the first quarter of the twenty-first century can be regarded as another phase in the continual process of stabilization and destabilization, of normativity and transgression, of embracing change and fretting about change, leading to the reassertion of norms that, to a significant extent, end up accommodating change. In the eighteenth century, the early proponents of establishing Russian as a language of culture had been centrally concerned with grounding its dignity in authoritative norms. Since that time, norms have been sources both of frustration and of reassurance. And in such cycles of tension, the norms themselves have evolved. That is why the culture and cultivation of the language have a history and are not merely the repetitive swinging of a pendulum. The history does not end just because of some current legislation. This book is historical, not prophetic, but the history does show that, if at any stage anybody had assumed that the arguments and solutions of their own time were permanent, they would have been wrong.

APPENDIX:

Chronological List of Printed Dictionaries Mentioned in the Text

1700: [I. Kopievskii], *Nomenklator na russkom, latinskom i nemetskom iazyke*, and *Nomenklator na russkom, nemetskom i gollandskom iazykakh* (Amsterdam)

1704: [F. Polikarpov], *Leksikon treiazychnyi, sirech' rechenii slavenskikh, ellinogre-cheskikh i latinskikh sokrovishche* (Moscow)

1717: Ia. V. Brius, *Kniga leksikon ili Sobranie rechei po Alfavitu c Rossiiskogo na Gollandskii iazyk* (St Petersburg)

1731: *Teutsch-Lateinisch- und Russisches Lexicon, samt denen Anfangs-Gründen der Russischen Sprache. Nemetsko-latinskii i russkii leksikon kupno s pervymi nachalami russkogo iazyka* (St Petersburg)

1755: Samuel Johnson, *A Dictionary of the English Language* (London; also 2nd edn, 1773)

1755–64: Sergei Volchkov, *Novyi leksikon na frantsuzskom, nemetskom, latinskom i rossiiskom iazykakh*, 2 vols (St Petersburg)

1763: [Grigorii Poletika], *Slovar' na shesti iazykakh: rossiiskom, grecheskom, latinskom, frantsuzskom, nemetskom i angliiskom* (St Petersburg)

1784: I. Sots, *Nouveau dictionnaire françois, italien, allemand, latin et russe. Novyi leksikon ili slovar' na frantsuzskom, ital'ianskom, nemetskom, latinskom i rossi-iskom iazykakh* (Moscow)

1789–94: *Slovar' Akademii rossiiskoi*, 6 vols (St Petersburg)

1815: G. Harmonière, *Vocabulaire français et russe* (Paris)

1828: Noah Webster, *An American Dictionary of the English Language* (New York)

1852: A. Vostokov, ed., *Opyt oblastnogo velikorusskogo slovaria* (St Petersburg)

1863–6: V. I. Dal', *Tolkovyi slovar' zhivogo velikorusskogo iazyka*, 4 vols (Moscow; 2nd edn, 1880–82)

1950–65: *Slovar' sovremennogo russkogo literaturnogo iazyka*, 17 vols (Moscow and Leningrad)

1971: *Novye slova i znacheniia. Slovar'-spravochnik po materialam pressy i literatury 60-kh godov*, ed. N. Z. Kotelova and Iu. S. Sorokin (Moscow)

1973: A. Flegon, *Beyond the Russian Dictionary. Za predelami russkogo slovaria* (London)

1977: D. I. Alekseev, ed., *Slovar' sokrashchenii russkogo iazyka* (Moscow)

1980–[2008]: *Novoe v russkoi leksike. Slovarnye materialy – 1977*; then in a sequence of eighteen issues covering each year to 1994 (Leningrad, then St Petersburg)

1984: *Novye slova i znacheniia. Slovar'-spravochnik po materialam pressy i literatury 70-kh godov*, ed. N. Z. Kotelova (Moscow)

1990: A. I. Solzhenitsyn, *Russkii slovar' iazykovogo rasshireniia*, 2nd edn (Moscow, 2015)

1992: D. S. Baldaev, V. K. Belko, I. M. Isupov, *Slovar' tiuremno-lagerno-blatnogo zhargona (rechevoi i graficheskii portret sovetskoi tiur'my)* (Moscow)

1995: V. M. Mokienko, *Slovar' russkoi brannoi leksiki (matizmy, obstsenizmy, evfemizmy* (Berlin, 1995)

1996: *Novye slova i znacheniia. Slovar'-spravochnik po materialam pressy i literatury 80-kh godov*, ed. E. A. Levashov (St Petersburg)

1998: S. A. Kuznetsov, ed., *Bol'shoi tolkovyi slovar' russkogo iazyka* (St Petersburg)

1998: V. M. Mokienko, T. G. Nikitina, *Tolkovyi slovar' iazyka Sovdepii* (St Petersburg)

2001: V. M. Mokienko, T. G. Nikitina, *Bol'shoi slovar' russkogo zhargona* (St Petersburg)

2001, 2005: A. Plutser-Sarno, *Bol'shoi slovar' mata*, vols I–II (St Petersburg)

2003: Gasan Guseinov, *D.S.P. Materialy k russkomu slovariu obshchestvenno-politicheskogo iazyka XX veka* (Moscow)

2003: V. M. Mokienko, T. G. Nikitina, *Slovar' russkoi brani (matizmy, obstsenizmy, evfemizmy* (St Petersburg)

2004–[2024]: *Bol'shoi akademicheskii slovar' russkogo iazyka*, vols I–[XXVIII] (Moscow and St Petersburg)

2004–: *Slovar' obikhodnogo iazyka Moskovskoi Rusi XVI–XVII vekov*, vols I– (St Petersburg)

2006: G. N. Skliarevskii, *Tolkovyi slovar' russkogo iazyka nachala XXI veka. Aktual'naia leksika* (St Petersburg)

2006–12: E. V. Ivantsova, ed., *Polnyi slovar' dialektnoi iazykovoi lichnosti*, 4 vols (Tomsk)

2007: V. M. Mokienko, T. G. Nikitina, *Bol'shoi slovar' russkikh pogovorok* (Moscow)

2008: V. M. Mokienko, T. G. Nikitina, *Bol'shoi slovar' russkikh narodnykh sravnenii* (Moscow)

2009: *Rossiia. Bol'shoi lingvostranovedcheskii slovar'*, ed. Iu. E. Prokhorov (Moscow)

2009: E. N. Shagalova, ed., *Slovar' noveishikh inostrannykh slov (konets XX–nachalo XXI vv.)* (Moscow)

2009, 2014: T. I. Butsev, E. A. Levashov, eds, *Novye slova i znacheniia. Slovar'-spravochnik po materialam pressy i literatury 90-kh godov XX veka*, 3 vols (St Petersburg)

2011: D. I. Keselovich, *Samyi polnyi slovar' nenormativnoi leksiki* (Moscow)

2014–22: L. P. Krysin, ed., *Tolkovyi slovar' russkoi razgovornoi rechi*, vols I–V (Moscow)

2018: *Novoe v russkoi leksike. Slovarnye materialy – 2016* (St Petersburg)

2019: *Novoe v russkoi leksike. Slovarnye materialy – 2017* (St Petersburg)

2019: Vladimir Lebedev, *Etimologicheskii slovar' mirovogo russkogo iazyka*, 4 vols [Ekaterinburg]
2020: *Novoe v russkoi leksike. Slovarnye materialy – 2015* (St Petersburg)
2020: *Novoe v russkoi leksike. Slovarnye materialy – 2018* (St Petersburg)
2021: *Novoe v russkoi leksike. Slovarnye materialy – 2019* (St Petersburg)
2021: *Novoe v russkoi leksike. Slovarnye materialy – 2020* (St Petersburg)
2021: M. N. Priemysheva et al., eds, *Slovar' russkogo iazyka koronavirusnoi epokhi* (St Petersburg)
2022: *Novoe v russkoi leksike. Slovarnye materialy – 2021* (St Petersburg)
2023: *Novoe v russkoi leksike. Slovarnye materialy – 2022* (St Petersburg)
2024: T. A. Golikova, *Lingvokul'turologicheskii slovar' sovremennogo russkogo iazyka (2000–2024 gg.)*, 2nd edn; 2 vols (Moscow)
2025: N. M. Kropachev, S. A. Belov, S. A. Kuznetsov, eds, *Tolkovyi slovar' gosudarstvennogo iazyka Rossiiskoi federatsii*, 2 vols (St Petersburg)
2025: *Orfoepicheskii slovar' russkogo iazyka kak gosudarstvennogo iazyka Rossiiskoi federatsii* (Moscow)
2025: *Orfograficheskii slovar' russkogo iazyka kak gosudarstvennogo iazyka Rossiiskoi federatsii* (Moscow)
2025: *Slovar' inostrannykh slov* (St Petersburg)

REFERENCES

Introduction

1 Gerry Knowles, *A Cultural History of the English Language* (London, 1997), p. ix.
2 See, for example, Juan Manuel Hernández-Campoy and Juan Camilo Conde-Silvestre, eds, *The Handbook of Historical Sociolinguistics* (Malden, MA, Oxford and Chichester, 2012); also the website of the Historical Sociolinguistics Network, founded in 2005: https://hison.org.
3 Dick Leith, *A Social History of English*, 2nd edn (London and New York, 1997).
4 For example, Farzad Sharifian, ed., *Advances in Cultural Linguistics* (Singapore, 2017); Judit Baranyiné Kóczy and Veronika Szelid, eds, *Cultural Linguistics and (Re)conceptualized Tradition* (Singapore, 2024).
5 See, for example, Iu. E. Prokhorov, ed., *Rossiia. Bol'shoi lingvostranovedcheskii slovar'* (Moscow, 2009).
6 Michael S. Gorham, *After Newspeak: Language Culture and Politics in Russia from Gorbachev to Putin* (Ithaca, NY, and London, 2014), pp. x–xi.
7 V. M. Zhivov, *Istoriia iazyka russkoi pis'mennosti*, 2 vols (Moscow, 2017), vol. 1, p. 9.
8 For example, E. A. Galinskaia, *Istoricheskaia grammatika russkogo iazyka: Fonetika. Morfologiia* (Moscow, 2015).
9 For example, A. I. Gorshkov, *Teoriia i istoriia russkogo literaturnogo iazyka* (Moscow, 1984); A. M. Kamchatnov, *Istoriia russkogo literaturnogo iazyka XI–pervaia polovina XIX veka* (Moscow, 2008).
10 Tore Nesset, *How Russian Came to Be the Way It Is: A Student's Guide to the History of the Russian Language* (Bloomington, IN, 2015); see also, among works in English, G. O. Vinokur, *The Russian Language: A Brief History*, trans. Mary A. Forsyth (Cambridge, 1971); A. P. Vlasto, *A Linguistic History of Russia to the End of the Eighteenth Century* (Oxford, 1986); also Paul Cubberley, *Russian: A Linguistic Introduction* (Cambridge, 2002), pp. 12–52.
11 Samuel Johnson, *A Dictionary of the English Language* (London, 1755), Preface [p. viii].
12 Samuel Johnson, *A Dictionary of the English Language*, 4th edn (London, 1773), Preface [p. viii].

1 Prehistories

1 For a succinct summary see Tore Nesset, *How Russian Came to Be the Way It Is: A Student's Guide to the History of the Russian Language* (Bloomington, IN, 2015), pp. 207–13.

2 See Alexander M. Schenker, *The Dawn of Slavic: An Introduction to Slavic Philology* (New Haven, CT, and London, 1995), pp. 185–90; Roman Krivko, 'Church Slavic, Canonical', in *Encyclopedia of Slavic Languages and Linguistics Online*, ed. Mark L. Greenberg and Lenore A. Grenoble, available at https://referenceworks.brill.com/display/db/eslo.

3 See the summary in Simon Franklin, *Writing, Society and Culture in Early Rus, c. 950–1300* (Cambridge, 2002), pp. 93–100.

4 For a critical study of the foundational myths of the Cyrillo-Methodian tradition see Mirela Ivanova, *Inventing Slavonic: Cultures of Writing between Rome and Constantinople* (Oxford, 2024).

5 For example, on the period from the late nineteenth century to the end of the USSR see A. G. Kravetskii and A. A. Pletneva, *Istoriia tserkovnoslavianskogo iazyka v Rossii. Konets XIX–XX v.* (Moscow, 2001).

6 See, for example, O. V. Maikova, 'Drevnerusskoe liturgicheskoe proiznoshenie v iuzhnoi Rusi v XII–XIII vv.', in *Drevnerusskii literaturnyi iazyk v ego otnoshenii k staroslavianskomu*, ed. L. P. Zhukovskaia (Moscow, 1987), pp. 129–43; for a summary of the early modern Russian tradition, see V. Iu. Grigor'eva, *Normy liturgicheskogo proiznosheniia. Tserkovnoslavianskie teksty v istochnikakh XVI–XVII vv.* (Moscow, 2024).

7 Nesset, *How Russian Came to Be the Way It Is*, pp. 10–11.

8 See the distribution map in Jos Schaeken, *Voices on Birchbark: Everyday Communication in Medieval Russia* (Leiden and Boston, MA, 2019), p. 18.

9 A. A. Zalizniak, *Drevnenovgorodskii dialekt*, 2nd edn (Moscow, 2004).

10 See, for example, V. M. Zhivov, *Istoriia iazyka russkoi pis'mennosti*, 2 vols (Moscow, 2017), vol. 1, pp. 250–71.

11 For a collection of around 2,000 such 'false friends' see O. A. Sedakova, *Tserkovnoslaviano-russkie paronimy. Materialy k slovariu* (Moscow, 2005).

12 Jaap Kamphuis, *Verbal Aspect in Old Church Slavonic: A Corpus-Based Approach* (Leiden and Boston, MA, 2020).

13 Nesset, *How Russian Came to Be the Way It Is*, pp. 135–54.

14 On the implications of the loss of reduced vowels see, for example, V. V. Ivanov, *Istoricheskaia fonologiia russkogo iazyka* (Moscow, 1968), pp. 289–353; Vlasto, *A Linguistic History of Russia*, pp. 50–70; Nesset, *How Russian Came to Be the Way It Is*, pp. 246–60.

15 On this, plus annotated thematic lists of around 1,600 such words, see James Cracraft, *The Petrine Revolution in Russian Culture* (Cambridge, MA, 2004), pp. 276–83, 377–485.

16 Simon Franklin, *The Russian Graphosphere, 1450–1850* (Cambridge, 2019), pp. 116–42.

17 See Nikolaos A. Chrissidis, *An Academy at the Court of the Tsar: Greek Scholars and Jesuit Education in Early Modern Russia* (DeKalb, IL, 2016).

18 Further on the 'look' of Russian see below, Chapter Six.

19 The word is introduced by Zhivov, *Istoriia iazyka russkoi pis'mennosti*, vol. II, pp. 836–47. On such 'de-adaptation' spanning the late fourteenth and fifteenth centuries and following South Slav precedent, see Harvey Goldblatt, *Orthography and Orthodoxy: Constantine Kostenečki's Treatise on the Letters* (Florence, 1987); P. E. Lukin, *Pis'mena i pravoslavie. Istoriko-filologicheskoe issledovanie 'Skazaniia o pis'menakh' Konstantina Filosofa Kostenetskogo* (Moscow, 2001).

20 See, for example, Nicholas Lupinin, *Religious Revolt in the XVIIth Century: The Schism of the Russian Church* (Princeton, NJ, 1984).

21 In complete facsimile: *'Azbuka friaskaia' 1604 g.*, ed. I. M. Basov et al. (St Petersburg, 2023); scanned version available at https://scriptum.spbiiran.ru/wp-content/uploads/2024/07/azbukovnik_azbuka_fryaskaya.pdf; also the Supplement with a description of the manuscript: from the same site (add 'prilozhenie' to the link).

22 See, for example, Angelina A. Kalashnikova and Maria E. Proskuryakova, 'The Visual Markup of the Text in Russian Chancellery Documents from the Fifteenth to the Seventeenth Centuries', in *Cyrillic Manuscripts: From Medieval to Digital*, ed. Viacheslav Lytvynenko et al. (New York and Lausanne, 2025), pp. 63–85.

23 See D. O. Tsypkin, 'O formirovanii estetiki drevnerusskoi skoropisi (po rezul'tatam issledovaniia SPbII RAN, F. 115, No. 160)', *Aktual'nye problemy teorii i istorii iskusstva*, 11 (2021), pp. 907–24, colour illustrations on p. 994; D. O. Tsypkin, '"Azbuka friaskaia" 1604 g.: drevnerusskaia kalligrafiia na zare epokhi tirazhirovaniia', in *Pol'za zelo velikaia. Sbornik nauchnykh statei k 60-letiiu Andreia Vladimirovicha Voznesenskogo*, ed. S. A. Davydova (St Petersburg, 2022), pp. 21–36.

24 Facsimile edition with introduction: *Simeon Polotskii, Orel rossiiskii*, ed. L. I. Sazonova (Moscow, 2015).

25 Karion Istomin, *Bukvar' sostavlen Karionom Istominym, gravirovan Leontiem Buninym, otpechatan v 1694 v Moskve* (Leningrad, 1981); see Gary Marker, 'A World of Visual Splendor: The Illustrated Texts of Karion Istomin', in *Seeing Muscovy Anew: Politics – Institutions – Culture. Essays in Honor of Nancy Shields Kollmann*, ed. Michael S. Flier et al. (Bloomington, IN, 2017), pp. 173–88.

26 See V. K. Bylinin and A. A. Iliushin, 'Nachalo russkogo virshepisaniia', in *Virshevaia poeziia (pervaia polovina XVII veka)* (Moscow, 1980), pp. 5–19; also the collection of seventeenth-century verse in *Biblioteka literatury Drevnei Rusi*, vol. XVIII, ed. D. S. Likhachev, L. A. Dmitriev and N. V. Ponyrko (St Petersburg, 2014).

27 A. M. Panchenko, *Russkaia stikhotvornaia kul'tura XVII veka* (Leningrad, 1973); for the later seventeenth and early eighteenth centuries, see L. I. Sazonova, *Literaturnaia kul'tura Rossii. Ranee Novoe vremia* (Moscow, 2006).

28 On the earliest theatre see Claudia Jensen, Ingrid Maier, Stepan Shamin and Daniel C. Waugh, *Russia's Theatrical Past: Court Entertainment in the Seventeenth Century* (Bloomington, IN, 2021). On verse components see *Artakserksovo deistvo. Pervaia p'esa russkogo teatra XVII v.*, ed. I. M. Kudriavsteva (Moscow and Leningrad, 1957), pp. 75–6.

29 Simeon Polotskii, *Izbrannye sochineniia* (Moscow and Leningrad, 1955), pp. 161–202.

30 See Zhivov, *Istoriia iazyka russkoi pis'mennosti*, vol. II, pp. 865–87; Stefan Schneck, *Wissen und Wissenschaft im Russland der Frühen Neuzeit: Mathematik, Medezin, die Grammatik und der intellektuelle Wander vor Peter dem Großen* (Zurich, 2025), esp. pp. 69–148.

31 See Walker Riggs Thompson, *Epifanii Slavinetskii's Greek–Slavonic–Latin Lexicon between East and West* (Heidelberg, 2024).

32 Cited in A. M. Panchenko, 'Epifanii Slavinetskii', in *Slovar' knizhnikov i knizhnosti Drevnei Rusi. vyp 3. XVII v., ch. 1*, ed. D. S. Likhachev (St Petersburg, 1992), p. 313.

33 Cited in Zhivov, *Istoriia iazyka russkoi pis'mennosti*, vol. II, p. 873.

34 See Gary Marker, 'Primers and Literacy in Muscovy: A Taxonomic Investigation', *Russian Review*, XLVIII/1 (1989), pp. 1–19; also Max Okenfuss, *The Discovery of Childhood in Russia: The Evidence of the Slavic Primer* (Newtonville, MA, 1980), pp. 1–42.

35 For an illustrated overview of the primers mentioned here, see Marat Botvinnik, *Otkuda est' poshel bukvar'* (Minsk, 1983). For a full bibliography see E. L. Nemirovskii and Iu. E. Shustova, 'Kirillicheskie Azbuki i Bukvari XVI–XVIII vv.: bibliograficheskii svod izdanii', in *V Rossii nado zhit' po knige. Nachal'noe obuchenie chteniiu i pis'mu. Stanovlenie uchebnoi knigi*, ed. M. V. Tendriakova and V. G. Bezrogov (Moscow, 2015), pp. 185–338. For illustrated descriptions of primers from the mid-sixteenth to the mid-twentieth century see A. G. Goretskii and G. V. Karpiuk, *Ot azbuki Ivana Fedorova do sovremennogo bukvaria* (Moscow, 1974).

36 See Ingrid Maier, 'Wer war der Autor von *Alfabetum Rutenorum* (Stockholm ohne Jahr)?', in *Schnittpunkt Slavistik. Ost und West im wissenschaftlichen Dialog. Teil 3* (Göttingen, 2012), pp. 333–57.

37 Ingrid Maier, 'A Unique Copy of *Alphabetum Russarum*, Printed in Stockholm by Peter van Selow', *Scandoslavica*, LXIX (2023), pp. 322–40; Ingrid Maier, 'A Lutheran Catechism in Russian Translation (Stockholm, 1628)', in *Katekhizisy u slavian v XVI–XVIII vekakh: ikh retseptsiia, rasprostranenie, kul'turoobrazuiushchee i prosvetitel'skoe znachenie*, ed. Svetlana Mengel (Berlin, 2024), pp. 149–233.

38 '. . . *imushchim uchitisia otrokom i otrokovitsam muzhem i zhenam pisati*': Karion Istomin, *Bukvar'* [p. 2].

39 For a collected edition of such verses from primers (but not including Burtsov's 1637 preface) see D. N. Ramazanova and Iu. E. Shustova, *Kirillicheskie bukvari XVI–XVIII vv.* (Moscow, 2018), pp. 247–313.

40 On its sources see D. N. Ramazanova, 'Slaviano-greko-latinskii bukvar' Fedora Polikarpova (1701 g.): istoriia sozdaniia i istochniki', *Vestnik PSTGU IV: Pedagogika. Psikhologiia*, 4 (2013), pp. 78–88.

41 [F. Polikarpov], *Leksikon treiazychnyi, sirech' rechenii slavenskikh, ellinogrecheskikh i latinskikh sokrovishche* (Moscow, 1704).

42 *Slovar' obikhodnogo iazyka Moskovskoi Rusi XVI–XVII vekov. Vypusk 1. A-Biaz'* (St Petersburg, 2004), p. 4.

43 *Pustozerskii sbornik. Avtografy sochinenii Avvakuma i Epifaniia*, ed. N. S. Demkova, N. F. Droblenkova and L. I. Sazonova (Leningrad, 1975), p. 112.

44 Avvakum, 'Kniga tolkovanii i nravouchenii', in *Biblioteka literatury Drevnei*

Rusi, vol. XVII, ed. D. S. Likhachev, L. A. Dmitriev and N. V. Ponyrko (St Petersburg, 2013), p. 156.
45 V. A. Chernov, 'Na kakom iazyke pisal Avvakum?', *Trudy Otdela drevnerusskoi literatury*, XLII (1989), pp. 369–73.
46 *Povest' vremennykh let*, ed. D. S. Likhachev and V. P. Adrianova-Peretts, 2nd edn (St Petersburg, 1999), p. 16.
47 See Chapter Two.
48 Adelisa Malena, '"Promoting the Common Interest of Christ": H. W. Ludolf's "Impartial" Projects and the Beginnings of the SPCK', in *Protestant Missions and the Conversion of Europe, 1600–1900*, ed. Simone Maghenzani and Stefano Villani (New York and London, 2021), pp. 140–63.
49 Heinrich Wilhelm Ludolf, *Grammatica russica* (Oxford, 1696), fol. A2.
50 Ibid., fol. A1v.
51 Cited in Zhivov, *Istoriia iazyka russkoi pis'mennosti*, vol. II, p. 950; also Cracraft, *The Petrine Revolution in Russian Culture*, pp. 205–8.
52 Zhivov, *Istoriia iazyka russkoi pis'mennosti*, vol. II, pp. 952–9.
53 Ibid., p. 950.
54 Note, however, that administrative language in Peter's time did in fact acquire more Slavonisms: see L. V. Rudnev and T. S. Sadova, 'Delovaia rech' petrovskoi epokhi: nasledie proshlogo ili radikal'noe preobrazovanie', in *Literaturnaia kul'tura Rossii XVIII veka*, 8 (St Petersburg, 2019), pp. 169–88.
55 See below, Chapter Six.
56 See, for example, the trilogy by James Cracraft: *The Petrine Revolution in Russian Architecture* (Chicago, IL, 1988); *The Petrine Revolution in Russian Imagery* (Chicago, IL, 1997); as well as his 2004 volume, *The Petrine Revolution in Russian Culture*.
57 See, for example, Nancy Shields Kollmann, *The Russian Empire, 1450–1801* (Oxford, 2017); Donald Ostrowski, *Russia in the Early Modern World: The Continuity of Change* (Lanham, MD, Boulder, CO, New York and London, 2022).

2 A Language Worthy of Empire

1 On varieties of written usage in the mid-eighteenth century, see Thomas Rosén, *Russian in the 1740s* (Boston, MA, 2022).
2 See Aphra Behn, *Lycidus: or the Lover in Fashion: Being an Account from Lycidus to Lysander of the Voyage from the Island of Love* (London, 1688).
3 V. K. Trediakovskii, *Ezda v ostrov liubvi* (St Petersburg, 1730), [p. 4]; translation adapted from Marcus Levitt, 'The Age of Classicism', in *The New Cambridge History of Russian Literature*, ed. Simon Franklin, Rebecca Reich and Emma Widdis (Cambridge, 2024), p. 54.
4 B. A. Uspenskii, *Vokrug Trediakovskogo. Trudy po istorii russkogo iazyka i russkoi kul'tury* (Moscow, 2008), p. 87.
5 Vasilii Trediakovskii, *Sochineniia i perevody*, ed. N. Iu. Alekseeva (St Petersburg, 2009), p. 145.
6 Ibid., p. 147.
7 V. T. Tatishchev, *Zapiski. Pis'ma. 1717–1750 gg.*, ed. A. I. Iukht (Moscow, 1990), pp. 221–30.
8 Ibid., p. 224.

9 V. K. Trediakovskii, *Razgovor mezhdu chuzhestrannym chelovekom i rossiiskom ob ortografii starinnoi i novoi i o vsem chto prinadlezhit k sei materii* (St Petersburg, 1748).

10 On Sumarokov see especially the dozen studies in Marcus C. Levitt, *Early Modern Russian Letters: Texts and Contexts. Selected Essays by Marcus C. Levitt* (Boston, MA, 2009), pp. 3–264; Amanda Ewington, *A Voltaire for Russia: A. P. Sumarokov's Journey from Poet-Critic to Russian Philosophe* (Evanston, IL, 2010).

11 Marcus C. Levitt, 'Sumarokov's Russianized "Hamlet": Texts and Contexts', *Slavic and East European Journal*, XXXVIII/2 (1994), pp. 319–41.

12 S. I. Nikolaev, 'A. P. Sumarokov – perevodchik s russkogo iazyka na russkii', in Nikolaev, *Razyskaniia o russkikh poetakh pervoi poloviny XVIII veka* (Moscow and St Petersburg, 2023), pp. 211–19.

13 A. P. Sumarokov, 'Dve epistoly', in A. P. Sumarokov, *Izbrannye sochineniia* (Leningrad, 1957), pp. 112–25. On these, see Kirill Ospovat, *Pridvornaia slovesnost'. Institut literatury i konstruktsii absoliutizma v Rossii serediny XVIII veka* (Moscow, 2020), pp. 108–79.

14 Sumarokov, 'Dve epistoly', p. 116.

15 Ibid., pp. 112, 125.

16 Ibid., p. 113.

17 Ospovat, *Pridvornaia slovesnost'*, pp. 152–73.

18 Sumarokov, 'Dve epistoly', p. 115.

19 M. V. Lomonosov, 'Predislovie o pol'ze knig tserkovnykh v rossiiskom iazyke', in Lomonosov, *Polnoe sobranie sochinenii*, vol. VII: *Trudy po filologii* (Moscow and Leningrad, 1952), pp. 587–92.

20 Ibid., p. 589.

21 See B. A. Uspenskii, *Istoriia russkogo literaturnogo iazyka (XI–XVII vv.)*, 3rd edn (Moscow, 2002), pp. 401–2; Salvatore Del Gaudio, 'Rol' "slavenorosskogo iazyka" v istorii razvitiia ukrainskogo i russkogo iazykov', *Wiener Slawistischer Almanach*, LXIV (2009), pp. 227–46.

22 Karion Istomin, *Bukvar' sostavlen Karionom Istominym, gravirovan Leontiem Buninym, otpechatan v 1694 v Moskve*, p. 2.

23 V. M. Zhivov, *Istoriia iazyka russkoi pis'mennosti*, 2 vols (Moscow, 2017), vol. II, pp. 954–61; see above, Chapter One.

24 Lomonosov, 'Predislovie', p. 591.

25 A. S. Pushkin, *Polnoe sobranie sochinenii v 17 tomakh. T. 11: kritika i publitsistika 1819–1834* (Moscow, 1996), p. 31.

26 Zhivov, *Istoriia iazyka russkoi pis'mennosti*, vol. II, pp. 950–51.

27 See also D. M. Bulanin and V. K. Ziborov, 'Feodor Polikarpov Orlov', in *Slovar' knizhnosti i knizhnikov Drevnei Rusi. Vyp. 3 (XVII v.), Chast' 4*, ed. D. M. Bulanin (St Petersburg, 2004), pp. 105–30 (esp. pp. 108–10).

28 See Svetlana Mengel', ed., *Al'ternativnye puti formirovaniia russkogo literaturnogo iazyka v kontse XVII – pervoi treti XVIII veka. Vklad inostrannykh uchenykh i perevodchikov* (Moscow, 2021).

29 Just two surviving copies are known: see S. V. Vlasov and L. V. Moskovkin, *Pervyi v Rossii pechatnyi uchebnik russkogo iazyka kak inostrannogo* (St Petersburg, 2023).

30 [Martin Schwanwitz], *Nemetskaia grammatika iz raznykh avtorov sobrana i rossiiskoi iunosti v pol'zu izdana* (St Petersburg, 1730).

31 Helmut Keipert, *Compendium grammaticae russicae (1731). Die erste Akademie-Grammatik der russischen Sprache* (Munich, 2002).
32 *Teutsch-Lateinisch- und Russisches Lexicon, samt denen Anfangs-Gründen der Russischen Sprache. Nemetsko-latinskii i russkii leksikon kupno s pervymi nachalami russkogo iazyka* (St Petersburg, 1731). On this in context see H. Keipert, 'Die Petersburger *Teutsche Grammatica* und die Anfänge der Russistik in Russland', in *Lomonosov und grammatische Beschreibung im 18. Jahrhundert*, ed. G. Freidhof, P. Kosta and M. Schütrumpf (Munich, 1983), pp. 77–140.
33 Mikhail Lomonosov, *Rossiiskaia grammatika* (St Petersburg, 1755 [1757]), pp. 5–6.
34 Ibid., p. 8.
35 Ibid., pp. 9–10.
36 For example, ibid., pp. 134–5, on reflexive verbs.
37 On the representation of the morphology of the past in eighteenth-century grammars see V. M. Zhivov, *Ocherki istoricheskoi morfologii russkogo iazyka XVII–XVIII vekov* (Moscow, 2004), pp. 578–601.
38 Feofan Prokopovich, *Sochineniia*, ed. I. P. Eremin (Moscow and Leningrad, 1961), pp. 224 and (for the Latin) 494.
39 See V. P. Vomperskii, *Slovari XVIII veka* (Moscow, 1986), pp. 8–10; I. E. Kuznetsova, 'Ob istochnike "Nomenklatora na russkom, nemetskom i latinskom iazyke" Il'i Kopievskogo', in *Indoevropeiskoe iazykoznanie i klassicheskaia filologiia – XIII*, ed. N. A. Bondarko and N. N. Kazanskii (St Petersburg, 2009), pp. 319–25. For a scanned copy of the original in the Russian National Library (lacking the first few leaves), see kp.rusneb.ru/item/reader/nomenklator-na-russkom-latinskom-i-nemeckom-yazykah, accessed 13 April 2026.
40 Ia. V. Brius, *Kniga leksikon ili Sobranie rechei po Alfavitu c Rossiiskogo na Gollandskii iazyk* (St Petersburg, 1717); see Vomperskii, *Slovari XVIII veka*, p. 14.
41 [Grigorii Poletika], *Slovar' na shesti iazykakh: rossiiskom, grecheskom, latinskom, frantsuzskom, nemetskom i angliiskom* (St Petersburg, 1763).
42 Sergei Volchkov, *Novyi leksikon na frantsuzskom, nemetskom, latinskom i rossiiskom iazykakh*, 2 vols (St Petersburg, 1755, 1764).
43 I Sots, *Nouveau dictionnaire françois, italien, allemand, latin et russe. Novyi leksikon ili slovar' na frantsuzskom, ital'ianskom, nemetskom, latinskom i rossiiskom iazykakh* (Moscow, 1784).
44 This survey is limited to printed dictionaries. There were many initiatives in the production of dictionaries in manuscript: see, for example, A. M. Safronova, *Vasilii Tatishchev i pervye inoiazychnye shkoly Ekaterinburga (1735–1750-e gody)* (St Petersburg and Ekaterinburg, 2024), pp. 343–57. For an online reference resource on early dictionaries of Russian, curated by the Institute of the Russian Language, see http://83.149.210.98:81.
45 Iu. V. Stennik, ed., *Russkaia satiricheskaia proza XVIII veka* (Leningrad, 1986), pp. 143–92.
46 Ibid., pp. 168, 169, 179, 185.
47 *Slovar' Akademii rossiiskoi. Chast' I. Ot A do G* (St Petersburg, 1789), p. viii.
48 Ibid., pp. ix–x.
49 Ibid., p. xiv.
50 Ibid.

51 Sumarokov, 'Dve epistoly', p. 122: '*poem shutlivykh sklad dvoiak*'.
52 *Devich'ia igrushka, ili Sochineniia gospodina Barkova*, ed. A. Zorin and N. Sapov (Moscow, 1992).
53 *Slovar' sovremennogo russkogo literaturnogo iazyka*, vol. I (Moscow and Leningrad, 1950), p. iii.
54 *Bol'shoi akademicheskii slovar' russkogo iazyka*, vol. I (Moscow and St Petersburg, 2004), p. 3; on this dictionary see Chapter Nine.

3 True Feeling, Gallicism and the Authority of Taste

1 See Simon Karlinsky, 'Russian Comic Opera in the Age of Catherine the Great', *19th-Century Music*, VII/3 (April 1984), pp. 318–25.
2 Semantically calqued in Russian by the cluster of words that includes *chuvstennost'*, *chuvstvitel'nost'*, *chuvstvie*: see May Smith, *The Influence of French on Eighteenth-Century Literary Russian: Semantic and Phraseological Calques* (Oxford et al., 2006), pp. 107–21.
3 A. P. Sumarokov, 'O istreblenii chuzhikh slov iz russkogo iazyka', in *Polnoe sobranie sochinenii v stikhakh i proze pokoinogo Deistvitel'nogo Statskogo Sovetnika, Ordena Sv. Anny Kavalera i Leiptsigskogo Uchenogo Sobraniia Chlena, Aleksandra Petrovicha Sumarokova*, ed. Nikolai Novikov (Moscow, 1781), vol. IX, p. 274.
4 Ibid., p. 276.
5 Ibid., p. 277.
6 See Derek Offord, Vladislav Rjéoutski and Gesine Argent, *The French Language in Russia: A Social, Cultural and Literary History* (Amsterdam, 2018), pp. 173–261.
7 V. T. Tatishchev, *Zapiski. Pis'ma. 1717–1750 gg.*, ed. A. I. Iukht (Moscow, 1990), p. 224; see also in Kirill Ospovat, *Pridvornaia slovesnost'. Institut literatury i konstruktsii absoliutizma v Rossii serediny XVIII veka* (Moscow, 2020), p. 134.
8 Derek Offord, 'Linguistic Gallophobia in Russian Comedy', in *French and Russian in Imperial Russia*, vol. II: *Language Attitudes and Identity*, ed. Derek Offord, Lara Ryazanova-Clarke, Vladislav Rjéoutski and Gesine Argent (Edinburgh, 2015), pp. 79–99.
9 May Smith, in a review of a French translation of Fonvizin's *Letters from France*, in *Slavonic and East European Review*, LXXIV/3 (1996), p. 497.
10 Derek Offord, 'Beware the Garden of Earthly Delights: Fonvizin and Dostoevskii on Life in France', *Slavonic and East European Review*, LXXVIII/4 (2000), pp. 625–42; V. I. Moriakov, 'D. I. Fonvizin o Frantsii poslednei treti XVIII v.', *Vestnik Moskovskogo universiteta. Seriia 8. Istoriia*, (2011/3), pp. 52–68.
11 N. M. Karamzin, 'Otchego v Rossii malo avtorskikh talantov?', in Karamzin, *Izbrannye sochineniia v dvukh tomakh* (Moscow and Leningrad, 1964), vol. II, p. 185.
12 A. G. Cross, *N. M. Karamzin: A Study of His Literary Career (1783–1803)* (Carbondale and Edwardsville, IL, 1971).
13 For example, August Wilhelm Tappe, *Russisches historishes Lesebuch aus Karamsins Geschichte Russlands, für Schulen und den Selbstunterricht . . .* (St Petersburg and Riga, 1819): with title pages in German, French and Russian, accented texts, specimen translations, and grammatical notes; see also several

of the specimen passages from Karamzin in James Heard, *Key to the Themes in Heard's Russian Grammar* (St Petersburg, 1827).
14 Maurice B. Line, *Bibliography of Russian Literature in English Translation to 1900* (London, 1963), p. 23.
15 *Tales from the Russian of Nicolai Karamsin* (London, 1804), p. vi.
16 [Vasilii Protopopov], *Rassuzhdenie o vychishchenii, udobrenii i obogashchenii rossiiskogo iazyka* (Moscow, 1786); see A. M. Kamchatnov, *Russkii drevoslov Aleksandra Shishkova. Lingvisticheskoe nasledie A. S. Shishkova v nauchnom i kul'turnom kontekste epokhi* (St Petersburg, 2018), pp. 31–2.
17 A. S. Shishkov, *Rassuzhdenie o starom i novom sloge rossiiskogo iazyka* (St Petersburg, 1813). On the polemic with Karamzin, see Kamchatnov, *Russkii drevoslov Aleksandra Shishkova*, pp. 42–152; Offord, Rjéoutski and Argent, *The French Language in Russia*, pp. 484–94.
18 Shishkov, *Rassuzhdenie*, p. 1.
19 Ibid., p. 353.
20 Ibid., p. 4.
21 Ibid., pp. 22–5.
22 Sumarokov, 'O istreblenii chuzhikh slov', p. 275.
23 See Thomas B. Gilmour Jr, 'Johnson's Attitudes towards French Influence on the English Language', *Modern Philology*, LXXVIII/3 (1981), pp. 243–60 (quotation on p. 243); see also the remarks of John Gallagher, 'What a Spalage', *London Review of Books*, XLVII/4 (6 March 2025), pp. 7–8.
24 Shishkov, *Rassuzhdeniia*, pp. 170–207, 208–334.
25 Kamchatnov, *Russkii drevoslov Aleksandra Shishkova*, pp. 166–86.
26 Ibid., pp. 187–211.
27 Stephen K. Batalden, *Russian Bible Wars: Modern Scriptural Translation and Cultural Authority* (Cambridge, 2013); also Simon Franklin, *The Russian Graphosphere, 1450–1850* (Cambridge, 2019), pp. 260–67.
28 See his pamphlets and letters in 'K istorii Bibleiskogo obshchestva v Rossii', *Sbornik istoricheskikh materialov, izvlechennykh iz arkhiva sobstvennoi Ego Imperatorskogo Velichestva kantseliarii*, vol. XII, ed. N. Dubrovin (St Petersburg, 1903), pp. 325–76.

4 The Authority of the Writer

1 See Rudolf Neuhäuser, *The Romantic Age in Russian Literature: Poetic and Aesthetic Norms* (Munich, 1975), p. 30.
2 A. P. Sumarokov, 'Dve epistoly', in Sumarokov, *Izbrannye sochineniia* (Leningrad, 1957), p. 112.
3 M. Iu. Lermontov, *Polnoe sobranie sochinenii v chetyrekh tomakh*, vol. I: *Stikhotvoreniia 1828–1841* (St Petersburg, 2014), p. 107.
4 Ibid., p. 235.
5 See V. M. Zhivov, *Istoriia iazyka russkoi pis'mennosti*, 2 vols (Moscow, 2017), vol. II, p. 1122.
6 For example, N. A. Meshcherskii, *Istoriia russkogo literaturnogo iazyka* (Leningrad, 1981), pp. 193–207.
7 For a succinct overview of Pushkin and his reputation, see Robert Chandler, *Alexander Pushkin* (London, 2009); for a comprehensive account of the life,

see T. J. Binyon, *Pushkin: A Biography* (London, 2002). For aspects of the posthumous mythology of Pushkin, see Stephanie Sandler, *Commemorating Pushkin: Russia's Myth of a National Poet* (Stanford, CA, 2004).

8 Aleksandr Pushkin, *Evgenii Onegin. Roman v stikhakh* [Book I] (St Petersburg, 1825), p. viii.

9 See Simon Franklin, 'Novels without End: Notes on *Eugene Onegin* and *Dead Souls*', *Modern Language Review*, LXXIX (1984), pp. 372–83.

10 *Eugene Onegin*, Book VIII, stanza 14.

11 Ibid., Book III, stanza 29.

12 Ibid., Book VII, stanza 24.

13 Ibid., Book VIII, stanza 46.

14 Ibid., stanza 48.

15 V. G. Belinskii, *Polnoe sobranie sochinenii v 13 tomakh* (Moscow, 1953–8), vol. VII (1955), p. 503.

16 N. G. Chernyshevskii, *Ocherki gogolevskogo perioda russkoi literatury*, in Chernyshevskii, *Polnoe sobranie sochinenii v 15-i tomakh* (Moscow, 1939–53), vol. III (1947), pp. 8–309.

17 *Eugene Onegin. A Novel in Verse by Aleksandr Pushkin, Translated from the Russian and with a Commentary by Vladimir Nabokov. In Four Volumes* (London, 1964), vol. I, p. 7.

5 The Authority of the People

1 See G. O. Vinokur, *The Russian Language: A Brief History*, trans. Mary A. Forsyth (Cambridge, 1971), pp. 122–5, on evidence for colloquial speech in salon society.

2 See Iu. A. Bel'chikov, *Russkii literaturnyi iazyk vo vtoroi polovine XIX veka* (Moscow, 1974), pp. 54–122; Gabriella Safran, *Recording Russia: Trying to Listen in the Nineteenth Century* (Ithaca, NY, and London, 2022).

3 N. V. Gogol', *Polnoe sobranie sochinenii*, 14 vols (Moscow and Leningrad, 1937–52), vol. I, p. 105.

4 Ibid., p. 137.

5 Ibid., p. 138.

6 A. Kopiev, *Chto nashe tovo nam i ne nada* (St Petersburg, 1794).

7 *Severnaia pchela*, 137; 22 June 1842, pp. 346–7.

8 For an overview of the figure of the peasant in Russian literature see Alexey Vdovin, 'The Peasant', in *The New Cambridge History of Russian Literature*, ed. Simon Franklin, Rebecca Reich and Emma Widdis (Cambridge, 2024), pp. 737–55.

9 Safran, *Recording Russia*, pp. 103–5.

10 Ibid., p. 117.

11 V. G. Belinskii, [review of] V. A. Vasil'ev, *Grammaticheskie razyskaniia* (1845), in Belinskii, *Polnoe sobranie sochinenii v 13 tomakh* (Moscow, 1953–8), vol. IX, p. 224.

12 Safran, *Recording Russia*, pp. 20–21, 107.

13 N. G. Chernyshevskii, 'Ne nachalo li peremeny?', in Chernyshevskii, *Polnoe sobranie sochinenii v 15 tomakh*, vol. VII (Moscow, 1950), p. 865.

14 See L. L. Kasatkin, ed., *Russkaia dialektologiia* (Moscow, 2005), pp. 6–7.

15 For a relatively simple version, see the Russian dialect map available at https://en.wikipedia.org/wiki/File:Russian_dialects.png, accessed 13 April 2026. For a

data-rich interactive atlas with information at the level of individual settlements, see https://da.ruslang.ru, accessed 30 July 2025.

16 Thus, for example, in the seminal *Thoughts on the History of the Russian Language* by Izmail Sreznevskii (1812–80), first published in 1849 and much reprinted: see I. I. Sreznevskii, *Mysli ob istorii russkogo iazyka* (Moscow, 1959).

17 See, for example, the sayings and proverbs collected by Vasilii Tatishchev: A. M. Safronova, *Vasilii Tatishchev i pervye inoiazychnye shkoly Ekaterinburga (1735–1750-e gody)* (St Petersburg and Ekaterinburg, 2024), p. 344.

18 *Opyt oblastnogo velikorusskogo slovaria* (St Petersburg, 1852); V. I. Dal', *Tolkovyi slovar' zhivogo velikorusskogo iazyka* (Moscow, 1863–6); the most widely used version is the posthumously published second edition of 1880–82.

19 *Opyt oblastnogo velikorusskogo slovaria*, pp. v–xii.

20 Ibid., p. xii.

21 See Alexander D. Nakhimovsky, *The Language of Russian Peasants in the Twentieth Century: A Linguistic Analysis and Oral History* (Lanham, MD, 2020).

22 *Opyt oblastnogo velikorusskogo slovaria*, p. IV.

23 For a succinct account of Dal's life and works see G. P. Matvievskaia and I. K. Zubova, *Vladimir Ivanovich Dal', 1801–1872* (Moscow, 2002).

24 *Otechestvennye zapiski*, 1846, no. 2, pp. 263–428 (Dostoevskii, *The Double*); no. 4, pp. 155–92 (Herzen); no. 5, pp. 1–60 and no. 6, pp. 151–90 (Luganskii/Dal); no. 10, pp. 151–78 (Dostoevskii, 'Mr Prokharchin'), 249–70 (Turgenev); no. 12, pp. 177–229 (Grigorovich).

25 V. I. Dal', *Poslovitsy russkogo naroda. Sbornik poslovits, pogovorok, rechenii, prislovii, chistogovorok, pribautok, zagadok, poverii i proch* (Moscow, 1862).

26 V. I. Dal', *Tolkovyi slovar' zhivogo velikorusskogo iazyka. Chast' pervaia, A–Z* (Moscow, 1863), p. 88. The stresses are as marked in the original.

27 *Opyt oblastnogo velikorusskogo slovaria*, p. 11.

28 Published among several related pieces in the preface to the second edition (St Petersburg and Moscow, 1880), pp. lxxxvi–lxxxvii.

29 Ibid., p. xxvi.

30 See Simon Franklin, 'Reading the Streets: Encounters with the Public Graphosphere, *c.* 1700–1950', in *Reading Russia: A History of Reading in Modern Russia*, vol. 1, ed. Damiano Rebecchini and Rafaella Vassena (Milan, 2021), pp. 259–91 (esp. pp. 276–80).

31 Fedor Distribuendi, *Vzgliad na moskovskie vyveski* (Moscow, 1836), p. 57.

32 V. G. Belinskii, ed., *Fiziologiia Peterburga* (Moscow, 1984), p. 132.

33 Ibid., pp. 123–4.

34 'Peterburgskie vyveski', *Illiustratsiia*, no. 30 (28 August 1848), pp. 81–2; available at https://tiam-tula.ru, accessed 20 March 2026.

6 Language beyond Language

1 See Simon Franklin, *The Russian Graphosphere, 1450–1850* (Cambridge, 2019), pp. 37–51.

2 On the visual sources of civil type, see A. G. Shitsgal, *Russkii grazhdanskii shrift 1708–1958* (Moscow, 1959), pp. 21–114.

3 See, for example, V. M. Zhivov, 'Azbuchnaia reforma Petra I kak semioticheskoe preobrazovanie', *Trudy po znakovym sistemam*, XIX (1986), pp. 54–67. The

authoritative modern catalogue of printed material from the Petrine period has separate volumes for materials in the two typefaces: T. A. Bykova and M. M. Gurevich, *Opisanie izdanii, napechatannykh pri Petre Pervom. Svodnyi katalog: Opisanie izdanii grazhdanskoi pechati, 1708–ianvar' 1725 g* (Moscow and Leningrad, 1955); *Opisanie izdanii, napechatannykh kirillitsei. 1689–ianvar' 1725 g.* (Moscow and Leningrad, 1958); plus a later supplementary volume: *Dopolneniia i prilozheniia* (Leningrad, 1972).

4 See, for example, *Rossiiskaia azbuka dlia obucheniia iunoshestva chteniiu* (St Petersburg, n.d. [*c.* 1781]), p. 13. The heading is printed in the civil typeface.

5 Bykova and Gurevich, *Opisanie izdanii grazhdanskoi pechati*, no. 272; *Opisanie izdanii, napechatannykh kirillitsei*, no. 111.

6 Equivalent to 5 January and 14 January 1918 according to the Gregorian calendar, to which Russia officially switched only at the start of the following month. For details of the reform, see Bernard Comrie, Gerald Stone and Maria Polinsky, *The Russian Language in the Twentieth Century* (Oxford, 1996), pp. 283–95.

7 Michael G. Smith, *Language and Power in the Creation of the USSR, 1917–1953* (Berlin and New York, 1998), pp. 103–19.

8 Franklin, *The Russian Graphosphere*, pp. 74, 79–83.

9 See A. G. Shitsgal, *Russkii tipografskii shrift. Voprosy istorii i praktika primeneniia*, 2nd edn (Moscow, 1985), pp. 89–144.

10 For examples see, e.g., Roman Biske, ed., *Russian Handwriting. Original Specimens Contributed by 55 Different Persons* (London, 1919); on the importance of specimen books see Alison Smith, 'Handwriting and Bureaucracy', *Slavic Review*, LXXXV (2026) [forthcoming].

11 Franklin, 'Reading the Streets', pp. 273–5.

12 From E. I. Rastorguev, *Progulki po Nevskomu prospektu* (St Petersburg, 1846), repr. in *Chuvstvitel'nye progulki po Nevskomu prospektu*, ed. A. M. Konechnyi (St Petersburg, 2009), pp. 139–41. Very little seems to be known about Rastorguev, including the dates of his birth and death.

13 See, for example, Stephen White, *The Bolshevik Poster* (New Haven, CT, and London, 1988) and Victoria E. Bonnell, *Iconography of Power: Soviet Political Posters under Lenin and Stalin* (Berkeley, Los Angeles, CA, and London, 1997).

14 See, for example, Eleonora Glinternik, *Reklama v Rossii XVIII–pervoi poloviny XX veka* (St Petersburg, 2007), pp. 292, 296.

15 See, for example, Shitsgal, *Russkii tipografskii shrift*, pp. 184–5.

16 I. A. Fomin, ed., *Shrifty i ikh postroenie* (Leningrad, 1927).

17 See, for example, Glinternik, *Reklama v Rossii*, p. 293.

18 *Obraztsy gazetnykh shriftov (matrits) linotipnogo otdeleniia tipografii gazety Pravda* (Moscow, 1929).

19 On the legislation for this in the mid-1930s, see Franklin, 'Reading the Streets', pp. 286–7.

20 Iurii Olesha, *Ni dnia bez strochki* (Moscow, 1965), pp. 257–8.

21 For examples, see Franklin, 'Reading the Streets', pp. 269–77.

22 Shitsgal, *Russkii tipografskii shrift*, p. 186.

23 For a collection ('museum') of everyday signs see Alexei Plutser-Sarno, *Notes from Russia* (London, 2007).

24 N. V. Nikolaev, 'Dostatochno li bukv v russkom alfavite?', in *Tri stoletiia russkogo grazhdanskogo shrifta (1708–2008)*, ed. Iu. D. Samarin et al. (Moscow, 2008), pp. 182–7; Valentina Iepuri, 'What Makes Russian Advertisements Russian? Contemporary Russian Advertising as a Sociocultural Phenomenon', *Russian Language Journal*, LXVII (2017), pp. 55–76.
25 F. I. Tiutchev, *Polnoe sobranie sochinenii i pis'ma v shesti tomakh*, vol. I (Moscow, 2002), p. 123.
26 See Yuri Corrigan, 'Symbolism and the *Fin de Siècle*', in *The New Cambridge History of Russian Literature*, ed. Simon Franklin, Rebecca Reich and Emma Widdis (Cambridge, 2024), pp. 107–24; Thomas Seifrid, *The Word Made Self: Russian Writings on Language, 1860–1930* (Ithaca, NY, and London, 2005), pp. 53–81.
27 D. Burliuk et al., *Poshchechina obshchestvennomu vkusu* (Moscow, 1912); English version in Anna Lawton, ed., *Russian Futurism through Its Manifestoes* (Ithaca, NY, and London, 1988), pp. 51–2.
28 For illustration of imitation of handwriting in Futurist books see, for example, Susan P. Compton, *The World Backwards: Russian Futurist Books, 1912–16* (London, 1978); Nancy Perloff, *Explodity: Sound, Image and Word in Russian Futurist Book Art* (Los Angeles, CA, 2016).
29 Vasilii Kamenskii, *Tango s korovami. Zhelezobetonnye poemy* (Moscow, 1914).
30 As has been accomplished in the remarkable version by Daniel Mellis and Eugene Ostashevsky – an 'artist's book' in its own right: *'Tango with Cows': Translation, Facsimile, and Commentary* (Chicago, IL, 2022). See also the section 'picturing speed in verse', in Tim Harte, *Fast Forward: The Aesthetics and Ideology of Speed in Russian Avant-Garde Culture, 1910–1930* (Madison, WI, 2009), pp. 87–97.
31 For example, Luciano Caruso and Stelio M. Martini, eds, *Tavole parolibere futuriste (1912–1944)*, 2 parts (Naples, 1974, 1977). See also some similarities in Wyndham Lewis's 1914 Vorticist manifesto in *Blast* 1 (1914), esp. pp. 11–28, accessible at the Modernist Journals Project, https://modjourn.org/issue/bdr430555; see Olga Sokolova, *'Shtyk-iazyk ostri i tri!' Iazykovye politiki poeticheskogo avangarda* (Moscow, 2024), pp. 280–308.
32 Aleksei Kruchenykh's much reprinted 1913 leaflet, *Deklaratsiia slova kak takovogo* ('Declaration of the Word as Such'): translation in *Russian Futurism through Its Manifestoes*, ed. Lawton, pp. 67–8.
33 In *Pomada* (Moscow, 1913), [p. 12].
34 On Khlebnikov on language see Raymond Cooke, *Velimir Khlebnikov: A Critical Study* (Cambridge, 1987), pp. 67–103.

7 Sovietspeak

1 See Orlando Figes and Boris Kolonitskii, *Interpreting the Russian Revolution: The Language and Symbols of 1917* (New Haven, CT, and London, 1999).
2 See Michael S. Gorham, *Speaking in Soviet Tongues: Language Culture and the Politics of Voice in Revolutionary Russia* (DeKalb, IL, 2003).
3 Ibid., p. 39.
4 Ibid., p. 80; see also Catriona Kelly, '"How to Write to the Newspaper": Language and Power at the Birth of Soviet Public Language', in *Public Debate in*

Russia: Matters of (Dis)order, ed. Nikolai Vakhtin and Boris Firsov (Edinburgh, 2017), pp. 101–26.

5 Gorham, *Speaking in Soviet Tongues*, pp. 111–14.

6 [V. I. Lenin], 'Lev Tolstoi, kak zerkalo russkoi revoliutsii', first published anonymously in the Bolshevik newspaper *Proletarii*, XXXV (11/24 September 1908).

7 See Bernard Comrie, Gerald Stone and Maria Polinsky, *The Russian Language in the Twentieth Century* (Oxford, 1996).

8 For example, Francoise Thom, *Newspeak: The Language of Soviet Communism* (London, 1989); Gorham, *After Newspeak*.

9 On nuances of similarity and differentiation between Orwellian 'Newspeak' and Russia usage of the word *novoiáz*, see Maksim Krongauz, 'Russian and Newspeak: Between Myth and Reality', in *Public Debate in Russia*, ed. Vakhtin and Firsov, pp. 31–51.

10 For a glossary of some two hundred such key words, see Il'ia Zemtsov, *Sovetskii politicheskii iazyk* (London, 1985). For an attempt at a thorough dictionary of vocabulary that typifies the Soviet period, see V. M. Mokienko and T. G. Nikitina, *Tolkovyi slovar' iazyka Sovdepii* (St Petersburg, 1998). For summary of changes in vocabulary over the Soviet period see Comrie, Stone and Polinsky, *The Russian Language in the Twentieth Century*, pp. 205–25.

11 Comrie, Stone and Polinsky, *The Russian Language in the Twentieth Century*, pp. 139–43, 198–9.

12 *Slovar' sokrashchenii russkogo iazyka*, ed. D. I. Alekseev (Moscow, 1977).

13 Ibid., pp. 226, 104.

14 See N. A. Kupina, *Totalitarnyi iazyk: slovar' i rechevye reaktsii* (Ekaterinburg and Perm, 1995), pp. 18–19.

15 For example, see Ludmila Pöppel, *The Rhetoric of 'Pravda' Editorials: A Diachronic Study of a Political Genre* (Stockholm, 2007), esp. pp. 20–37; see Andreas Ventsel, 'The Role of Political Rhetoric in the Development of Soviet Totalitarian Language', *Russian Journal of Communication*, II (2009), pp. 9–25.

16 For essays on Soviet uses of media, especially through the 1920s and '30s, see Khans Giunter and Sabina Khensgen [that is, Hans Günther and Sabine Hänsgen], eds, *Sovetskaia vlast' i media* (St Petersburg, 2006).

17 Stephen Lovell, *Russia in the Microphone Age: A History of Soviet Radio, 1919–1970* (Oxford, 2015), p. 72.

18 Ibid., pp. 78–93.

19 Ibid., pp. 134–59.

20 Ibid., p. 104.

21 Z. N. Liustrova, L. I. Skvortsov and V. Ia. Deriagin, *Druz'iam russkogo iazyka Kniga o razvitii sovremennogo russkogo iazyka, o ego meste v sotsialisticheskoi kul'ture* (Moscow, 1982), p. 3.

22 Ibid., p. 154.

23 Pöppel, *The Rhetoric*.

24 *Russia Today*, 6 (New Series) (June 1936), p. 13.

25 V. P. Adrianova-Peretts, 'Osnovnye zadachi izucheniia drevnerusskoi literatury v issledovaniiakh 1917–1947 gg.', *Trudy Otdela drevnerusskoi literatury*, VI (1948), pp. 5–14.

26 Adrianova-Peretts, 'Osnovnye zadachi', pp. 6, 14. On the denigration of the pursuit of merely 'professional interests', see, for example, Lenin's 1903 essay 'The Tasks of Revolutionary Youth', in V. I. Lenin, *Polnoe sobranie sochinenii. Izdanie piatoe* (Moscow, 1967), vol. VII, p. 343.

27 *Novyi mir* 1963.10, p. 198.

28 Ibid., p. 193. Despite decades of preparatory work, the project was never completed.

29 *Voronezhskie chekisty rasskazyvaiut...* (Voronezh, 1976), pp. 24–5, 315–16.

30 On ritualization of Pravda editorials see Pöppel, *The Rhetoric*, p. 256; on sacralization of the language of power see Gorham, *Speaking in Soviet Tongues*, pp. 119–24; for a theoretical contextualization of Sovietspeak as ritual see Konstantin Bogdanov, 'Ritorika rituala. Sovetskii sotsiolekt v etnolingvisticheskom osveshchenii', *Antropologicheskii forum*, 8 (2008), pp. 300–337.

31 Note, however, that this can be consistent with the technical notion of an 'empty signifier': see Ventsel, 'The Role of Political Rhetoric'.

32 Marina Frolova-Walker, 'Stalin and the Art of Boredom', *Twentieth-Century Music*, I/1 (March 2004), pp. 101–24 (p. 103).

33 A. Blok, 'Intelligentsiia i revoliutsiia': first in *Znamia truda*, 19 January 1918; available at https://dugward.ru, accessed 20 April 2025.

34 Gorham, *Speaking in Soviet Tongues*, pp. 84–6.

35 See Igal Halfin, 'The Bolsheviks' Gallows Laughter', *Journal of Political Ideologies*, XI/3 (2006), pp. 247–68.

36 Vasilii Shukshin, *Sobranie sochinenii v shesti knigakh*, vol. III (Moscow, 1998), pp. 101–4.

37 The catchphrase entered political folklore so recognizably that even in 2006 it needed no explanation as the title of a three-part documentary about Brezhnev: *I lichno Leonid Il'ich*, available at www. youtube.com, accessed 20 April 2025.

38 Kupina, *Totalitarnyi iazyk*, pp. 98–123; also on linguistic strategies of resistance, with more focus on literature, N. A. Kupina, *Iazykovoe soprotivlenie v kontekste totalitarnoi kul'tury. Izbrannye trudy* (Moscow and Ekaterinburg, 2020); on late Soviet *anekdoty* in a wider context of late Soviet modes of ironic reframing of ritual discourse (broadly labelled *stiob*) see also Alexei Yurchak, *Everything Was Forever until It Was No More: The Last Soviet Generation* (Princeton, NJ, and Oxford, 2005), pp. 273–6.

8 Russian beyond Russia

1 For a more granular breakdown of the pre-Soviet period see Aneta Pavlenko, 'Linguistic Russification in the Russian Empire: Peasants into Russians?', *Russian Linguistics*, XXXV/3 (2011), pp. 331–50.

2 Simon Franklin, *The Russian Graphosphere, 1450–1850* (Cambridge, 2019), pp. 128–34.

3 *The Twenty-Seventh Report of the British and Foreign Bible Society* (London, 1831), pp. 110–11.

4 *Polnoe sobranie zakonov Rossiiskoi imperii s 1649 goda*, vol. VI: *1720–1722* (St Petersburg, 1830), pp. 244–5 (no. 3653).

5 On this overlapping sequence of functional varieties of language use in Ukraine see Andrii Danylenko and Halyna Naienko, 'Linguistic Russification in Russian

Ukraine: Languages, Imperial Models, and Policies', *Russian Linguistics*, XLIII (2019), pp. 19–39.

6 See Anatolii Remnev, 'Colonization and "Russification" in the Imperial Geography of Asiatic Russia: From the Nineteenth to the Early Twentieth Centuries', in *Asiatic Russia: Imperial Power in Regional and International Contexts*, ed. Uyama Tomohiko (London, 2012), pp. 102–28.

7 Pavlenko, 'Linguistic Russification', pp. 337–44.

8 Summary figures in Pavlenko, 'Linguistic Russification', p. 340; for more detailed analysis of literacy data from 1897 and other censuses see A. G. Rashin, *Naselenie Rossii za 100 let (1811–1913 gg.) Statisticheskie ocherki* (Moscow, 1956), pp. 284–311. On the complexity of interpretation see A. A. Safronov, 'Pervaia vseobshchaia perepis' naseleniia Rossii 1897 g.: razrabotka dannykh o gramotnosti, ikh informatsionnyi potentsial i dostovernost'', in *Dokument. Arkhiv. Istoriia. Sovremennost'*, III (2002), pp. 203–20.

9 Full text of the circular is available at ru.wikisource.org/wiki/Валуевский_циркуляр (in English: en.wikisource.org/wiki/Translation:Valuyev_Circular), accessed 20 March 2025. For an analysis of its implementation see Johannes Remy, 'The Valuev Circular and Censorship of Ukrainian Publications in the Russian Empire (1863–1876): Intention and Practice', *Canadian Slavonic Papers*, XLIX/1–2 (March–June 2007), pp. 87–110.

10 Wayne Dowler, *Classroom and Empire: The Politics of Schooling Russia's Eastern Nationalities, 1860–1917* (Montreal, 2001), pp. 63–84.

11 Dowler, *Classroom and Empire*, pp. 47–8. See Oxana Zemtsova, *Russification and Educational Policies in the Middle Volga Region (1860–1914)* (EUI dissertation, Florence, 2014), pp. 81–109.

12 M. Vol'per, *Russkaia rech'. Uchebnoe posobie, primenennoe k obucheniiu russkomu iazyku v tekh shkolakh, v kotorykh deti pri postuplenii ne umeiut govorit' po-russki* (St Petersburg, 1886–7).

13 *Volper's Russian Accidence in Tables . . . Adapted for English Students and Provided with a Full Index and Grammatical Glossary by Mark Sieff* (London and New York, 1916).

14 Lenore A. Grenoble, *Language Policy in the Soviet Union* (New York, Boston, Dordrecht, London and Moscow, 2003), p. vii; also Michael G. Smith, *Language and Power in the Creation of the USSR, 1917–1953* (Berlin and New York, 1998).

15 Grenoble, *Language Policy*, p. 39.

16 Ibid., p. 47, Table 5.

17 Ibid., pp. 41–2.

18 Ibid., p. 52. On Sovietspeak see above, Chapter Seven.

19 Smith, *Language and Power*, pp. 121–42; Grenoble, *Language Policy*, pp. 48–51.

20 E. Iu. Tokareva, 'Russkie familii tiurkskogo proiskhozhdeniia v "revizskikh skazkakh" g. Tobol'ska XVIII v.', *Istoriia, kul'tura, ekonomika urala i zaural'ia* (11 November 2015), pp. 94–7.

21 See Nicholas Poppe Jr., 'A Survey of Studies of Turkic Loan-Words in the Russian Language', *Central Asiatic Journal*, XI/4 (December 1966), pp. 298–310. On historical phases see Mainura Abil'taevna Buribaeva, *Tiurkizmy v russkom iazyke: ot variantov k norme* (Moscow, 2014), and, in summary, the same author's 'Tiurkskie slova v russkom iazyke kak rezul'tat iazykovykh kontaktov',

Vestnik Irkutskogo gosudarstvennogo lingvisticheskogo universiteta (2013), pp. 99–105.

22 On 'imperiality' in Russian literature see Vitaly Chernetsky, 'Empire', in *The New Cambridge History of Russian Literature*, ed. Simon Franklin, Rebecca Reich and Emma Widdis (Cambridge, 2024), pp. 423–40.

23 On the resonances of the conquest of the Caucasus in literature, see Susan Layton, *Russian Literature and Empire: Conquest of the Caucasus from Pushkin to Tolstoy* (Cambridge, 2009).

24 See Daniel Schreier, Marianne Hundt and Edgar Schneider, *The Cambridge Handbook of World Englishes* (Cambridge, 2020); on Russian English in the 'expanding circle' of World Englishes see Zoya G. Proshina and Anna A. Eddy, eds, *Russian English: History, Functions, and Features* (Cambridge, 2016).

25 G. Harmonière, *Vocabulaire français et russe* (Paris, 1815); *Dialogues russes et français à l'usage des deux nations* (Paris, 1816); *Grammaire russe* (Paris, 1817).

26 See Ralph Cleminson, 'Boris Godunov and the Vicar of Woolley: A Tale of the Unexpected', *Slavonic and East European Review*, LXV/3 (July 1987), pp. 399–403.

27 Albert Baiburin, *The Soviet Passport: The History, Nature and Uses of the Internal Passport in the USSR*, trans. Stephen Dalziel (Cambridge, 2021).

28 Mark Tolts, 'A Half Century of Jewish Emigration from the Former Soviet Union', in *Migration from the Newly Independent States 25 Years after the Collapse of the USSR*, ed. Mikhail Denisenko, Salvatore Strozza and Matthew Light (Cham, 2020), pp. 323–44.

29 See Constantin Katsakioris, 'Return from the USSR: Soviet-Educated Africans, Politics and Work, 1960s to 2000s', *Canadian Journal of African Studies*, LV/2 (2021), pp. 267–86.

30 See, for example, the summary information at https://tamizdatproject.org.

31 See Kevin M. F. Platt, ed., *Global Russian Cultures* (Madison, WI, 2019); also the contributions to A. Byford, C. Doak and S. Hutchings, eds, *Transnational Russian Studies* (Liverpool, 2019).

32 See, for example, Arto Mustajoki, Ekaterina Protassova and Maria Yelenevskaya, eds, *The Soft Power of the Russian Language: Pluricentricity, Politics and Policies* (Abingdon, 2020); Christian Noack, ed., *Politics of the Russian Language beyond Russia* (Edinburgh, 2021); Olesya Kisselev, Oksana Laleko and Irina Dubinina, eds, *Russian as a Heritage Language: From Research to Classroom Applications* (Abingdon, 2024).

33 For a spectrum of attitudes to linguistic identity even in a small sample of users, see, for example, Lara Ryazanova-Clarke, 'Transnational Self and Community in the Talk of Russophone Cultural Leaders in the UK', in *Transnational Russian Studies*, ed. Byford, Doak and Hutchings, pp. 318–39.

34 See the editors' introductory first chapter in Kisselev, Laleko and Dubinina, eds, *Russian as a Heritage Language*.

35 For the exceptional case of Kazakhstan, see Akbota Alisharieva, Zhanar Irbaeva and Ekaterina Protassova, 'Kazakhstanskii russkii: vzgliad so storony', *Ab imperio*, 4 (2017), pp. 231–63.

36 See Marco Puleri, 'Russophonia as an Epistemic Challenge', *Ab Imperio*, 1 (2023), pp. 76–98.

37 See https://totaldict.ru/about, accessed 10 March 2026.
38 See https://gramota.ru/o-portale, accessed 10 April 2026.
39 See https://rs.gov.ru/about-foiv and https://rsgov.ru/activities, both accessed 13 April 2026.
40 As of December 2025 the Rossotrudnichestvo website (rs.gov.ru) listed the addresses of 'Russian Houses' in dozens of countries. Most gave no Internet links except to the relevant embassies. Email addresses tended to be in the 'gov.ru' domain.
41 See https://russkiymir.ru/rucenter/catalogue.php, accessed 13 April 2026.

9 Disruptions and Reactions in Post-Soviet Russia

1 For surveys of the period, see L. P. Krysin, ed., *Sovremennyi russkii iazyk. Aktivnye protsessy na rubezhe XX–XXI vekov* (Moscow, 2008); also Michael S. Gorham, *After Newspeak: Language Culture and Politics in Russia from Gorbachev to Putin* (Ithaca, NY, and London, 2014); and the essays in Ingunn Lunde and Tina Roesen, eds, *Landslide of the Norm: Language Culture in Post-Soviet Russia* (Bergen, 2006); Ingunn Lunde and Martin Paulsen, eds, *From Poets to Padonki: Linguistic Authority and Norm Negotiation in Modern Russian Culture* (Bergen, 2009); and, with a focus on literature, Ingunn Lunde, *Language on Display: Writers, Fiction and Linguistic Culture in Post-Soviet Russia* (Edinburgh, 2017); Michael S. Gorham, Ingunn Lunde and Martin Paulsen, eds, *Digital Russia: The Language, Culture and Politics of New Media Communication* (Abingdon, 2014). See also the ambitious attempt at a lexicographical juxtaposition of Soviet and immediate post-Soviet vocabularies: Gasan Guseinov, *D.S.P. Materialy k russkomu slovariu obshchestvenno-politicheskogo iazyka XX veka* (Moscow, 2003).
2 M. Krongauz, *Russkii iazyk na grani nervnogo sryva* (Moscow, 2007).
3 On distinct periods in Russian digital culture see Gasan Guseinov, 'Blogosfera kak kommunikativnoe prostranstvo', in *Russkii iazyk i novye tekhnologii*, ed. G. Ch. Guseinov (Moscow, 2014), pp. 27–57.
4 Most of the word-forms here are from E. N. Shagalova, ed., *Slovar' noveishikh inostrannykh slov (konets XX–nachalo XXI vv.)* (Moscow, 2009). The Academy's dictionaries of new words are discussed later in this chapter.
5 Benjamin Peters, *How Not to Network a Nation: The Uneasy History of the Soviet Internet* (Cambridge, MA, and London, 2016).
6 See, for example, Maksim Krongauz, *Samouchitel' olbanskogo* (Moscow, 2013), pp. 253–65.
7 For examples see Martin Paulsen, 'Translit – novaia orfografiia russkogo iazyka', in *Russkii iazyk i novye tekhnologii*, ed. Guseinov, pp. 58–73; Paulsen, 'Translit: Computer-Mediated Digraphia on the Runet', in *Digital Russia*, ed. Gorham, Lunde and Paulsen, pp. 156–73.
8 For an extensive account see Krongauz, *Samouchitel' olbanskogo*, pp. 21–125.
9 Ibid., p. 88.
10 Gasan Guseinov, 'Instrumenty opisaniia nepolnoi kommunikatsii v blogosfere', in Guseinov, *Russkii iazyk i novye tekhnologii*, pp. 227–38.
11 Krongauz, *Samouchitel' olbanskogo*, pp. 61–7.
12 For deeper analysis of some linguistic practices in the mature blogosphere see, for example, V. M. Shaklein and I. V. Kovtunenko, *Russkaia blogosfera.*

Pragmaticheskaia i lingvokul'turnaia spetsifika realizatsii kategorii sviaznosti (Moscow, 2023).

13 For example, D. S. Baldaev, V. K. Belko and I. M. Isupov, *Slovar' tiuremno-lagerno-blatnogo zhargona (rechevoi i graficheskii portret sovetskoi tiur'my)* (Moscow, 1992).

14 For example, V. M. Mokienko and T. G. Nikitina, *Bol'shoi slovar' russkikh pogovorok* (Moscow, 2007); Mokienko and Nikitina, *Bol'shoi slovar' russkikh narodnykh sravnenii* (Moscow, 2008).

15 V. M. Mokienko and T. G. Nikitina, *Bol'shoi slovar' russkogo zhargona* (St Petersburg, 2001), with 25,000 headwords.

16 G. N. Skliarevskii, *Tolkovyi slovar' russkogo iazyka nachala XXI veka. Aktual'naia leksika* (St Petersburg, 2006).

17 L. P. Krysin, ed., *Tolkovyi slovar' russkoi razgovornoi rechi*, vols I–V (Moscow, 2014–22).

18 See Tatiana Kosmeda, 'Gendernaia leksikografiia: formirovanie novogo napravleniia (slovari feminitivov russkogo i ukrainskogo iazykov)', *Wiener Slawistischer Almanach*, LXXXVIII (2022 [published 2023]), pp. 135–47.

19 E. V. Ivantsova, ed., *Polnyi slovar' dialektnoi iazykovoi lichnosti*, 4 vols (Tomsk, 2006–12).

20 Vladimir Lebedev, *Etimologicheskii slovar' mirovogo russkogo iazyka*, 4 vols ([Ekaterinburg], 2019).

21 V. A. Chudinov, *Vernem etruskov Rusi. Rasshifrovka nadpisei drevnei tsivilizatsii* (Moscow, 2006).

22 Felix Dreizin and Tom Priestly, 'A Systematic Approach to Russian Obscene Language', *Russian Linguistics*, VI (1982), pp. 233–49 (esp. p. 233).

23 Iu. E. Prokhorov, ed., *Rossiia. Bol'shoi lingvostranovedcheskii slovar'* (Moscow, 2009), pp. 349–50.

24 The blurb to Anatolii Baranov and Dmitrii Dobrovol'skii, *Zapretnye slova. Zametki lingvistov o russkom mate* (Moscow, 2025).

25 Dreizin and Priestly, 'A Systematic Approach', pp. 237–9.

26 A. Plutser-Sarno, *Bol'shoi slovar' mata*, vols I–II (St Petersburg, 2001, 2005).

27 The example is given by Valerii Otiakovskii, 'Barkov, Prutkov i prochie: o "stikhakh poezii" leitenanta Pidorenko V. P.', *Matica Srbska Review of Slavic Studies*, C (2021), pp. 847–62 (p. 850).

28 On the necessity of norms in the idiomatic use of obscenities see Anatoly Baranov, Dmitrij Dobrovol'skij, 'Printsipy opisaniia obstsennoi idiomatiki', *Russian Linguistics*, XLVII/1 (2023), pp. 1–14.

29 *Brannye slova oskorbliaiut usta, iz kotorykh iskhodiat, stol'ko zhe, skol'ko i ushi, v kotorye vkhodiat*: in *Rossiiskaia azbuka dlia obucheniia iunoshestva chteniiu* (St Petersburg, n.d. [*c.* 1781]), p. 27.

30 See Manuela Kovalev, 'The Function of Russian Obscene Language in Late Soviet and Post-Soviet Prose', PhD, University of Manchester, 2014, pp. 33–7.

31 S. A. Kuznetsov, ed., *Bol'shoi tolkovyi slovar' russkogo iazyka* (St Petersburg, 1998), p. 3.

32 N. M. Kropachev, S. A. Belov. S. A. Kuznetsov, eds, *Tolkovyi slovar' gosudarstvennogo iazyka Rossiiskoi federatsii*, 2 vols (St Petersburg, 2025), vol. I, p. 770.

33 Interview with Sokurov in *Argumenty i fakty*, no. 27 (4 July 2014).
34 D. I. Keselovich, *Samyi polnyi slovar' nenormativnoi leksiki* (Moscow, 2011).
35 Michael Gorham, 'Language Culture and Identity in Post-Soviet Russia: The Economies of *Mat*', in *Soviet and Post-Soviet Identities*, ed. Mark Bassin and Catriona Kelly (Cambridge, 2012), pp. 237–53.
36 For example, in fairly extreme form, T. Nikitina, *Pravda o skvernoslovii i kurenii* (Moscow, 2022), pp. 3–32.
37 Daniel E. Collins, 'Reconstructing the Pragmatics of a Medieval Marriage Negotiation (Novgorod 955)', *Russian Linguistics*, XXXV/1 (2011), pp. 33–61. Note the form *yabem* (probably reflecting a first-person plural of the verb *ebat'*) reported in a grammatical study composed in Hebrew (in England) in the late twelfth or early thirteenth century: see Alexander Kulik, 'Jews from Rus in Medieval England', *Jewish Quarterly Review*, CII/3 (2012), pp. 380–81.
38 See letter no. 531 from the early thirteenth century: text and translation on the website gramoty.ru; on this insult as punishable by a fine, see Daniel E. Kaiser, *The Laws of Rus': Tenth to Fifteenth Centuries* (Salt Lake City, UT, 1992), p. 48.
39 Adam Olearius, *Vermehrete Newe Beschreibung Der Muscowitischen und Persischen Reise* (Schleswig, 1656), pp. 190–91.
40 'Tsar' Nikita i ego sorok docherei', in A. S. Pushkin, *Polnoe sobranie sochinenii v 17 tomakh*, vol. II.1 (Moscow, 1994), pp. 222–6.
41 Hamlet, III.2: note that this is followed by Hamlet's reference to the 'nothing' that lies 'between maid's legs' ('nothing' was a common euphemism for vagina). Pushkin's equivalent juxtaposition of the euphemistic 'nothing' and the punning *bezdelki* may well be no coincidence.
42 Krongauz, *Russkii iazyk na grani nervnogo sryva*, p. 111.
43 The first printed version is a bibliographical mystification: it is attributed (spuriously) to Ivan Barkov, is designated the 'second edition' and is ostensibly published in Moscow in 1969, by the Central Committee of the Communist Party of the Soviet Union. None of this is true: see Ivan Barkov, *Luka Mudishchev. 2-e izdanie* (Moscow, 1969). The real place of publication is either Paris or London (where Flegon Press subsequently claimed credit).
44 A. N. Afanas'ev, *Narodnye russkie skazki ne dlia pechati, zavetnye poslovitsy i pogovorki*, ed. O. V. Alekseeva, V. I. Eremina, E. A. Kostiukhin and L. V. Bessmertnykh (Moscow, 1997), including (pp. 485–519) the sayings collected by Dal, headed 'Russkie zavetnyi poslovitsy i pogovorki'.
45 On aspects of late Soviet and early post-Soviet *mat* see G. Ch. Guseinov, *D.S.P. Sovetskie ideologemy v russkom diskurse 1990-kh* (Moscow, 2004), pp. 145–235. See also Jasmina Savic, 'Porno Ludens: Soviet Literary Pornography, 1970s–1990s', PhD, University of Illinois Urbana–Champaign, 2019.
46 Dreizin and Priestly, 'A Systematic Approach', p. 233.
47 A. Flegon, *Beyond the Russian Dictionary. Za predelami russkogo slovaria* (London, 1973).
48 V. M. Mokienko, *Slovar' russkoi brannoi leksiki (matizmy, obstsenizmy, evfemizmy)* (Berlin, 1995).
49 V. M. Mokienko and T. G. Nikitina, *Slovar' russkoi brani (matizmy, obstsenizmy, evfemizmy)* (St Petersburg, 2003).
50 Kovalev, 'The Function of Russian Obscene Language', pp. 163–7.

51 See Ellen Rutten, 'Oshibka kak novoe pravilo? Iazykovaia identichnost' v blogakh rossiiskikh pisatelei', in *Russkii iazyk i novye tekhnologii*, ed. Guseinov, pp. 74–86.
52 On anti-obscenity legislation in 2014 and reaction to it, see Ingunn Lunde, '"Abanamat": Reactions from the Cultural Field to the 2014 Anti-Obscenity Law', *Zeitschrift für slavische Philologie*, LXXIII/1 (2017), pp. 1–29. For a range of studies on contemporary obscenity see *Skvernoslovie v sovremennykh rossiiskikh mass-media, kul'ture i politike*: a special issue of the online journal *Palladium*, XVI (2025), https://freeuniversity.press/palladium.
53 *Federal'nyi zakon o vnesenii izmenenii v Federal'nyi zakon "Ob informatsii, informatsionnykh tekhnologiiakh i o zashchite informatsii*, available at http://publication.pravo.gov.ru, document no. 0001202012300062.
54 Cited from a post of 22 June 2023 on legalacademy.ru, specifically at legalacademy.ru/sphere/post/sledite-zayazykom-v-rossii-usilivayut-kontrol-za-brannoi-leksikoi, accessed 20 March 2025. The original announcement was on the Roskomnadzor site and could be found at 16.rkn.gov.ru/directions/mass-communications/control-nadzor-smi/spravka/p15638, but, at the time of writing, outside access to this site appears to have been blocked.
55 As reported on the news site *Moskva24* on 5 February 2021: m24.ru/articles/obshchestvo/05022021/157685.
56 Ibid.
57 Nikolai Kozin, Tat'iana Shishkina, '750 protokolov na mat v SMI sostavil za chetyre goda Roskomnadzor', *Parlamentskaia gazeta*, pnp.ru, 23 January 2025.
58 For a survey of reactions that might broadly be labelled conservative, see Gorham, *After Newspeak*, pp. 98–130.
59 First issued by the Academy of Sciences publishing house ('Nauka') in 1990; cited here from: A. I. Solzhenitsyn, *Russkii slovar' iazykovogo rasshireniia* (Moscow, 2015).
60 Solzhenitsyn, *Russkii slovar'*, p. 3
61 See www.english-corpora.org/coca, accessed 13 April 2025.
62 See https://ruscorpora.ru, accessed 13 April 2025.
63 *Novye slova i znacheniia. Slovar'-spravochnik po materialam pressy i literatury 90-kh godov XX veka v dvukh tomakh*, vol. I (St Petersburg, 2009). The publication was originally conceived in two volumes, but expanded to three.
64 *Novye slova i znacheniia*, vols II, III (St Petersburg, 2014).
65 *Novoe v russkoi leksike. Slovarnye materialy – 2015* (St Petersburg, 2020), p. 3.
66 *Novoe v russkoi leksike. Slovarnye materialy – 2016* (St Petersburg, 2018), pp. 5–6.
67 *Novoe v russkoi leksike. Slovarnye materialy – 2020* (St Petersburg, 2021), p. 10.
68 *Novoe v russkoi leksike. Slovarnye materialy – 2018* (St Petersburg, 2020), pp. 89–90.
69 *Novoe v russkoi leksike. Slovarnye materialy – 2021* (St Petersburg, 2022), p. 10.
70 M. N. Priemysheva et al., eds, *Slovar' russkogo iazyka koronavirusnoi epokhi* (St Petersburg, 2021).
71 Ibid., pp. 182–3.
72 T. A. Golikova, *Lingvokul'turologicheskii slovar' sovremennogo russkogo iazyka (2000–2024 gg.)*, 2nd edn, revised and supplemented, 2 vols (Moscow, 2024). On potential criteria for lexicographic normativity in dealing with

foreign imports see, for example, L. P. Krysin, *Slovo v sovremennykh tekstakh i slovariakh: Ocherki o russkoi leksike i leksikografii* (Moscow, 2008), pp. 83–97.

73 *Bol'shoi akademicheskii slovar' russkogo iazyka*, vol. I (Moscow and St Petersburg, 2004), p. 4.

74 For the online version, see iling.spb.ru/departments/13.

75 *Bol'shoi akademicheskii slovar' russkogo iazyka*, vol. I, pp. 3–5.

76 Roman L. Vorontsov, Marina N. Priemysheva and Elizaveta V. Puritskaia, 'Printsipy normativnosti i istorizma v russkoi akademicheskoi leksikografii: eshche raz o tipe bol'shogo tolkovogo slovaria', *Voprosy leksikografii*, XXVIII (2023), pp. 5–27.

77 *Bol'shoi akademicheskii slovar' russkogo iazyka*, vol. I, p. 6.

78 See Michael S. Gorham and Daniel Weiss, eds, *The Culture and Politics of Verbal Prohibition in Putin's Russia*: special issue of *Zeitschrift für Slavische Philologie*, LXXII/2 (2016).

79 *O gosudarstvennom iazyke Rossiiskoi Federatsii*: see the texts on the site ivo.garant.ru/#/document/12140387/paragraph/1:0, which track both the 2005 version and the amendments. For analysis and critique, see *The 2005 Federation Law on the Russian Language*, a special issue of *Russian Language Journal*, LVI (2006).

80 Order no. 1197 of 8 August 2020: *O pravitel'stvennoi komissii po russkomu iazyku*: publication.pravo.gov.ru, document no. 0001202008110005.

81 See also the processes approved in a supplementary regulation of 1 July 2023: ivo.garant.ru/#/document/407133128/paragraph/1:0.

82 Affirmed in more detail on 25 December 2024: see the link to the document from government.ru/news/53894.

83 *Orfograficheskii slovar' russkogo iazyka kak gosudarsvennogo iazyka Rossiiskoi federatsii* (Moscow, 2025), and *Orfoepicheskii slovar' russkogo iazyka kak gosudarsvennogo iazyka Rossiiskoi federatsii* (Moscow, 2025).

84 *Slovar' inostrannykh slov* (St Petersburg, 2025).

85 Kropachev, Belov and Kuznetsov, eds, *Tolkovyi slovar' gosudarstvennogo iazyka Rossiiskoi federatsii*. This initial version presented itself as provisional, a work in progress; and indeed, reviewers noted deficiencies, omissions and inconsistencies: see e.g. Gasan Guseinov, 'Gosudarstvoobrazuiushchii iazyk i sovetskaia antropologiia', online and as a podcast on Radio France Internationale (RFI): rfi.fr/ru, accessed 1 December 2025.

86 All four were on the websites of two of the issuing institutions: ruslang.ru/normativnyje_slovari, and spbu.ru/sveden/normativnye-slovari.

87 The preface to the explanatory dictionary declared that it paid special attention to 'key concepts' which, according to a presidential decree of 2022, 'formed the basis of the traditional values of the peoples of Russia': Kropachev, Belov and Kuznetsov, eds, *Tolkovyi slovar' gosudarstvennogo iazyka Rossiiskoi federatsii*, p. 4.

88 *Rossiiskaia gazeta*, 20 June 2025, p. 2.

89 See publication.pravo.gov.ru, document no. 0001202506240035, pp. 2–3.

SELECT BIBLIOGRAPHY

Dictionaries are listed in the Appendix

Adrianova-Peretts, V. P., 'Osnovnye zadachi izucheniia drevnerusskoi literatury v issledovaniiakh 1917–1947 gg.', *Trudy Otdela drevnerusskoi literatury*, VI (1948), pp. 5–14

Afanas'ev, A. N., *Narodnye russkie skazki ne dlia pechati, zavetnye poslovitsy i pogovorki*, ed. O. V. Alekseeva et al. (Moscow, 1997)

Alisharieva, Akbota, Zhanar Irbaeva and Ekaterina Protassova, 'Kazakhstanskii russkii: vzgliad so storony', *Ab imperio*, IV (2017), pp. 231–63

Artakserksovo deistvo. Pervaia p'esa russkogo teatra XVII v., ed. I. M. Kudriavsteva (Moscow and Leningrad, 1957)

Avvakum, 'Iz "Knigi tolkovanii i nravouchenii"', in *Biblioteka literatury Drevnei Rusi*, vol. XVII, pp. 147–59

——, *Pustozerskii sbornik. Avtografy sochinenii Avvakuma i Epifaniia*, ed. N. S. Demkova, N. F. Droblenkova and L. I. Sazonova (Leningrad, 1975)

Baiburin, Albert, *The Soviet Passport: The History, Nature and Uses of the Internal Passport in the USSR*, trans. Stephen Dalziel (Cambridge, 2021)

Baranov, Anatolii, and Dmitrii Dobrovol'skii, *Zapretnye slova. Zametki lingvistov o russkom mate* (Moscow, 2025)

——, 'Printsipy opisaniia obstsennoi idiomatiki', *Russian Linguistics*, XLVII/1 (2023), pp. 1–14

[Barkov, Ivan], *Devich'ia igrushka, ili Sochineniia gospodina Barkova*, ed. A. Zorin and N. Sapov (Moscow, 1992)

——, *Luka Mudishchev*, 2nd edn (Moscow, 1969) [= Paris or London]

[Basov, Fedor], *'Azbuka friaskaia' 1604 g.*, ed. I. M. Basov, E. A. Liakhovitskii, A. V. Sirenov and D. O. Tsypkin (St Petersburg, 2023)

Batalden, Stephen K., *Russian Bible Wars: Modern Scriptural Translation and Cultural Authority* (Cambridge, 2013)

Behn, Aphra, *Lycidus: or the Lover in Fashion. Being an Account from Lycidus to Lysander of the Voyage from the Island of Love* (London, 1688)

Bel'chikov, Iu. A., *Russkii literaturnyi iazyk vo vtoroi polovine XIX veka* (Moscow, 1974)

Belinskii, V. G., ed., *Fiziologiia Peterburga* (Moscow, 1984)

——, *Polnoe sobranie sochinenii v 13 tomakh* (Moscow, 1953–8)

[Bible Society], *The Twenty-Seventh Report of the British and Foreign Bible Society* (London, 1831)

Biblioteka literatury Drevnei Rusi, 20 vols, ed. D. S. Likhachev et al. (St Petersburg, 1997–2020)

Binyon, T. J., *Pushkin: A Biography* (London, 2002)

Biske, Roman, ed., *Russian Handwriting, Original Specimens Contributed by 55 Different Persons* (London, 1919)

Blok, A., 'Intelligentsiia i revoliutsiia', *Znamia truda*, 19 January 1918

Bogdanov, Konstantin, 'Ritorika rituala. Sovetskii sotsiolekt v etnolingvisticheskom osveshchenii', *Antropologicheskii forum*, 8 (2008), pp. 300–337

Bonnell, Victoria E., *Iconography of Power: Soviet Political Posters under Lenin and Stalin* (Berkeley, Los Angeles, CA, and London, 1997)

Botvinnik, Marat, *Otkuda est' poshel bukvar'* (Minsk, 1983)

Bulanin, D. M. and V. K. Ziborov, 'Feodor Polikarpov Orlov', in *Slovar' knizhnosti i knizhnikov Drevnei Rusi. Vyp. 3 (XVII v.), Chast' 4*, ed. D. M. Bulanin (St Petersburg, 2004), pp. 105–30

Buribaeva, Mainura Abil'taevna, *Tiurkizmy v russkom iazyke: ot variantov k norme* (Moscow, 2014)

——, 'Tiurkskie slova v russkom iazyke kak rezul'tat iazykovykh kontaktov', *Vestnik Irkutskogo gosudarstvennogo lingvisticheskogo universiteta* (2013), pp. 99–105

Burliuk, D. et al., *Poshchechina obshchestvennomu vkusu* (Moscow, 1912)

Bykova, T. A., and M. M. Gurevich, *Opisanie izdanii, napechatannykh pri Petre Pervom. Svodnyi katalog: Opisanie izdanii grazhdanskoi pechati, 1708-ianvar' 1725 g* (Moscow and Leningrad, 1955); *Opisanie izdanii, napechatannykh kirillitsei. 1689–ianvar' 1725 g.* (Moscow and Leningrad, 1958); *Dopolneniia i prilozheniia* (Leningrad, 1972)

Bylinin, V. K., and A. A. Iliushin, 'Nachalo russkogo virshepisaniia', in *Virshevaia poeziia (pervaia polovina XVII veka)* (Moscow, 1980), pp. 5–19

Caruso, Luciano and Stelio M. Martini, eds, *Tavole parolibere futuriste (1912–1944)*, 2 parts (Naples, 1974, 1977)

Chandler, Robert, *Alexander Pushkin* (London, 2009)

Chernetsky, Vitaly, 'Empire', in *The New Cambridge History of Russian Literature*, ed. Franklin, Reich and Widdis, pp. 423–40

Chernov, V. A., 'Na kakom iazyke pisal Avvakum?', *Trudy Otdela drevnerusskoi literatury*, XLII (1989), pp. 369–73

Chernyshevskii, N. G., *Polnoe sobranie sochinenii v 15-i tomakh* (Moscow, 1939–53)

Chrissidis, Nikolaos A., *An Academy at the Court of the Tsar: Greek Scholars and Jesuit Education in Early Modern Russia* (DeKalb, IL, 2016)

Chudinov, V. A., *Vernem etruskov Rusi. Rasshifrovka nadpisei drevnei tsivilizatsii* (Moscow, 2006)

Cleminson, Ralph, 'Boris Godunov and the Vicar of Woolley: A Tale of the Unexpected', *Slavonic and East European Review*, LXV/3 (July 1987), pp. 399–403

Collins, Daniel E., 'Reconstructing the Pragmatics of a Medieval Marriage Negotiation (Novgorod 955)', *Russian Linguistics*, XXXV/1 (2011), pp. 33–61

Compton, Susan P., *The World Backwards: Russian Futurist Books 1912–16* (London, 1978)

Comrie, Bernard, Gerald Stone and Maria Polinsky, *The Russian Language in the Twentieth Century* (Oxford, 1996)

Cooke, Raymond, *Velimir Khlebnikov: A Critical Study* (Cambridge, 1987)

Corrigan, Yuri, 'Symbolism and the *Fin de Siècle*', in *The New Cambridge History of Russian Literature*, ed. Franklin, Reich and Widdis, pp. 107–24

Cracraft, James, *The Petrine Revolution in Russian Architecture* (Chicago, IL, 1988)

——, *The Petrine Revolution in Russian Culture* (Cambridge, MA, 2004)

——, *The Petrine Revolution in Russian Imagery* (Chicago, IL, 1997)

Cross, A. G., *N. M. Karamzin: A Study of His Literary Career (1783–1803)* (Carbondale and Edwardsville, IL, 1971)

Cubberley, Paul, *Russian: A Linguistic Introduction* (Cambridge, 2002)

Dal', V. I., *Poslovitsy russkogo naroda. Sbornik poslovits, pogovorok, rechenii, prislovii, chistogovorok, pribautok, zagadok, poverii i proch.* (Moscow, 1862)

——, 'Russkie zavetnye poslovitsy i pogovorki', in A. N. Afanas'ev, *Narodnye russkie skazki ne dlia pechati*, pp. 485–519

Danylenko, Andrii, and Halyna Naienko, 'Linguistic Russification in Russian Ukraine: Languages, Imperial Models, and Policies', *Russian Linguistics*, XLIII (2019), pp. 19–39

Del Gaudio, Salvatore, 'Rol' "slavenorosskogo iazyka" v istorii razvitiia ukrainskogo i russkogo iazykov', *Wiener Slawistischer Almanach*, LXIV (2009), pp. 227–46

Distribuendi, Fedor, *Vzgliad na moskovskie vyveski* (Moscow, 1836)

Dowler, Wayne, *Classroom and Empire: The Politics of Schooling Russia's Eastern Nationalities, 1860–1917* (Montreal, 2001)

Dreizin, Felix, and Tom Priestly, 'A Systematic Approach to Russian Obscene Language', *Russian Linguistics*, VI (1982), pp. 233–49

Ewington, Amanda, *A Voltaire for Russia: A. P. Sumarokov's Journey from Poet-Critic to Russian Philosophe* (Evanston, IL, 2010)

Figes, Orlando, and Boris Kolonitskii, *Interpreting the Russian Revolution: The Language and Symbols of 1917* (New Haven, CT, and London, 1999)

Fomin, I. A., ed., *Shrifty i ikh postroenie* (Leningrad, 1927)

Franklin, Simon, 'Novels without End: Notes on *Eugene Onegin* and *Dead Souls*', *Modern Language Review*, LXXIX (1984), pp. 372–83

——, 'Reading the Streets: Encounters with the Public Graphosphere, *c.* 1700–1950', in *Reading Russia: A History of Reading in Modern Russia*, 3 vols, ed. Damiano Rebecchini and Rafaella Vassena (Milan, 2021), vol. I, pp. 259–91

——, *The Russian Graphosphere, 1450–1850* (Cambridge, 2019)

——, *Writing, Society and Culture in Early Rus, c. 950–1300* (Cambridge, 2002)

——, Rebecca Reich and Emma Widdis, eds, *The New Cambridge History of Russian Literature* (Cambridge, 2024)

Frolova-Walker, Marina, 'Stalin and the Art of Boredom', *Twentieth-Century Music*, I/I (March 2004), pp. 101–24

Galinskaia, E. A., *Istoricheskaia grammatika russkogo iazyka: Fonetika. Morfologiia* (Moscow, 2015)

Gallagher, John, 'What a Spalage', *London Review of Books*, LXXVII/4 (6 March 2025), pp. 7–8

Gilmour, Thomas B. Jr, 'Johnson's Attitudes towards French Influence on the English Language', *Modern Philology*, LXXVIII/3 (1981), pp. 243–60

Giunter, Khans, and Sabina Khensgen [i.e. Hans Günther and Sabine Hänsgen], eds, *Sovetskaia vlast' i media* (St Petersburg, 2006)
Glinternik, Eleonora, *Reklama v Rossii XVIII-pervoi poloviny XX veka* (St Petersburg, 2007)
Gogol', N. V., *Polnoe sobranie sochinenii*, 14 vols (Moscow and Leningrad, 1937–52)
Goldblatt, Harvey, *Orthography and Orthodoxy: Constantine Kostenečki's Treatise on the Letters* (Florence, 1987)
Goretskii, A. G., and G. V. Karpiuk, *Ot azbuki Ivana Fedorova do sovremennogo bukvaria* (Moscow, 1974)
Gorham, Michael S., *After Newspeak: Language Culture and Politics in Russia from Gorbachev to Putin* (Ithaca, NY, and London, 2014)
—, 'Language Culture and Identity in Post-Soviet Russia: The Economies of *Mat*', in *Soviet and Post-Soviet Identities*, ed. Mark Bassin and Catriona Kelly (Cambridge, 2012), pp. 237–53
—, *Speaking in Soviet Tongues: Language Culture and the Politics of Voice in Revolutionary Russia* (DeKalb, IL, 2003)
Gorham, Michael S., and Daniel Weiss, eds, *The Culture and Politics of Verbal Prohibition in Putin's Russia*: special issue of *Zeitschrift für Slavische Philologie*, LXXII/2 (2016)
Gorham, Michael S., Ingunn Lunde and Martin Paulsen, eds, *Digital Russia: The Language, Culture and Politics of New Media Communication* (Abingdon, 2014)
Gorshkov, A. I., *Teoriia i istoriia russkogo literaturnogo iazyka* (Moscow, 1984)
Grenoble, Lenore A., *Language Policy in the Soviet Union* (New York, Boston, Dordrecht, London and Moscow, 2003)
Grigor'eva, V. Iu., *Normy liturgicheskogo proiznosheniia. Tserkovnoslavianskie teksty v istochnikakh XVI–XVII vv.* (Moscow, 2024)
Guseinov, Gasan, 'Blogosfera kak kommunikativnoe prostranstvo', in G. Ch. Guseinov, ed., *Russkii iazyk i novye tekhnologii* (Moscow, 2014), pp. 27–57
—, *D.S.P. Materialy k russkomu slovariu obshchestvenno-politicheskogo iazyka XX veka* (Moscow, 2003)
—, *D.S.P. Sovetskie ideologemy v russkom diskurse 1990-kh* (Moscow, 2004)
—, 'Gosudarstvennoobrazuiushchii iazyk i sovetskaia antropologiia', online and as a podcast on Radio France International (RFI) (1 December 2025), rfi.fr/ru
—, 'Instrumenty opisaniia nepolnoi kommunikatsii v blogosfere', in Guseinov, *Russkii iazyk i novye tekhnologii*, pp. 227–38
Halfin, Igal, 'The Bolsheviks' Gallows Laughter', *Journal of Political Ideologies*, XI/3 (2006), pp. 247–68
Harte, Tim, *Fast Forward: The Aesthetics and Ideology of Speed in Russian Avant-Garde Culture, 1910–1930* (Madison, WI, 2009)
Heard, James, *Key to the Themes in Heard's Russian Grammar* (St Petersburg, 1827)
Hernández-Campoy, Juan Manuel and Juan Camilo Conde-Silvestre, eds, *The Handbook of Historical Sociolinguistics* (Malden, MA, Oxford and Chichester, 2012)
Iepuri, Valentina, 'What Makes Russian Advertisements Russian? Contemporary Russian Advertising as a Sociocultural Phenomenon', *Russian Language Journal*, LXVII/1 (2017), pp. 55–76

[Istomin, Karion], *Bukvar' sostavlen Karionom Istominym, gravirovan Leontiem Buninym, otpechatan v 1694 v Moskve* (Leningrad, 1981)
Ivanov, V. V., *Istoricheskaia fonologiia russkogo iazyka* (Moscow, 1968)
Ivanova, Mirela, *Inventing Slavonic: Cultures of Writing between Rome and Constantinople* (Oxford, 2024)
Jensen, Claudia, Ingrid Maier, Stepan Shamin and Daniel C. Waugh, *Russia's Theatrical Past: Court Entertainment in the Seventeenth Century* (Bloomington, IN, 2021)
Kaiser, Daniel E., *The Laws of Rus': Tenth to Fifteenth Centuries* (Salt Lake City, UT, 1992)
Kalashnikova, Angelina A., and Maria E. Proskuryakova, 'The Visual Markup of the Text in Russian Chancellery Documents from the Fifteenth to the Seventeenth Centuries', in *Cyrillic Manuscripts: From Medieval to Digital*, ed. Viacheslav Lytvynenko et al. (New York and Lausanne, 2025), pp. 63–85
Kamchatnov, A. M., *Istoriia russkogo literaturnogo iazyka XI–pervaia polovina XIX veka* (Moscow, 2008)
——, *Russkii drevoslov Aleksandra Shishkova. Lingvisticheskoe nasledie A. S. Shishkova v nauchnom i kul'turnom kontekste epokhi* (St Petersburg, 2018)
Kamenskii, Vasilii, *Tango s korovami. Zhelezobetonnye poemy* (Moscow, 1914)
——, *'Tango with Cows': Translation, Facsimile, and Commentary* by Daniel Mellis and Eugene Ostashevsky (Chicago, IL, 2022): see tangowithcows.com
Kamphuis, Jaap, *Verbal Aspect in Old Church Slavonic: A Corpus-Based Approach* (Leiden and Boston, MA, 2020)
Karamzin, N. M., *Izbrannye sochineniia v dvukh tomakh* (Moscow and Leningrad, 1964)
——, *Tales from the Russian of Nicolai Karamsin* (London, 1804)
Karlinsky, Simon, 'Russian Comic Opera in the Age of Catherine the Great', *19th-Century Music*, VII/3 (April 1984), pp. 318–25
Kasatkin, L. L., ed., *Russkaia dialektologiia* (Moscow, 2005)
Katsakioris, Constantin, 'Return from the USSR: Soviet-Educated Africans, Politics and Work, 1960s to 2000s', *Canadian Journal of African Studies*, LV/2 (2021), pp. 267–86
Keipert, Helmut, *Compendium grammaticae russicae (1731). Die erste Akademie-Grammatik der russischen Sprache* (Munich, 2002)
——, 'Die Petersburger *Teutsche Grammatica* und die Anfänge der Russistik in Russland', in *Lomonosov und grammatische Beschreibung im 18. Jahrhundert*, ed. G. Freidhof, P. Kosta and M. Schütrumpf (Munich, 1983), pp. 77–140
Kelly, Catriona, '"How to Write to the Newspaper": Language and Power at the Birth of Soviet Public Language', in *Public Debate in Russia*, ed.Vakhtin and Firsov, pp. 101–26
Kisselev, Olesya, Oksana Laleko and Irina Dubinina, eds, *Russian as a Heritage Language: From Research to Classroom Applications* (Abingdon, 2024)
Knowles, Gerry, *A Cultural History of the English Language* (London, 1997)
Kóczy, Judit Baranyiné, and Veronika Szelid, eds, *Cultural Linguistics and (Re)-Conceptualized Tradition* (Singapore, 2024)
Kollmann, Nancy Shields, *The Russian Empire, 1450–1801* (Oxford, 2017)
Konechnyi, A. M., ed., *Chuvstvitel'nye progulki po Nevskomu prospektu* (St Petersburg, 2009)
Kopiev, A., *Chto nashe tovo nam i ne nada* (St Petersburg, 1794)

Kosmeda, Tatiana, 'Gendernaia leksikografiia: formirovanie novogo napravleniia (slovari feminitivov russkogo i ukrainskogo iazykov)', *Wiener Slawistischer Almanach*, LXXXVIII (2022 [published 2023]), pp. 135–47

Kovalev, Manuela, 'The Function of Russian Obscene Language in Late Soviet and Post-Soviet Prose', PhD, University of Manchester, 2014

Kozin, Nikolai, and Tat'iana Shishkina, '750 protokolov na mat v SMI sostavil za chetyre goda Roskomnadzor', *Parlamentskaia gazeta*, 23 January 2025: online at pnp.ru/social/750-protokolov-na-mat-v-smi-sostavil-za-chetyre-goda-roskomnadzor.html

Kravetskii, A. G., and Pletneva, A. A., *Istoriia tserkovnoslavianskogo iazyka v Rossii. Konets XIX–XX v.* (Moscow, 2001)

Krivko, Roman, 'Church Slavic, Canonical', in *Encyclopedia of Slavic Languages and Linguistics Online*, ed. Mark L. Greenberg and Lenore A. Grenoble: referenceworks.brill.com/display/db/eslo

Krongauz, Maksim, 'Russian and Newspeak: Between Myth and Reality', in *Public Debate in Russia*, ed. Vakhtin and Firsov, pp. 31–51

——, *Russkii iazyk na grani nervnogo sryva* (Moscow, 2007)

——, *Samouchitel' olbanskogo* (Moscow, 2013)

Krysin, L. P., *Slovo v sovremennykh tekstakh i slovariakh. Ocherki o russkoi leksike i leksikografii* (Moscow, 2008)

——, ed., *Sovremennyi russkii iazyk. Aktivnye protsessy na rubezhe XX–XXI vekov* (Moscow, 2008)

Kulik, Alexander, 'Jews from Rus in Medieval England', *Jewish Quarterly Review*, CII/3 (2012), pp. 371–403

Kupina, N. A., *Iazykovoe soprotivlenie v kontekste totalitarnoi kul'tury. Izbrannye trudy* (Moscow and Ekaterinburg, 2020)

——, *Totalitarnyi iazyk: slovar' i rechevye reaktsii* (Ekaterinburg and Perm, 1995)

Kuznetsova, I. E., 'Ob istochnike "Nomenklatora na russkom, nemetskom i latinskom iazyke" Il'i Kopievskogo', in *Indoevropeiskoe iazykoznanie i klassicheskaia filologiia – XIII* (St Petersburg, 2009), pp. 319–25

Lawton, Anna, ed., *Russian Futurism through Its Manifestoes* (Ithaca, NY, and London, 1988)

Layton, Susan, *Russian Literature and Empire: Conquest of the Caucasus from Pushkin to Tolstoy* (Cambridge, 2009)

Leith, Dick, *A Social History of English*, 2nd edn (London and New York, 1997)

Lenin, Vladimir, 'Lev Tolstoi, kak zerkalo russkoi revoliutsii', *Proletarii*, XXXV (11/24 September 1908)

Lermontov, M. Iu., *Polnoe sobranie sochinenii v chetyrekh tomakh*, vol. I: *Stikhotvoreniia 1828–1841* (St Petersburg, 2014)

Levitt, Marcus, 'The Age of Classicism', in *The New Cambridge History of Russian Literature*, ed. Franklin, Reich and Widdis, pp. 52–70

——, *Early Modern Russian Letters: Texts and Contexts. Selected Essays by Marcus C. Levitt* (Boston, MA, 2009)

——, 'Sumarokov's Russianized "Hamlet": Texts and Contexts', *Slavic and East European Journal*, XXXVIII/2 (1994), pp. 319–41

Line, Maurice. B., *Bibliography of Russian Literature in English Translation to 1900* (London, 1963)

Liustrova, Z. N., L. I. Skvortsov and V. Ia. Deriagin, *Druz'iam russkogo iazyka (Kniga o razvitii sovremennogo russkogo iazyka, o ego meste v sotsialisticheskoi kul'ture* (Moscow, 1982)

Lomonosov, M. V., *Polnoe sobranie sochinenii*, vol. VII: *Trudy po filologii* (Moscow and Leningrad, 1952)

——, *Rossiiskaia grammatika* (St Petersburg, 1755 [1757])

Lovell, Stephen, *Russia in the Microphone Age: A History of Soviet Radio, 1919–1970* (Oxford, 2015)

Ludolf, Heinrich Wilhelm, *Grammatica russica* (Oxford, 1696)

Lukin, P. E., *Pis'mena i pravoslavie. Istoriko-filologicheskoe issledovanie 'Skazaniia o pis'menakh' Konstantina Filosofa Kostenetskogo* (Moscow, 2001)

Lunde, Ingunn, '"Abanamat": Reactions from the Cultural Field to the 2014 Anti-Obscenity Law', *Zeitschrift für Slavische Philologie*, LXXIII/1 (2017), pp. 1–29

——, *Language on Display: Writers, Fiction and Linguistic Culture in Post-Soviet Russia* (Edinburgh, 2017)

Lunde, Ingunn, and Martin Paulsen, eds, *From Poets to Padonki: Linguistic Authority and Norm Negotiation in Modern Russian Culture* (Bergen, 2009)

Lunde, Ingunn, and Tina Roesen, eds, *Landslide of the Norm: Language Culture in Post-Soviet Russia* (Bergen, 2006)

Lupinin, Nicholas, *Religious Revolt in the XVIIth Century: The Schism of the Russian Church* (Princeton, NJ, 1984)

Maier, Ingrid, 'A Lutheran Catechism in Russian Translation (Stockholm, 1628)', in *Katekhizisy u slavian v XVI–XVIII vekakh: ikh retseptsiia, rasprostranenie, kul'turoobrazuiushchee i prosvetitel'skoe znachenie*, ed. Svetlana Mengel (Berlin, 2024), pp. 149–233

——, 'A Unique Copy of *Alphabetum Russarum*, Printed in Stockholm by Peter van Selow', *Scandoslavica*, LXIX (2023), pp. 322–40

——, 'Wer war der Autor von *Alfabetum Rutenorum* (Stockholm ohne Jahr)?', in *Schnittpunkt Slavistik. Ost und West im wissenschaftlichen Dialog. Teil 3* (Göttingen, 2012), pp. 333–57

Maikova, O. V., 'Drevnerusskoe liturgicheskoe proiznoshenie v iuzhnoi Rusi v XII–XIII vv.', in *Drevnerusskii literaturnyi iazyk v ego otnoshenii k staroslavianskomu*, ed. L. P. Zhukovskaia (Moscow, 1987), pp. 129–43

Malena, Adelisa, '"Promoting the Common Interest of Christ": H. W. Ludolf's "Impartial" Projects and the Beginnings of the SPCK', in *Protestant Missions and the Conversion of Europe, 1600–1900*, ed. Simone Maghenzani and Stefano Villani (New York and London, 2021), pp. 140–63

Marker, Gary J., 'Primers and Literacy in Muscovy: A Taxonomic Investigation', *Russian Review*, XLVIII/1 (1989), pp. 1–19

——, *Publishing, Printing and the Origins of Intellectual Life in Russia, 1700–1800* (Princeton, NJ, 1985)

——, 'A World of Visual Splendor: The Illustrated Texts of Karion Istomin', in *Seeing Muscovy Anew: Politics – Institutions – Culture. Essays in Honor of Nancy Shields Kollmann*, ed. Michael S. Flier et al. (Bloomington, IN, 2017), pp. 173–88

Matvievskaia, G. P., and I. K. Zubova, *Vladimir Ivanovich Dal', 1801–1872* (Moscow, 2002)

Mengel', Svetlana, ed., *Al'ternativnye puti formirovaniia russkogo literaturnogo iazyka v kontse XVII–pervoi treti XVIII veka. Vklad inostrannykh uchenykh i perevodchikov* (Moscow, 2021)

Meshcherskii, N. A., *Istoriia russkogo literaturnogo iazyka* (Leningrad, 1981)

Moriakov, V. I., 'D. I. Fonvizin o Frantsii poslednei treti XVIII v.', *Vestnik Moskovskogo universiteta. Seriia 8. Istoriia*, 3 (2011), pp. 52–68

Mustajoki, Arto, Ekaterina Protassova and Maria Yelenevskaya, eds, *The Soft Power of the Russian Language: Pluricentricity, Politics and Policies* (Abingdon, 2020)

[Nabokov, Vladimir], *Eugene Onegin: A Novel in Verse by Aleksandr Pushkin, Translated from the Russian and with a Commentary by Vladimir Nabokov. In Four Volumes* (London, 1964)

Nakhimovsky, Alexander D., *The Language of Russian Peasants in the Twentieth Century: A Linguistic Analysis and Oral History* (Lanham, MD, 2020)

Nemirovskii, E. L., and Iu. E. Shustova, 'Kirillicheskie Azbuki i Bukvari XVI–XVIII vv.: bibliograficheskii svod izdanii', in *V Rossii nado zhit' po knige. Nachal'noe obuchenie chteniiu i pis'mu. Stanovlenie uchebnoi knigi*, ed. M. V. Tendriakova and V. G. Bezrogov (Moscow, 2015), pp. 185–338

Nesset, Tore, *How Russian Came to Be the Way It Is: A Student's Guide to the History of the Russian Language* (Bloomington, IN, 2015)

Neuhäuser, Rudolf, *The Romantic Age in Russian Literature: Poetic and Aesthetic Norms* (Munich, 1975)

Nikitina, T., *Pravda o skvernoslovii i kurenii* (Moscow, 2022)

Nikolaev, N. V., 'Dostatochno li bukv v russkom alfavite?', in *Tri stoletiia russkogo grazhdanskogo shrifta (1708–2008)*, ed. Iu. D. Samarin et al. (Moscow, 2008), pp. 182–7

Nikolaev, S. I., *Razyskaniia o russkikh poetakh pervoi poloviny XVIII veka* (Moscow and St Petersburg, 2023)

Noack, Christian, ed., *Politics of the Russian Language beyond Russia* (Edinburgh, 2021)

Obraztsy gazetnykh shriftov (matrits) linotipnogo otdeleniia tipografii gazety Pravda (Moscow, 1929)

Offord, Derek, 'Beware the Garden of Earthly Delights: Fonvizin and Dostoevskii on Life in France', *Slavonic and East European Review*, LXXVIII/4 (2000), pp. 625–42

——, 'Linguistic Gallophobia in Russian Comedy', in *French and Russian in Imperial Russia*, vol. II: *Language Attitudes and Identity*, ed. Derek Offord, Lara Ryazanova-Clarke, Vladislav Rjéoutski and Gesine Argent (Edinburgh, 2015), pp. 79–99

——, Vladislav Rjéoutski and Gesine Argent, *The French Language in Russia: A Social, Cultural and Literary History* (Amsterdam, 2018)

O gosudarstvennom iazyke Rossiiskoi Federatsii, ivo.garant.ru/#/document/12140387/

Okenfuss, Max, *The Discovery of Childhood in Russia: The Evidence of the Slavic Primer* (Newtonville, MA, 1980)

Olearius, Adam, *Vermehrete Newe Beschreibung Der Muscowitischen und Persischen Reise* (Schleswig, 1656)

Olesha, Iurii, *Ni dnia bez strochki* (Moscow, 1965)

Ospovat, Kirill, *Pridvornaia slovesnost'. Institut literatury i konstruktsii absoliutizma v Rossii serediny XVIII veka* (Moscow, 2020)

Ostrowski, Donald, *Russia in the Early Modern World: The Continuity of Change* (Lanham, MD, Boulder, CO, New York and London, 2022)
Otiakovskii, Valerii, 'Barkov, Prutkov i prochie: o "stikhakh poezii" leitenanta Pidorenko V. P.', *Matica srbska Review of Slavic Studies*, C (2021), pp. 847–62
Palladium, 16 (2025): https://freeuniversity.press/palladium/16/
Panchenko, A. M., 'Epifanii Slavinetskii', in *Slovar' knizhnikov i knizhnosti Drevnei Rusi. vyp 3. XVII v., ch. 1*, ed. D. S. Likhachev (St Petersburg, 1992), pp. 309–14
——, *Russkaia stikhotvornaia kul'tura XVII veka* (Leningrad, 1973)
Paulsen, Martin, 'Translit – Computer-Mediated Digraphia on the Runet', in *Digital Russia*, ed. Gorham, Lunde and Paulsen, pp. 156–73
—, 'Translit – novaia orfografiia russkogo iazyka,' in *Russkii iazyk i novye tekhnologii*, ed. Guseinov, pp. 58–73
Pavlenko, Aneta, 'Linguistic Russification in the Russian Empire: Peasants into Russians?', *Russian Linguistics*, XXXV/3 (2011), pp. 331–50
Perloff, Nancy, *Explodity: Sound, Image and Word in Russian Futurist Book Art* (Los Angeles, CA, 2016)
Peters, Benjamin, *How Not to Network a Nation: The Uneasy History of the Soviet Internet* (Cambridge, MA, and London, 2016)
Platt, Kevin M. F., ed., *Global Russian Cultures* (Madison, WI, 2019)
Plutser-Sarno, Alexei, *Notes from Russia* (London, 2007)
Polnoe sobranie zakonov Rossiiskoi imperii s 1649 goda (St Petersburg, 1830)
Poppe, Nicholas, Jr, 'A Survey of Studies of Turkic Loan-Words in the Russian Language', *Central Asiatic Journal*, XI/4 (December 1966), pp. 298–310
Pöppel, Ludmila, *The Rhetoric of 'Pravda' Editorials: A Diachronic Study of a Political Genre* (Stockholm, 2007)
Povest' vremennykh let, ed. D. S. Likhachev and V. P. Adrianova-Peretts, 2nd edn (St Petersburg, 1999)
Prokopovich, Feofan, *Sochineniia*, ed. I. P. Eremin (Moscow and Leningrad, 1961)
Proshina, Zoya G., and Anna A. Eddy, eds, *Russian English: History, Functions, and Features* (Cambridge, 2016)
[Protopopov, Vasilii], *Rassuzhdenie o vychishchenii, udobrenii i obogashchenii rossiiskogo iazyka* (Moscow, 1786)
Puleri, Marco, 'Russophonia as an Epistemic Challenge', *Ab Imperio*, 2023.1, pp. 76–98
Pushkin, A. S., *Evgenii Onegin. Roman v stikhakh* [Book 1] (St Petersburg, 1825)
——, *Polnoe sobranie sochinenii v 17 tomakh*, vol. II.1: *stikhotvoreniia 1817–1825* (Moscow, 1994)
——, *Polnoe sobranie sochinenii v 17 tomakh*, vol. XI: *kritika i publitsistika 1819–1834* (Moscow, 1996)
Ramazanova, D. N., 'Slaviano-greko-latinskii bukvar'' Fedora Polikarpova (1701 g.): istoriia sozdaniia i istochniki', *Vestnik PSTGU IV: Pedagogika. Psikhologiia*, 2013/4, pp. 78–88
——, and Iu. E. Shustova, *Kirillicheskie bukvari XVI–XVIII vv.* (Moscow, 2018)
Rashin, A. G., *Naselenie Rossii za 100 let (1811–1913 gg.) Statisticheskie ocherki* (Moscow, 1956)
Rastorguev, E. I., 'Progulki po Nevskomu prospektu', in *Chuvstvitel'nye progulki*, ed. Konechnyi, pp. 121–210

Remnev, Anatolii, 'Colonization and "Russification" in the Imperial Geography of Asiatic Russia: From the Nineteenth to the Early Twentieth Centuries', in *Asiatic Russia: Imperial Power in Regional and International Contexts*, ed. Uyama Tomohiko (London, 2012), pp. 102–28
Remy, Johannes, 'The Valuev Circular and Censorship of Ukrainian Publications in the Russian Empire (1863–1876): Intention and Practice', *Canadian Slavonic Papers*, XLIX/1–2 (March–June 2007), pp. 87–110
Rosén, Thomas, *Russian in the 1740s* (Boston, MA, 2022)
Rossiiskaia azbuka dlia obucheniia iunoshestva chteniiu (St Petersburg, n.d. [*c.* 1781])
Rudnev, L. V., and T. S. Sadova, 'Delovaia rech' petrovskoi epokhi: nasledie proshlogo ili radikal'noe preobrazovanie', in *Literaturnaia kul'tura Rossii XVIII veka*, 8 (St Petersburg, 2019), pp. 169–88
Russkaia satiricheskaia proza XVIII veka, ed. Iu. V. Stennik (Leningrad, 1986)
Rutten, Ellen, 'Oshibka kak novoe pravilo? Iazykovaia identichnost' v blogakh rossiiskikh pisatelei', in *Russkii iazyk i novye tekhnologii*, ed. Guseinov, pp. 74–86
Ryazanova-Clarke, Lara, 'Transnational Self and Community in the Talk of Russophone Cultural Leaders in the UK', in *Transnational Russian Studies*, ed. A. Byford, C. Doak and S. Hutchings (Liverpool, 2019), pp. 318–39
Safran, Gabriella, *Recording Russia: Trying to Listen in the Nineteenth Century* (Ithaca, NY, and London, 2022)
Safronov, A. A., 'Pervaia vseobshchaia perepis' naseleniia Rossii 1897 g.: razrabotka dannykh o gramotnosti, ikh informatsionnyi potentsial i dostovernost'', in *Dokument. Arkhiv. Istoriia. Sovremennost'*, III (2002), pp. 203–20
Safronova, A. M., *Vasilii Tatishchev i pervye inoiazychnye shkoly Ekaterinburga (1735–1750-e gody)* (St Petersburg and Ekaterinburg, 2024), pp. 343–57
Sandler, Stephanie, *Commemorating Pushkin: Russia's Myth of a National Poet* (Stanford, CA, 2004)
Savic, Jasmina, 'Porno Ludens: Soviet Literary Pornography, 1970s–1990s', PhD, University of Illinois Urbana–Champaign, 2019
Sazonova, L. I., *Literaturnaia kul'tura Rossii. Ranee Novoe vremia* (Moscow, 2006)
Schaeken, Jos, *Voices on Birchbark: Everyday Communication in Medieval Russia* (Boston, MA, and Leiden 2019)
Schenker, Alexander M., *The Dawn of Slavic: An Introduction to Slavic Philology* (New Haven, CT, and London, 1995)
Schneck, Stefan, *Wissen und Wissenschaft im Russland der Frühen Neuzeit: Mathematik, Medezin, die Grammatik und der intellektuelle Wander vor Peter dem Großen* (Zurich, 2025)
Schreier, Daniel, Marianne Hundt and Edgar Schneider, *The Cambridge Handbook of World Englishes* (Cambridge, 2020)
[Schwanwitz, Martin], *Nemetskaia grammatika iz raznykh avtorov sobrana i rossiiskoi iunosti v pol'zu izdana* (St Petersburg, 1730)
Sedakova, O. A., *Tserkovnoslaviano-russkie paronimy. Materialy k slovariu* (Moscow, 2005)
Seifrid, Thomas, *The Word Made Self: Russian Writings on Language, 1860–1930* (Ithaca, NY, and London, 2005)
Shaklein, V. M., and I. V. Kovtunenko, *Russkaia blogosfera. Pragmaticheskaia i lingvokul'turnaia spetsifika realizatsii kategorii sviaznosti* (Moscow, 2023)

Sharifian, Farzad, ed., *Advances in Cultural Linguistics* (Singapore, 2017)
[Shishkov, A. S.] [letters and pamphlets], in *Sbornik istoricheskikh materialov, izvlechennykh iz arkhiva sobstvennoi Ego Imperatorskogo Velichestva kantseliarii*, vol. XII, ed. N. Dubrovin (St Petersburg, 1903), pp. 325–76
——, *Rassuzhdenie o starom i novom sloge rossiiskogo iazyka*, revised edn (St Petersburg, 1813)
Shitsgal, A. G., *Russkii grazhdanskii shrift 1708–1958* (Moscow, 1959)
——, *Russkii tipografskii shrift. Voprosy istorii i praktika primeneniia*, 2nd edn (Moscow, 1985)
Shukshin, Vasilii, *Sobranie sochinenii v shesti knigakh. Kniga III* (Moscow, 1998)
Simeon Polotskii, *Izbrannye sochineniia* (Moscow and Leningrad, 1955)
——, *Orel rossiiskii*, ed. L. I. Sazonova (Moscow, 2015)
——, *Psaltir' rifmotvornaia* (Moscow, 1680)
Skvernoslovie v sovremennykh rossiiskikh mass-media, kul'ture i politike: special issue of *Palladium*, XVI (2025): https://freeuniversity.press/palladium
Smith, Alison, 'Handwriting and Bureaucracy', *Slavic Review*, LXXXV (2026) [forthcoming].
Smith, May, *The Influence of French on Eighteenth-Century Literary Russian: Semantic and Phraseological Calques* (Oxford and Bern, 2006)
Smith, Michael G., *Language and Power in the Creation of the USSR, 1917–1953* (Berlin and New York, 1998)
Sokolova, Olga, *'Shtyk-iazyk ostri i tri!' Iazykovye politiki poeticheskogo avangarda* (Moscow, 2024)
Sreznevskii, I. I., *Mysli ob istorii russkogo iazyka* (Moscow, 1959)
Sumarokov, A. P., *Izbrannye sochineniia* (Leningrad, 1957)
——, *Polnoe sobranie sochinenii v stikhakh i proze pokoinogo Deistvitel'nogo Statskogo Sovetnika, Ordena Sv. Anny Kavalera i Leiptsigskogo Uchenogo Sobraniia Chlena, Aleksandra Petrovicha Sumarokova*, ed. Nikolai Novikov, 10 vols (Moscow, 1781–2)
'T', 'Peterburgskie vyveski', *Illiustratsiia*, 30 (28 August 1848), pp. 81–2
Tappe, August Wilhelm, *Russisches historishes Lesebuch aus Karamsins Geschichte Russlands, für Schulen und den Selbstunterricht*... (St Petersburg and Riga, 1819)
Tatishchev, V. T., *Zapiski. Pis'ma. 1717–1750 gg.*, ed. A. I. Iukht (Moscow, 1990)
The 2005 Federation Law on the Russian Language, special issue of *Russian Language Journal*, LVI (2006)
Thom, Francoise, *Newspeak: The Language of Soviet Communism* (London, 1989)
Thompson, Walker Riggs, *Epifanii Slavinetskii's Greek–Slavonic–Latin Lexicon between East and West* (Heidelberg, 2024)
Tiutchev, F. I., *Polnoe sobranie sochinenii i pis'ma v shesti tomakh*, vol. I (Moscow, 2002)
Tokareva, E. Iu., 'Russkie familii tiurkskogo proiskhozhdeniia v "revizskikh skazkakh" g. Tobol'ska XVIII v.', *Istoriia, kul'tura, ekonomika urala i zaural'ia*, 11 (November 2015), pp. 94–7
Tolts, Mark, 'A Half Century of Jewish Emigration from the Former Soviet Union', in *Migration from the Newly Independent States 25 Years after the Collapse of the USSR*, ed. Mikhail Denisenko, Salvatore Strozza and Matthew Light (Cham, 2020), pp. 323–44

Trediakovskii, V. K., *Ezda v ostrov liubvi* (St Petersburg, 1730)
——, *Razgovor mezhdu chuzhestrannym chelovekom i rossiiskom ob ortografii starinnoi i novoi i o vsem chto prinadlezhit k sei materii* (St Petersburg, 1748)
——, *Sochineniia i perevody*, ed. N. Iu. Alekseeva (St Petersburg, 2009)
Tsypkin, D. O., '"Azbuka friaskaia" 1604 g.: drevnerusskaia kalligrafiia na zare epokhi tirazhirovaniia', in *Pol'za zelo velikaia. Sbornik nauchnykh statei k 60-letiiu Andreia Vladimirovicha Voznesenskogo*, ed. S. A. Davydova (St Petersburg, 2022), pp. 21–36
——, 'O formirovanii estetiki drevnerusskoi skoropisi (po rezul'tatam issledovaniia SPBII RAN, F. 115, No. 160', in *Aktual'nye problemy teorii i istorii iskusstva*, 11 (St Petersburg and Moscow, 2021), pp. 907–24
Uspenskii, B. A., *Istoriia russkogo literaturnogo iazyka (XI–XVII vv.)*, 3rd edn (Moscow, 2002)
——, *Vokrug Trediakovskogo. Trudy po istorii russkogo iazyka i russkoi kul'tury* (Moscow, 2008)
Vakhtin, Nikolai, and Boris Firsov, eds, *Public Debate in Russia: Matters of (Dis)order* (Edinburgh, 2017)
Vdovin, Alexey, 'The Peasant', in *The New Cambridge History of Russian Literature*, ed. Franklin, Reich and Widdis, pp. 737–55
Ventsel, Andreas, 'The Role of Political Rhetoric in the Development of Soviet Totalitarian Language', *Russian Journal of Communication*, 11 (2009), pp. 9–25
Vinokur, G. O., *The Russian Language: A Brief History*, trans. Mary A. Forsyth (Cambridge, 1971)
Vlasov, S. V., and L. V. Moskovkin, *Pervyi v Rossii pechatnyi uchebnik russkogo iazyka kak inostrannogo* (St Petersburg, 2023)
Vlasto, A. P., *A Linguistic History of Russia to the End of the Eighteenth Century* (Oxford, 1986)
Vol'per, M., *Russkaia rech'. Uchebnoe posobie, primenennoe k obucheniiu russkomu iazyku v tekh shkolakh, v kotorykh deti pri postuplenii ne umeiut govorit' po-russki* (St Petersburg, 1886–7)
——, *Volper's Russian Accidence in Tables ... Adapted for English Students and Provided with a Full Index and Grammatical Glossary by Mark Sieff* (London and New York, 1916)
Vomperskii, V. P., *Slovari XVIII veka* (Moscow, 1986)
Voronezhskie chekisty rasskazyvaiut ... (Voronezh, 1976)
Vorontsov, Roman L., Marina N. Priemysheva and Elizaveta V. Puritskaia, 'Printsipy normativnosti i istorizma v russkoi akademicheskoi leksikografii: eshche raz o tipe bol'shogo tolkovogo slovaria', *Voprosy leksikografii*, XXVIII (2023), pp. 5–27
White, Stephen, *The Bolshevik Poster* (New Haven, CT, and London, 1988)
Yurchak, Alexei, *Everything Was Forever until It Was No More: The Last Soviet Generation* (Princeton, NJ, and Oxford, 2005)
Zalizniak, A. A., *Drevnenovgorodskii dialekt*, 2nd edn (Moscow, 2004)
Zemtsov, Il'ia, *Sovetskii politicheskii iazyk* (London, 1985)
Zemtsova, Oxana, *Russification and Educational Policies in the Middle Volga Region (1860–1914)*, EUI dissertation, Florence, 2014
Zhivov, V. M., 'Azbuchnaia reforma Petra I kak semioticheskoe preobrazovanie', *Trudy po znakovym sistemam*, XIX (1986), pp. 54–67

——, *Istoriia iazyka russkoi pis'mennosti*, 2 vols (Moscow, 2017)
——, *Ocherki istoricheskoi morfologii russkogo iazyka* XVII–XVIII *vekov* (Moscow, 2004)

ACKNOWLEDGEMENTS

I am grateful to Michael Leaman for prompting me to write this book, and to those who have commented on draft chapters or given feedback at various 'preview' talks: Ksenia Zanon and colleagues in Slavonic Studies at the University of Cambridge and at the European University at St Petersburg; the hospitable members of CamRuss; Susana Torres Prieto of IE University in Madrid. Many, many more have contributed to the book's long gestation through the decades before I was even aware that it was somehow forming at a level not yet discernible as a conscious plan. As an undergraduate student I was privileged (or otherwise) to be the only attendee at Alexis Vlasto's courses on Old Church Slavonic and the History of the Russian Language. Crucial was the experience of living for a year in a student hostel in the Soviet provinces in the mid-1970s, with linguistic immersion across the range from student parties, through diplomatic engagement with university authorities, to intelligentsia intensity on Moscow breaks in the company of Evgenii Evtushenko. I am grateful to all who were part of those formative encounters. In more academic mode, I owe a great deal to colleagues in Russia, particularly the pioneering cultural historian of language Viktor Zhivov and, in quite different ways, Andrei Zalizniak, Aleksei Gippius, Sergei Ivanov and Iuliia Khodko. I should also acknowledge generations of my own students, whose questions and interests helped to crystallize the notion that a book like this may be useful. The greatest debt is to my late wife, Natasha: for the intensity of her attachment to the language, her inspirational pedagogy and for showing that rigorous normativity and expressive non-normativity are sharpened by each other. This book is dedicated to her memory.

PHOTO ACKNOWLEDGEMENTS

The author and publishers wish to express their thanks to the sources listed below for illustrative material and/or permission to reproduce it. Some locations of artworks are also given below, in the interest of brevity:

Author's collection: 5, 6, 7, 10, 11, 12, 13, 14, 16, 22, 23, 24, 25, 29, 30 (and detail on cover), 31, 32, 33, 34, 35, 40 (and detail on cover), 41, 42, 43, 44, 45, 46, 47; The J. Paul Getty Museum, Los Angeles: 37, 38; © Natalia Goncharova/upravis, 2026: 36; Public Domain: 19, 26, 27 (and detail on cover), 28, 39; Russian Academy of Sciences Library, St Petersburg: 3, 4; Russian State Library, Moscow: 21; St Petersburg Institute of History: 1, 2 (and detail on cover); Wikimedia Commons (Public Domain): 8, 9, 15, 17, 18, 20.

INDEX

Page numbers in *italics* indicate illustrations